MW01534036

# The Trail Guide
# to NORTHERN
# ARIZONA

## by Bruce Grubbs

FALCON™

Falcon Press Publishing Co., Inc.
Helena, MT

Falcon Press is continually expanding its list of recreational guidebooks using the same general format as this book. All books include detailed descriptions, accurate maps, and all information necessary for enjoyable trips. You can order extra copies of this book and get information and prices for other Falcon books by writing Falcon Press, P.O. Box 1718, Helena, MT 59624. Also, please ask for a free copy of our current catalog.

Copyright © 1994 by Falcon Press Publishing Co., Inc.
Helena and Billings, Montana

Library of Congress Cataloging-in-Publication Data

Grubbs, Bruce (Bruce O.)
    The trail guide to northern Arizona / by Bruce Grubbs.
        p. cm.
    Includes bibliographical references.
    ISBN 1-56044-285-9
    1. Hiking—Arizona—Guidebooks. 2. Hiking—
Arizona—Flagstaff Region—Guidebooks. 3. Ari
zona—Guide- books. 4. Flagstaff Region (Ariz.)—
Guidebooks. I. Title
    GV199/42/A7G78  1994              94-21525
    796.5'1'09791—dc20                CIP

Printed in the United States of America.

Photos by author except as noted.
Cover photo by Gary Ladd, view of the
Grand Canyon of the Colorado River,
Grand Canyon National Park
Maps by Marita Martiniak

Text pages are printed on recycled paper.

# CONTENTS

Outdoor recreation activities are by their very nature potentially hazardous. All participants in such activities must assume the responsibility for their own actions and safety. The information contained in this guidebook cannot replace sound judgment and good decision-making skills, which help reduce risk exposure, nor does the scope of this book allow for disclosure of all the potential hazards and risks involved in such activities.

Learn as much as possible about the outdoor recreation activities you participate in, prepare for the unexpected, and be safe and cautious. The reward will be a safer and more enjoyable experience.

*A major avalanche path on the north side of Fremont Peak.*

# ACKNOWLEDGMENTS

Thanks go to all my hiking companions over the years who have made discovering the backcountry a joy, and special thanks to Duart Martin for invaluable proofreading and advice. Finally, I wish to thank Randall Green, my editor, for his patience and assistance, as well as the fine folks at Falcon Press who have made this book a reality.

*The red rocks of Bell Rock and Courthouse Butte catch the last rays of the evening sun in an aerial view.*

# OVERVIEW MAP

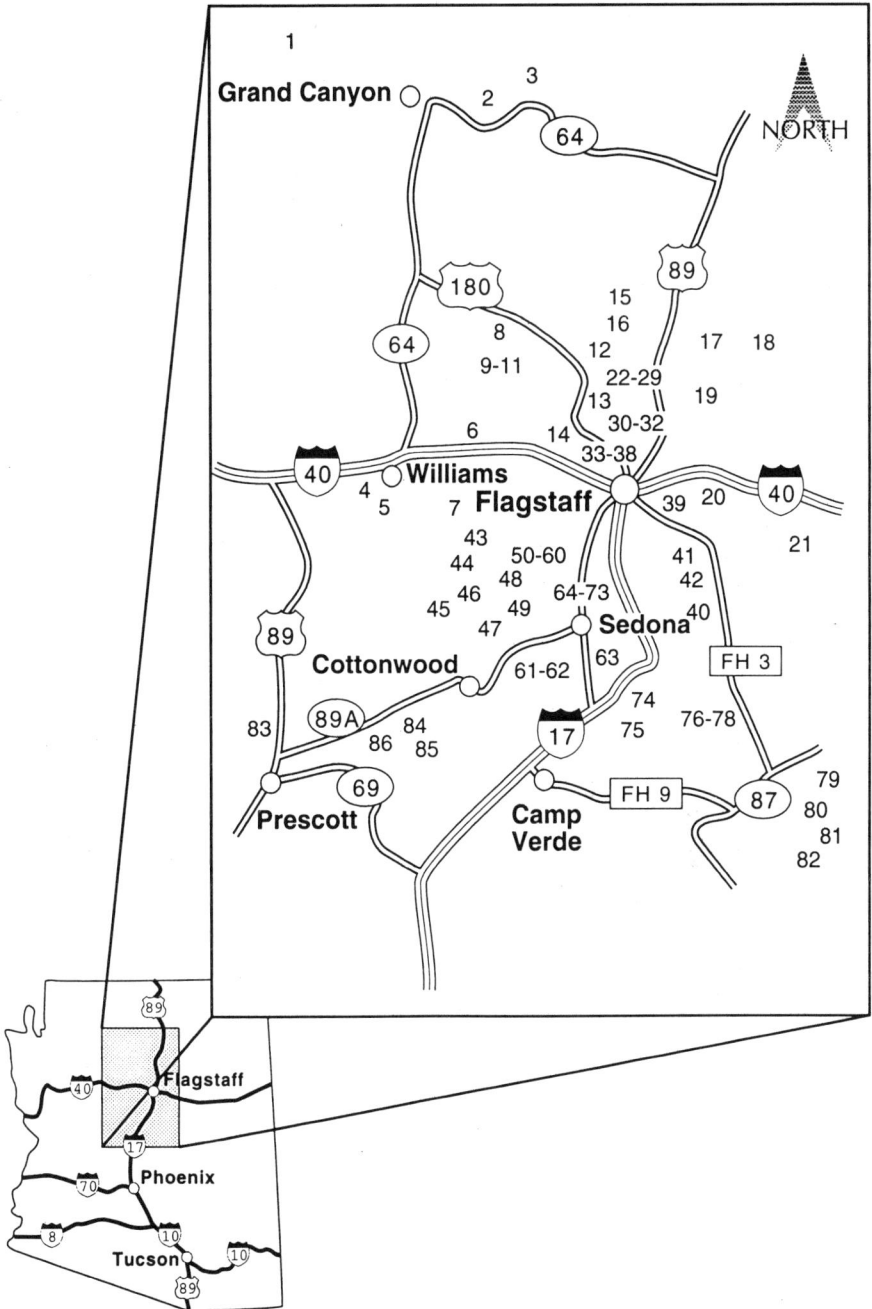

# MAP LEGEND

| | | | |
|---|---|---|---|
| Interstate |  | Featured Trail |  |
| Paved Roads | | Trail Head | |
| Unpaved Roads | 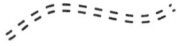 | Other Trail |  |
| Interstate | (00) | Cross Country Route | |
| U. S. Highway | (00) | Forest Trail | /0000/ |
| State Highway | (375) | River, Creek, | |
| Forest Road | [0000] | Drainage | |
| Pass | | Springs | |
| Mountain | | Scale of Miles | |
| Ranger Station | | | |
| Campground | | | |
| Building | | | |
| Ruin | | | |

Scale of Miles

MILE

Hike Location

NORTH

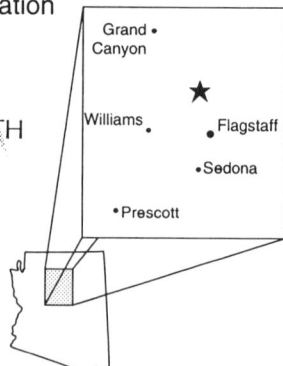

# INTRODUCTION

Northern Arizona offers almost unlimited opportunities for hiking and exploration. There are dense pine forests and sparse deserts, alpine peaks and desert sandstone canyons, trout streams and isolated springs, volcanic plateaus and rugged granite mountains. And Northern Arizona's friendly climate and great range in elevation allow hiking year-round. During summer, many desert dwellers from Phoenix and Tucson come north to explore the high plateaus, cool canyons, and towering peaks. During winter, residents of the high country can descend to the desert areas of Northern Arizona and enjoy pleasant hiking weather.

This region, bounded roughly by the Grand Canyon, Prescott, Camp Verde, Payson, Sedona, and Flagstaff, contains more than two hundred hiking trails and routes. This guidebook presents a selection of the best hiking in the region. The hikes range from short day hikes on paved trails to long multi-day backpack trips. Most of the hikes follow established trails, while a few involve cross-country hiking. Some hikes require walking for short distances on roads in order to complete a loop, but none of the hikes are entirely on roads. Trails in designated wilderness areas and in national parks and monuments are closed to bicycles and all motorized vehicles and provide the most serene hiking. Other trails are open to bicycles, and many are open to horses and pack stock. (By the way, mountain bikes are an excellent means of exploring backcountry roads that might be unappealing on foot.)

Readers of my previous book, *The Hiker's Guide to Arizona* (with Stewart Aitchison), may wonder what's new in this book. There's so much good hiking in Northern Arizona that we couldn't do it justice in the state-wide guide, so you'll find plenty of new hiking here. I have retained a few excellent hikes that are described in the Arizona book. In most cases, such hikes are presented here with new information—new trailhead directions or a way to do the hike as a loop, for example.

Of course, Northern Arizona boasts far more hikes than this book could encompass. Please regard *The Trail Guide to Northern Arizona* as an invitation to begin your personal discovery of this wonderful region. I hope you always travel with a light pack.

# THE MOSAIC OF NORTHERN ARIZONA

## *Canyons, Mountains, and Plateaus*
The geography of Northern Arizona is fascinating and varied. The Mogollon Rim begins north of Prescott and runs east nearly two hundred miles into New Mexico, dividing the state into two physiographic provinces. North of the Mogollon Rim, the Colorado Plateau province covers parts of Arizona, Utah, Colorado, and New Mexico.

1

*Hikers on the Tanner Trail, Grand Canyon National Park.*

Layer upon layer of sedimentary rocks have been laid down, some under water, some in Sahara-like deserts, over millions of years. Mountain-building forces raised the Plateau one to two-and-a-half miles above sea level, warping and fracturing the rocks. Running water from rain and snow melt has eroded these weaknesses into thousands of canyons. These range in length from a few miles to the 290 miles of the Grand Canyon. Volcanic forces have also intruded into the weak zones in the rock, creating hundreds of volcanic hills and mountains. Instead of a flat, featureless landscape, the Colorado Plateau is a region of narrow canyons, tall mountains, and vast vistas.

The fault escarpment of the Mogollon Rim faces generally south along its length. Below the Rim lies the most rugged portion of Arizona, the central mountains, which is part of the Basin and Range physiographic province. Numerous rugged mountain ranges rise more than 4,000 feet above the neighboring valleys. The Verde River, one of Arizona's last free-flowing rivers, drains this area. Numerous side canyons cutting into the mountains and the Mogollon Rim create a hiking paradise.

## Climate

The elevations in the area covered by this guide range from 2,400 feet along the Colorado River in the Grand Canyon and 3,000 feet along the Verde River to 12,633 feet at the summit of Humphreys Peak. Because of this, temperatures and climate vary greatly, and it is possible to hike all year. The wet seasons are December through March, when winter storms can be expected, and July through mid September, when summer thunderstorms are common. Fall and late spring are usually the best hiking seasons.

In winter, snow storms are not unusual, and there is often several feet of snow on the higher portions of the Colorado Plateau and much more in the mountains. Occasionally the first snowfall is delayed into January. Many high-elevation areas then remain open for hiking well into winter, but the late season traveler should be prepared for possible snow storms. The lower desert areas may experience an occasional snowfall, but the snow doesn't usually stay on the ground for more than a day or two. Between storms, the weather is normally bright and sunny, and any winter rains cause the streams to run and the grass to grow in areas recently parched by summer heat. As a result, the desert is a very rewarding place to hike in winter.

Spring weather is changeable as the storm pattern shifts toward summer. By April the weather is usually dry but still cool, good conditions for hiking. Fresh water springs, water pockets, and streams are usually full, making backpack trips easier to plan.

In May the weather usually begins to turn hot, with desert temperatures over 100 degrees Fahrenheit common by June. The high country, with high temperatures usually in the 80s, becomes attractive as the last of the snow melts. This is also a good time to explore desert canyons that require wading and swimming.

During early July, Arizona's summer season begins as moist air moves northwest from the Gulf of Mexico. Daily afternoon thunderstorms occur over the high country,

*The rim of the Dry Creek basin seen from Brins Mesa.*

and by August the storms start to migrate into the desert during the evening hours. Mornings dawn cool and clear, inviting early starts—a necessity for hikes into the highest mountains. To avoid the afternoon lightning hazard, leave exposed ridges and summits by noon. Also, the possibility of flash floods makes narrow canyons places to be avoided during the monsoon. The summer rains bring a resurgence of flowers to the forest country and are a welcome change from the hot, dry days of June.

The monsoon usually ends by mid September, and autumn is clear, cool, and dry. Although water sources may be harder to find, the stable weather and changing fall colors make hiking this time of year an absolute delight.

# WHY HIKE?

Hiking is an enjoyable activity for all ages and abilities, especially if the pace is set for the slowest member of the group. Faster hikers can use the extra time to explore or indulge in plant and animal identification, fishing, rock hounding, or loafing. Families and groups can find much to share in the outdoors as long as hiking is not allowed to become a competitive event.

Most Americans could do with more exercise, and hiking is a great way to get it. The brain has a chance to unwind from the stresses of modern life while the muscles carry the load for a change. The self reliance of being outdoors, away from the supporting but encumbering matrix of civilization, is a beneficial change for many people. In the outdoors, a person must provide his or her own shelter, food, and water. With modern equipment and techniques it is easy to do, and the natural world becomes a friendly and comfortable place to be enjoyed.

Despite our reliance on cars, roads don't go to the most interesting places. Where there are roads, especially paved roads, there are lots of people. And roads keep us isolated from the country. For example, check out the difference between the West Fork of Oak Creek with its quiet, streamside trail, and Oak Creek Canyon with its crowded campgrounds and resorts. To find the best places in Northern Arizona's natural world, you have to hike. Fortunately, getting there is most of the fun.

## Walking

Walking as a skill seems almost forgotten. Pace is probably the most important element; the group should hike at a speed that allows for easy conversation among all members with no one being out of breath. Long hikes, especially uphill, should be paced so that rest breaks are needed only about once an hour. That's not to say that you shouldn't stop at scenic viewpoints or when you find something else that is interesting. But too frequent breaks taken for rests are a sign that the pace is excessive. Hikes with young children should have very modest goals. A few hundred yards may be far enough. Children may find all sorts of interesting things that their parents would never see in such a small area.

At first, the novice hiker must consciously avoid stepping on sharp rocks or on cactus, but with practice the subconscious takes over most of this job. Still, the hiker must be aware of hazards such as slippery surfaces or shady rock overhangs that may

4

conceal a rattlesnake on hot days. While moving, it's best to keep an eye on the trail and the piece of ground immediately in front, and then stop to enjoy distant views or to plan the route of travel.

# EQUIPMENT

Day hiking has grown to become a highly popular activity. In comparison, only a small number of hikers make the transition to backpacking, staying out for two or more days. Day hiking is popular partly because it requires less time. Equipment for day hiking is also simpler—often beginners will find that they already have all the necessary gear. Backpacking and camping overnight require a few specialized items. A modest amount of good equipment—and the skill to use it—will make hiking more enjoyable and safer.

## Footwear

For short easy hikes on good trails, nearly any comfortable  footwear such as tennis shoes, running shoes, or boat shoes will work. Proper fit is most important—the shoe or boot should fit snugly but with plenty of toe room. To test for toe room, try the shoe on your largest foot wearing the socks you will hike in (see below), then, with it unlaced, stand up and slide your foot as far forward as it will go. You should be able to easily slip a finger behind your heel and wiggle it. With any less room, your toes will hit the end of the shoe, causing a lot of pain and nasty blisters. Fit is especially important with children because they can't determine the proper fit for themselves and won't complain until it is too late.

If hiking becomes a frequent activity, you may want to buy a pair of lightweight hiking boots. These are suitable for longer, rougher trails, and for cross-country hikes and backpack trips on the feet of an experienced hiker. There are many models available, in women's, men's, and children's sizes and widths. Most have uppers of nylon with leather reinforcing, and molded rubber soles. Some of the more sophisticated and expensive designs use waterproof/breathable fabrics. Again, fit is the most important consideration.

For difficult hiking with heavy loads, many hikers prefer all-leather boots with resolable soles. Be careful not to buy heavy, stiff boots intended for technical mountaineering. In fact, many of us prefer the lightweight approach to hiking boots even for very difficult cross-country hiking, trading durability for less weight on our feet. Even in mountaineering, the trend is toward much lighter boots.

Your choice of socks is critical. They provide not only insulation but also padding. A good combination is a light inner sock of cotton, wool, or polypropylene, with an outer medium- or heavy-weight sock of wool with nylon reinforcing. The outer sock will tend to slide on the inner sock, rather than directly on your skin, helping to prevent blisters. Inner socks of cotton are comfortable in warm weather, while polypropylene socks will wick moisture away from your skin in cool weather. Wool is still the best fiber for the outer, cushioning sock, though a small percentage of nylon extends its life. A small amount of Spandex[tm] will help the sock keep its shape and fluffiness, even on long hikes.

Incipient blisters should be treated before they actually blister. At the first sign of a hot spot or other discomfort on your feet, stop and check it out. A hot spot can be protected with a piece of felt moleskin (available at drug stores). Often a change of socks will help as well. Once a blister has fully developed, protect it with a piece of moleskin with the center cut out. A large or deep blister can be immobilizing, which is why prevention is important.

## Clothing

For day hikes in good, stable weather, nearly any durable clothing will do. In hot, sunny weather, keep your skin covered with long sleeves and long pants, or use a good sunscreen. Northern Arizona's strong sun and high altitudes can produce a painful sunburn in a short time, even on tanned skin. You may also want to wear long pants when hiking a brushy trail. In sunny weather, a sun hat with a brim is a good idea. There are a number of canvas hats that roll up and fit in your pack when they are not needed.

If the weather is cool, windy, or changeable—or if your trip will be overnight or longer—give a little more thought to clothing. Several layers of lightweight, flexible clothing work best.

Start with an inner layer of synthetic, wicking underwear. Over this don a pair of sturdy pants and a long-sleeved shirt (preferably of wool or synthetics) that can hold up to brush and rocks. The next layer consists of an insulating jacket or parka, which on most trips can be a down jacket. Down is unsurpassed for its warmth and light weight, but loses most of its insulating ability when wet. Substitute a synthetic pile jacket for the down if wet weather is expected. Synthetic pile is the warmest, driest insulator for very wet conditions. Even when soaked it can be wrung out and worn immediately. Pile pants are also available but are usually unnecessary on backpack trips. The outermost layer is a set of good rain pants and a jacket with hood. A waterproof and breathable fabric will shed wind as well as rain.

In cool weather, a warm wool or synthetic watch cap or balaclava will make an amazing difference in comfort. Up to half the body's heat is lost through the head. Your hands should be protected with wool or synthetic gloves or mittens.

While hiking, add or subtract layers as necessary to stay comfortable. Don't put up with being overheated or chilled for longer than it takes to do something about it.

## Food

Food should be brought on all but the shortest hikes. High calorie foods will keep your energy levels high. Sandwiches and other picnic items can be made up ahead of time, or fruit, cheese, crackers, nuts, and drink mixes can be carried.

Although a great deal of dehydrated food is made especially for backpacking and lightweight camping, it tends to be very expensive. A variety of items found in supermarkets make good backpacking food, and the cost is much lower. Using supermarket food, it is possible to do long backpack trips with no more than two pounds of food per person per day. Some suggestions—for breakfast: low bulk cold cereals with powdered milk, hot cereals, dried fruit, breakfast bars, hot chocolate, tea, and coffee bags.

For lunch: nuts, cheese, crackers, dried fruit, candy bars, athletic energy bars, dried soup, hard candy, beef or turkey jerky, sardines, and fruit-flavored drink mixes. For dinner: dried noodle or rice-based dishes supplemented with margarine and canned tuna, turkey, or chicken. Although canned food in general should be avoided because of its weight, a small can of tuna or chicken adds much-needed protein to dinner and still keeps the daily food weight under two pounds per person.

Redundant packaging such as cardboard boxes should be removed at home. Plastic bags with zipper closures make excellent food repackaging bags. Messy items should be double bagged. Margarine and peanut butter can be packed in reliable, wide mouth plastic jars (available from outdoor suppliers). Unless you really trust the seal, also put the container in a plastic bag!

## Pack

A good quality day pack that fits well will go a long way toward making short hikes a pleasant experience. Good packs are not cheap, but will last a long time. Look for foam padding on the back and on the shoulder straps. Larger day packs usually have a waist belt, which may or may not be padded. A reinforced bottom, made of heavy duty nylon, is a good idea. Children enjoy being included in the group, and will not mind a pack as long as it is small and light. Another possibility for small children is a small fanny pack. Fanny packs are gaining in popularity for adults as well. They are especially nice in warm weather because your back has free air circulation. The drawback is the limited capacity, which makes them unsuited for long hikes in remote areas, or in changeable weather.

Large packs for backpacking fall into two categories: internal frame and external frame. Internal frames are now the most common, but the choice is really one of personal preference. Internals give the best balance for cross-country hiking, and are better for airline travel. Externals are easier to pack and to overload for extended trips. They also give better back ventilation in hot weather, so are still preferred by many desert hikers. Any good backpack distributes the load between your shoulders, back, and hips, with most of the weight on your hips; and correct fit is critical. The best way to buy a pack is from an outdoor store staffed by someone knowledgeable in pack fitting. If you buy a pack by mail order, get the advice of an experienced friend, and make certain you can return the pack unused. Be cautious when buying a used pack. A poor fit negates any monetary savings. Women in particular should be very careful when thinking of buying or borrowing a pack from a male friend. Because of women's lesser average height and shorter torso length, it is rare for a man's pack to fit well. In the last few years the differences in anatomy have been recognized by pack designers and there are now a number of excellent packs designed specifically for women.

There are also packs designed for children. Backpacking parents can introduce their children to short hikes at an early age, gradually lengthening distances as they grow older and their stamina and interest increase. The first overnight hikes can be kept short, as they should be for any novice hiker. Once the child is old enough to carry a pack, keep its load light. If you progressively introduce your children to backpacking, by the time they are teenagers they'll both be addicted to hiking and more energetic than you, so you can get them to carry some of your load (at least in theory).

With a load, the pace must necessarily be slower, especially uphill. You may find a walking stick to be helpful, especially when the footing is uncertain. A hiking stick can also be used as a prop to turn a pack into a back rest. For those backpackers using a tarp for shelter instead of a tent, a hiking stick can be used as a support, which can be important in treeless desert.

## Sleeping Bags

Your sleeping bag is one of the most important items in your pack. A good sleeping bag will ensure a comfortable sleep, while a poor one will guarantee a miserable experience. A good indicator of quality is the length of the manufacturer's warranty. A well-made down sleeping bag will have a lifetime warranty, while an equivalent synthetic-fill bag will be guaranteed for several years. For occasional use, a backpacker's style mummy bag, insulated with one of the current synthetic fills, will do the job. Synthetic fills are also good in situations where getting the bag wet is unavoidable. Down-filled sleeping bags are a more expensive and lighter alternative. Good-quality down is still unsurpassed in insulating capability for it's weight. It is more durable than any of the synthetic fills, so in the long run, down is actually less expensive. Down is also more water resistant than commonly thought, as anyone who has tried to wash a down bag by hand can tell you. People who do a lot of backpacking, especially longer trips, tend to prefer down bags.

Sleeping bags are rated by temperature and sometimes by the number of recommended seasons. A three-season bag is good for most backpacking. If you sleep warm, you may wish to get a lighter, summer bag, and if you sleep cold, you'll probably like a winter bag.

## Sleeping Pads

Because lightweight sleeping bags don't provide much insulation or padding underneath, you'll need a sleeping pad. The best type currently available is the self-inflating, foam-filled air mattress. These are less prone to punctures than a traditional air mattress, are much warmer, and are at least as comfortable. A cheaper alternative is a closed-cell foam pad. They insulate very well but are not comfortable.

## Shelter

Most hikers depend on a tent for shelter. Good construction and high quality, as reflected in the warranty, is important. A three-season, two-person dome tent will be the most versatile. Larger tents are more awkward to carry and require more spacious campsites. Nearly all tents use a separate waterproof fly over the tent canopy, which provides rain protection and also allows moisture to escape from within the tent. Small children can share a three-person tent with their parents. As they get older, the kids will probably enjoy their own tent.

Many experienced Arizona hikers avoid the weight and expense of a tent by carrying a tarp and a separate groundsheet. A tarp can provide good weather protection and is versatile enough to use as a sun shade or wind break for lunch stops. Constructing a good shelter from a tarp does require more time and ingenuity than does a tent, and a tarp provides no protection from insects.

Avoid plastic tube tents. In the store they look simple and attractive, but in the field they're a nightmare. The plastic condenses body moisture, which then collects on the walls and runs down under your sleeping bag. It is impossible to close off the open ends against wind-driven rain without making the condensation problem worse.

## Sun Glasses

A good pair of sunglasses will protect your eyes from glare and invisible ultraviolet and infrared rays, reducing eyestrain and headaches. Hikers who are dependent on prescription glasses or contact lenses should carry a spare pair of glasses. A hard-shell plastic case will protect your expensive glasses.

## Sun Screen

Choose a sun screen with the level of protection you need. Use SPF fifteen or higher for the best protection. Remember that the summer sun is very intense because of the southern latitude and high altitude of northern Arizona. Waterproof and sweat proof brands are available.

## First Aid Kit

A good first aid kit may be the most neglected and yet the most important item in your pack. Chances are you'll never need more than a small bandage or some aspirin, but when you need it you'll really need it. A small first aid kit will do for day hikes; carry a wider array of bandages and medicines for extended trips. Well-stocked kits are commercially available (make sure you buy one intended for wilderness sports), or you can assemble your own from the shelves at your local pharmacy.

## Accessories

A good knife is more an essential than an accessory. Personal preference will dictate what type of knife to carry. Some hikers prefer the Swiss army type with scissors and other implements, while others like a simple, large-bladed knife such as a folding hunter. In any case, a good knife is necessary for many routine tasks, such as cutting rope, and is vital for emergency fire building.

A camera is probably the most common "extra" item carried on day hikes. Consider bringing a nylon ditty bag or plastic bag to protect it if rain is a possibility. Even the most water proof packs can let water in through seams and zippers. This advice also applies to other items in your pack that could be damaged by water, such as maps.

## Equipment Sources

If you have an outdoor shop nearby that sells hiking and lightweight camping equipment, then you may wish to buy locally. If the staff uses the gear they sell and are willing to spend time sharing their knowledge with you, then it will be worth paying higher prices. On the other hand, if there is no local shop, or no one carries the items you need, or the sales people don't know anything about the equipment, then mail order becomes an attractive option. Several established mail order companies have earned good reputations; check the ads in outdoor magazines for addresses and phone numbers.

# BACKCOUNTRY SKILLS

Most situations that arise in the backcountry are readily resolved with a dose of common sense and a willingness to adapt to your surroundings. But a few concerns are worth thinking about before you set foot on the trail, particularly if you are new to the art of backcountry travel or unfamiliar with Arizona's climate, terrain, and wildlife residents.

## Trip Planning

Maps and guidebooks are very useful for trip planning and should be obtained well in advance of the trip. Guidebooks are especially useful when you are unfamiliar with an area; they allow you to learn an area more quickly. Once you are comfortable with an area and have done many of the hikes in the guidebooks, you will be able to plan your own trip with the aid of maps and information from other hikers.

Desert backpack trips must be planned around water sources. It is convenient but not always possible to be near a spring or stream for lunch stops and at camps. Collapsible water bags that will hold up to two gallons are available and should be carried in addition to reliable plastic water bottles. Collapsible containers make it possible to carry water for a dry lunch or even a dry camp.

Contrary to common practice, it is not actually necessary to camp at a water source. Unless the weather is cool or you have experience in extended dry camping, plan to pass at least one reliable water source each day of the trip. If you have a collapsible water container, you can pick up a gallon or a two of water at your last source of the day, then continue on to a dry camp. Although dry camping does take some practice, the advantages are many. First of all, you can avoid heavily used campsites and their camp-robbing animal attendants. Insects are also less common at dry campsites. You'll find you have a much greater variety of campsites; ridges and mountaintops are scenic possibilities in good weather. Also, you'll avoid disturbing wildlife, which is often highly dependent on specific water sources. (It is actually illegal to camp within 0.25 mile of a spring in Arizona for this reason.)

Springs and streams shown on maps are often unreliable. Newer U.S. Geological Survey topographic maps no longer show the difference between permanent and seasonal stream beds. The best way to determine the reliability of desert water sources is from past first-hand experience in the area, or ask a trusted friend. Allowance must be made for springs and streams that may be dry—do not depend on any single water source. Be aware of reliable water sources that are off your route. Known water sources are listed in each hike description; there may be more water sources, but I have attempted to err on the side of caution.

*Lockett Tank reflects nearby quaking aspen.*

## Water Essentials

Water is the most important item in your pack in hot weather. Make certain you have enough. In cool weather, a quart may be enough for a short, easy hike, but a long, difficult hike in hot weather may require a gallon or more per person. The best water containers are plastic bottles with leak proof caps, carried inside your pack. Another popular arrangement is a fanny pack with external bottle carriers. Metal canteens carried on your belt or on a shoulder strap are very uncomfortable, and the metal rapidly gets hot in the sun.

All backcountry water sources should always be purified or filtered before use. Even sparkling clear water may contain dangerous parasites and disease organisms, many of which are spread by wildlife, domestic animals, and people. Of these, the most common is probably giardiasis, a severe gastrointestinal infection causing bloating, cramps, and diarrhea. The cysts that cause giardiasis are dispersed in the feces of mammals, including beaver, voles, deer, dogs, and people. No doubt improper disposal of human waste in the backcountry has contributed to the widespread contamination of water sources.

There are only three reliable methods for protecting yourself from contaminated drinking water:

**Carry treated water from home.** On day trips and short outings, it may be possible and preferable to carry tap water from home in plastic bottles and jugs. Keep containers tightly sealed and do not immerse them in streams or lakes for cold storage.

**Boil water for at least five minutes.** Giardia cysts are killed in water heated to 140 to 160 degrees F. Other bacteria and viruses are even more vulnerable to heat. Boil water for the allotted time before adding foods, powders, or flavorings to ensure sterilization. For drinking, boiled water tends to taste flat because the oxygen has been bubbled out of it. Make it palatable again by pouring it back and forth repeatedly between two clean containers.

**Filter water through an approved purifying device.** A number of effective water filters are now available for backcountry use, ranging in price from $30 to $300. Pocket filters tend to cost less and suffice for short backpack trips and parties of two or three people. Mid-range filters can clean a greater amount of water at a faster rate, and some boast ceramic filters that screen out a wider assortment of pathogens and inorganic compounds. Basecamp models are also available to purify large amounts of water for groups of six or more people. Always follow the manufacturer's instructions and keep water containers clean and free of contaminated water.

Other water treatment methods, such as disinfecting with iodine, Halazone, or chlorine, are less reliable and pose hazards of their own. These are not recommended. (Also see *Medicine for Mountaineering* in Further Reading.)

## Navigation

Backcountry navigation consists primarily of map reading. But a good, liquid-filled compass is important and should always be carried. You may only need it when there are no terrain features to match with your map. For example, suppose you climb out of a canyon and emerge on the rim of a pinyon-juniper flat on a cloudy day. Your car is parked along a road several miles across the flat, and the trees limit visibility to a hundred yards or less. Use your map and compass to determine the course, or bearing, that will take you to your car. Since it is impossible to walk a precise course, deliberately aim to the left or right of your car. Now use the compass to sight on a tree in the direction you wish to go. The farther away this object is, the more accurate your course will be. Hike to this object, then repeat the compass sighting on another object along your course. Keep track of the time; with experience, you'll know how fast you travel on a given terrain and will be able to predict your arrival with some accuracy. When you reach the road, you'll know which way to turn because of your deliberate offset to one side of your destination.

Good compasses come with instructions; refer to these for details on using your brand and model. There are several good books on compass work and orienteering. But keep in mind that classic orienteering techniques that emphasize travel in straight lines along compass courses are not usually appropriate in mountains and canyons.

The best way to learn map reading is to get a map of your local area, or a place you are familiar with, and then spend some time relating the symbols on the map to the terrain. The first step is to orient the map with the terrain. Most maps have north at the top; this includes all the USGS topographic maps and USDA Forest Service national forest maps referenced in this guide. As you gain experience, you'll be able to read the map and relate it to actual ground features without orienting it. The second step is to use a symbol key to learn the map symbols and compare them to the actual terrain features. Symbol keys are free from the USGS and map dealers, and Forest Service maps have a symbol key printed on the map.

Contour lines are the most important symbol on topographic maps. Each line represents a constant elevation above sea level. For example, if sea level rose to 4,000 feet, then the 4,000-foot contour would become the new shore line. Contour lines are spaced at regular intervals, usually twenty or forty feet in mountain country; the contour interval is specified on the map. Every fourth or fifth contour is printed darker for emphasis, and has the elevation printed along it. Contour lines spread out on gentle slopes and bunch up on steep slopes. Ridges show up as a series of V-shaped contours; drainages look similar but have a blue line representing the stream bed running through the apex of the V's. With a little practice, you'll be able to visualize the terrain in three dimensions.

The USGS series of topographic maps tend to be somewhat out of date because of the difficulty of maintaining all the maps (more than a thousand maps are required to cover northern Arizona). This means that man-made features, such as the edges of towns, may not be shown correctly, especially in rapidly growing areas. Foot trails may not be shown at all, and even roads may be incorrect. But the terrain represented by the contours doesn't change, and that is the most valuable feature of the topographic map for the hiker.

Forest Service maps generally cover a large section of a national forest. They are updated more often than the topographic maps, so roads and trails are shown more accurately, though at a smaller scale with less detail. Forest Service maps are usually planimetric and do not have contour lines. The two types of maps complement each other. You'll probably want to buy the Forest Service maps for general coverage of your hiking area, and the USGS topographic maps for your specific hike. Forest

Service and USGS maps are available from outdoor shops and bookstores. Forest Service maps are available from the Forest Service offices listed under Resources, and USGS maps and free state map catalogs and indexes can be ordered from the USGS address listed there.

Do not count on trail signs to tell you where you are in the backcountry. Signs may be vandalized or inaccurate. It is better to stay aware of your location at all times, and use signs to confirm what you already know. To stay oriented while hiking on a trail, refer to the map often and locate yourself in reference to visible landmarks. If you do this frequently as you hike then you will never be lost. Cross-country hiking is an extension of this process, using something other than a trail as a reference. Stream beds and ridge lines make good references. Before entering a given piece of country, establish a baseline by referring to your map. A baseline is a linear feature such as a major road or highway which forms a boundary along one side of your hiking area. If you then become totally disoriented while in the area, you can use your compass to follow a course toward your baseline. Traveling to your baseline may be out of your way, but it will get you out of the backcountry as a last resort. Of course, cross-country travel in some areas such as Grand Canyon is so difficult that travel to a baseline would be impractical.

## Trail Courtesy

Never cut switchbacks on trails. Short cutting actually takes more effort and increases erosion and trail maintenance needs. Give horses and other pack animals the right of way by stepping off the trail downhill. Don't make sudden movements or loud noises, which can spook an animal. Talk in a normal tone of voice.

Smokers should stop at a bare spot or rock ledge, then make certain that all smoking materials are out before continuing. Due to fire hazard, it is actually illegal to smoke while moving in a national forest. Never smoke, or light any kind of fire, on windy days or when the fire danger is high. When the fire danger is extreme, wildfires start easily and spread very rapidly.

Dogs are best left at home. Barking dogs disturb other hikers, and dogs can place stress on beleaguered wildlife. Dogs are not allowed on trails in national parks and monuments.

There are too many of us in the backcountry now for many outdated practices that were once reasonable. This includes cutting live trees or plants of any kind, blazing or carving initials on trees or rocks, picking wildflowers, and building rock campfire rings.

Never disturb ruins and other old sites and artifacts. These sites are protected by the federal Antiquities Act to preserve our historic and prehistoric heritage. Archaeologists study artifacts in place because the setting reveals much more information than the artifact alone. Once a site is disturbed, another piece of the puzzle is gone forever.

Motorized vehicles and bicycles, including mountain bikes, are prohibited in all wilderness areas and are allowed only on roads in national parks and monuments. State parks and other areas may also have restrictions.

# MAKING IT A SAFE TRIP

Wilderness is a safe place to be. Nature is indifferent to hikers, in the sense that there are neither malevolent or beneficial forces. The hiker must be self reliant, but there is no need to be paranoid. Once a hiker develops confidence in his or her techniques, abilities, and equipment, then operating in the backcountry becomes a welcome relief from the complex tangle of civilized living. Wilderness decisions are usually important but also basic in nature. While "out there," things that seemed important in civilization lose some of their urgency. In other words, we gain a sense of perspective.

Many wilderness accidents are caused when individuals or parties push too hard. Set reasonable goals, allowing for delays from weather, deteriorated trails, unexpectedly rough country, and dry springs. Be flexible enough to eliminate part of a hike if it appears that your original plans are too ambitious.

## Insects and Their Kin

Scorpions and spiders are actually a greater hazard in Arizona than are snakes. The small, straw-colored desert scorpion likes to lurk under rocks and logs and can give a sting that is life-threatening to children. The black widow spider, identifiable by the red hourglass-shaped mark on its underside, can inflict a dangerous bite. A brown spider bite causes extensive damage at the site but is not generally threatening. These stings or bites are not painful at first but may become very painful after several hours. More painful stings result from the less dangerous and more common scorpions. There is no specific field treatment; young children should be transported to a hospital as soon as possible.

Scorpions and spiders can be almost completely avoided by taking a few simple precautions. Avoid placing your hands and feet where you cannot see. Kick over rocks or logs before moving them with your hands. Don't unpack your sleeping bag before you need it in the evening, and always shake out clothing and footwear in the morning before putting it on.

Insects such as bees, wasps, and the like give painful but non-threatening stings. The exception is for people who suffer an allergic reaction to specific insect stings; about forty people die each year from allergic reactions to bee stings. If you know that you are allergic, carry an insect sting kit prescribed by your doctor.

A new hazard has recently appeared in the Southwest, the Africanized honey bee. These bees were accidentally introduced into Brazil in the 1960s and have since spread north to Texas and Arizona. As of this writing (December 1993) the bees had reached the Phoenix area. Because of their tropical origins, Africanized bees are sensitive to cold and will not likely become numerous in the mountains and on the Colorado Plateau. It is possible that a hiker could encounter Africanized bees in the southern, lower area of this book's coverage. Popularly known as "killer" bees, they have been responsible for about one thousand human deaths in the western hemisphere and one known death in the United States (in Texas). In comparison, the common European honey bees cause about one hundred deaths per year in the United States. Although the Africanized bee's venom is no more toxic than the

European honeybees, they are more aggressive in defending their hives and will sometimes swarm on or chase an intruder. The hazard to a person who is allergic to bee stings is obvious. Every documented fatal case in the Western hemisphere has involved such an allergic individual or someone who was infirm or otherwise unable to escape. Until we have more experience with the bees, the best advice seems to be to avoid all bee hives (including cultivated bees). Especially avoid swarming bees. If attacked, protect your eyes and run away (drop your pack if necessary). If shelter such as a tent, car, or building is available, use it. The bees don't pursue more than one-half mile.

## Snakes

Rattlesnakes easily can be avoided. They usually warn off intruders by rattling well before the person reaches striking range. Never handle or tease any snake. Since rattlesnakes can strike no further than half their body length, avoid placing your hands and feet in areas you cannot see, and walk several feet away from rock overhangs and shady ledges. Bites usually occur on the feet or ankles; ankle-high hiking boots and loose fitting long pants will stop most bites. Snakes prefer surfaces at about eighty degrees Fahrenheit, so during hot weather they prefer the shade of bushes or rock overhangs and in cool weather will be found sunning themselves on open ground.

The Sonoran coral snake is found only in the low desert and is so small that it would have difficulty biting a human. All other snakes in Arizona are nonpoisonous, though they may bite if handled. Rattlesnakes inject their venom through a pair of hollow

*The ponderosa pine forest on the Coconino Plateau is home to many different creatures.*

fangs, which will leave two puncture wounds in addition to the teeth marks.

A large lizard, the Gila monster, injects a venom similar to that of rattlesnakes. A rare and elusive reptile about a foot long, the Gila monster is only likely to bite if handled or molested. Don't let its torpid appearance fool you—it can move very fast. Gila monsters are also protected by state law.

You should carry a snake bite kit during the warm half of the year. Any time common lizards are active, then rattlesnakes probably are as well. Current medical opinion seems to agree that infection is as great a hazard as the venom. The amount of venom injected can vary greatly, and many bites, especially the warning bites most likely to be inflicted on a hiker, have no venom at all. A good snake bite kit containing a suction syringe can be used to remove some venom immediately after the bite and to disinfect the wound site. Follow the instructions included with the kit, then get the victim to a hospital as soon as possible.

## Wildlife

Wild animals will normally leave you alone unless molested or provoked. Don't ever feed any wild animals, as they rapidly get used to the handouts and then will vigorously defend their new food source. Around camp, problems with rodents can be avoided by hanging your food from rocks or trees. Even the toughest pack can be wrecked by a determined mouse or squirrel who has all night to work. Heavily used campsites present the worst problems.

*Poison ivy in Secret Canyon. It is easily recognized by its three glossy leaves and its favored habitat of cool, moist stream beds and dry washes.*

## Plants

Poison ivy is the only common plant in northern Arizona that is poisonous to the touch. It is easily recognized by its shiny leaves that grow in groups of three. Spiny plants like cactus are easy to avoid. Never eat any plant unless you know what you are doing. Many common plants, especially mushrooms, are deadly.

## Weather

During summer, hot weather can be a hazard. The lower desert areas may reach temperatures of 115 degrees Fahrenheit (45 degrees Celsius), and heat exhaustion and heat stroke are real possibilities. In very hot weather, it is best to hike in the higher, cooler areas or to do hikes near streams so that water is readily available. In hot weather, a gallon or more of drinking water will be needed by each hiker every day. To avoid dehydration, drink more water than required to quench your thirst. Electrolyte replacement drinks are also useful.

Protection from the heat and the sun is important. Most people find a lightweight sun hat vital for desert hiking. During hot weather hike early in the day to avoid the afternoon heat. Summer backpack trips can be planned to take advantage of the long days by hiking from first light to midmorning, taking a long, shady lunch break, and then finishing the day's walk in early evening when it cools off. At dusk, keep an eye out for rattlesnakes, because they are active in the evening during hot weather.

Summer thunderstorms commonly develop during the afternoons in July, August, and September in northern Arizona. Since much hiking is in the mountains, lightning can present a hazard. Less obvious are the hazards associated with sudden heavy rain, which include flash flooding and rapid temperature drops. Keep in mind that the mountains are eroded mostly during spring runoff and flash floods. Avoid camping in stream beds and dry washes.

Snow may fall at any time of year on the higher mountains. Be prepared by bringing more warm clothing than you think you will need. During the cooler season, wear synthetic garments made of polypropylene or polyester fibers. These fibers retain their insulating ability when wet better than any natural fiber, including wool. Avoid continuous exposure to chilling weather, which may subtly lower body temperature and cause sudden collapse from hypothermia, a life-threatening condition. Cool winds, especially with rain, are the most dangerous because the heat loss is insidious. Hypothermia may be prevented by wearing enough layers of clothing to avoid chilling, resting to prevent exhaustion, and by eating and drinking regularly to fuel the body.

For excellent information on outdoor health hazards and field treatment, refer to *Medicine for Mountaineering*, listed in Further Reading.

## Rescue

Anyone entering remote country should be self sufficient and be prepared to take care of problems like equipment failure and minor medical problems. Very rarely, circumstances may create a life-threatening situation that requires an emergency evacuation or a search effort. Always leave word of your hiking plans with a reliable individual or local ranger station. For multi-day trips, you should provide a written itinerary. The responsible person should be advised to contact the appropriate authority if you do not return on time. In your instructions, allow extra time for routine delays. In the region covered by this book, the authority responsible for search and rescue in all areas except national parks and monuments is the county sheriff. In the national parks and monuments, the authority is the National Park Service.

## Camping

Well before dark, start looking for a campsite, unless you are going to a familiar site. Campsites become harder to find as the group size increases, a good reason to avoid groups larger than five or six people. The best camps are on level sites with dry, sandy soil, on bare rock, or on pine needles. Avoid grassy meadows and other fragile sites, because grass takes a long time to grow in this dry climate. If bad weather threatens, look for a campsite sheltered from wind and blowing rain, with good drainage. Never dig drainage ditches or engage in extensive leveling of tent or bed sites. With modern sleeping bags and pads, it is possible to camp on gravel or even rock slabs in comfort. In hot weather, look for shade, especially from the morning sun. In ponderosa pine forest, check overhead for "widowmakers," large dead branches that may break off and crash down.

Dry camping is an art that can greatly expand your choice of camp sites. It's possible to camp overnight with two quarts per person as long as the weather isn't too warm. Food and cooking are the main water consumers. In warm weather, consider leaving the stove at home and eating only lunch-type munchies for all meals. In cool weather, where a hot meal will be appreciated, plan low water dinners for the nights

*Many times it is possible to camp without a tent and enjoy a bedroom with fifty-mile views.*

that will be spent at a dry camp. Stove cookery is much better than campfire cookery at dry camps, because dish washing takes much less water. Of course, no one is going to do much personal washing up at a dry camp, but wilderness bathing is much more pleasant during a sunny lunch stop than at a chilly night camp anyway.

## Campfires

Although many hikers enjoy the freedom and relaxation of cooking meals on a backpacker's stove, for others a campfire is an essential part of the experience. In some situations campfires should not be built. These include heavily used areas, near timberline or in the desert where wood is scarce, and where prohibited by regulation. During the summer the fire danger may be extreme, and no fire should be built on a windy day. Most of the time, it is possible to be a responsible hiker and still have a campfire. Use an established campfire ring if available. Otherwise look for a site in gravel, sand, or bare soil. Then dig a shallow pit, heaping the dirt around the edges to form a wind and fire break. Do not use stones, which become permanently blackened. Collect dead wood from the ground and take only sticks no thicker than your wrist. If you need an ax or a saw, then the wood is too large or too scarce. Keep your fire small, both to avoid using large amounts of wood and to keep the amount of ashes small. Backpacker's trash is so light it can be easily carried out; don't try to burn it. Note that many paper packages are lined with aluminum foil, which does not burn in any campfire, no matter how hot. Plastic also does not burn well and may give off highly toxic fumes.

When ready to leave camp, make certain the fire is cold by mixing in water or dirt and stirring until there is no obvious smoke or heat. Then check carefully with your bare hand. Last, cover the fire pit with the dirt from the original pit and scatter any remaining wood. After a short time, your fire site will again look natural.

## Trash

If you carried it in, you can also carry it out. Lightweight food that has been carefully repackaged to eliminate excess packaging produces little trash even after a week or more in the backcountry. Do not bury food or trash; animals will find it by smell shortly after you leave and dig it up.

## Sanitation

Wilderness sanitation is the most critical skill needed to keep the backcountry pristine. A walk in any popular recreation area will show that few people seem to know how to relieve themselves away from facilities. In some areas naturally occurring diseases such as giardiasis are being aggravated by poor human sanitation. Fortunately the rules are simple and easy to learn. If facilities are available, use them. Their presence means that the human population of the area is too large for the natural disposal systems of the soil. Where outhouses are absent, select a site at least one hundred yards from streams, lakes, and springs, and away from dry washes. Then dig a small "cat hole" about six inches into the organic layer of the soil. Some people carry a small plastic trowel for this purpose. Avoid barren, sandy soil if possible, but also do not unduly disturb vegetation. When finished, fill the hole, covering any toilet paper.

# USING THIS GUIDE

*Hike Descriptions*

Each hike description contains the following information:

The heading and the map both have the hike number and name. The hike number is also indicated on the Overview Map.

**General description**
This describes the type of hike (day hike or backpack trip), and the general area (mountain range, canyon, etc.).

**General location**
This is the approximate driving distance from the nearest major town.

**Maps**
Here are listed the topographic and planimetric maps that will be most useful for finding the trailhead and on the hike. In some cases the trail is not shown on the topographic map; this is noted later in the hike description.

**Difficulty**
All the hikes are rated as easy, moderate, or difficult. An easy hike is one with little elevation change, covering short distances, normally on a maintained trail. Nearly anyone should be able to do these hikes. Moderate hikes should also be within most people's abilities, but will be longer and have more elevation change, and so require more effort. The hiker should be prepared to spend part or all of a day on a moderate hike. Hikes rated difficult involve major elevation change, long distances, and possibly cross-country hiking. These hikes should be attempted only by experienced hikers. Please be aware that the perceived difficulty of a hike varies with the individual hiker, the load being carried, the season and weather, and the amount of recent trail maintenance.

**Length**
The length of a hike is the distance one way or around a loop in miles. Because trail distances are difficult to measure precisely in the field, the emphasis here is on landmarks for locating important features such as trail junctions, water sources, and campsites. Trail signs are noted if they were present when I last did the hike, but don't rely on any sign being in place.

**Elevation**
Here are listed the minimum and maximum elevations, in feet, that will be encountered on the hike. The minimum and maximum do not necessarily occur at the ends of the trail. If the hike is a descent (into a canyon, for example) that requires a climb

on the return, then the highest elevation is listed first. Keep in mind that some of the hikes are at elevations of 10,000 feet or more, and the thin air may affect your hiking ability.

## Special attractions
Reasons to do the hike!

## Water
This is a list of reliable water sources such as springs and streams. All backcountry water should be purified before use by boiling, treating with reliable chemicals, or filtering. Don't ever depend on a single water source, especially in hot weather.

## Best season
This is the recommended time of year to do the hike. In unusual years, the hiking season may be longer or shorter than indicated. Hikes which are noted as "all year" may be hot during midsummer; be certain to carry enough water.

## Information
This is the specific government office that manages the area of the hike. Refer to the Resources list on page 172 for the complete address and phone number.

## Permits
As of this writing, hiking permits are required only in Grand Canyon National Park. None of the other areas covered in this book require a hiking permit. During the dry seasons of April through June and in October, campfires, charcoal fires, and smoking may be prohibited on national forests and in national parks and monuments. Such restrictions are usually posted on Forest Service roads, but check with the office listed under "Information" for the current fire danger if you have any doubt.

## Finding the trailhead
Driving directions are given to the trailhead from the nearest large town (normally the same town mentioned under General Description). For one-way hikes requiring a car shuttle, both trailheads are described. Forest Service road numbers are noted, where present, as FR 234 and FH 3 (Forest Road 234 and Forest Highway 3, respectively).

## The hike
A description of the trail or cross-country route and any points of interest, as well as relevant natural and human history. Forest Service trail numbers, if mentioned, are abbreviated as FT 103, for example.

# GRAND CANYON

Nearly three hundred miles long and averaging ten miles wide, the Grand Canyon is truly the master canyon of the Colorado Plateau. A lifetime can easily be spent exploring its depths. Descending through the layered geology of the canyon, hikers will also travel southward in climate. On the South Rim, mixed ponderosa pine and pinyon-juniper forest mark the transition life zone. Midway in the descent, trails pass through the upper Sonoran life zone, identifiable by its pygmy forest of junipers. Near the river, hikers reach the lower Sonoran life zone, characterized by low desert shrubs and grasses.

Spanish conquistadors under the command of Coronado riding north from Mexico City in the early 1540s were the first Europeans to visit the Grand Canyon. They probably reached the South Rim somewhere between the present Tanner and Grandview trailheads. A number of days were spent trying to find a way to the Colorado River, without success. Undoubtedly their native guide knew of several routes, but chose to keep the information to himself. Over two hundred years would pass before Europeans would see the Canyon again. During the 1840s, mountain men roamed the Southwest in search of beaver, but apparently none got below the rims of the Canyon. The first scientific exploration of the great canyon was carried out by Major John Wesley Powell on two Colorado River float trips during 1869-71. His group, one of several government-sponsored surveys of the West, also extensively explored the region surrounding the Canyon. Major Powell named the Grand Canyon and many of its features. After Major Powell's explorations, miners and prospectors began to establish trails into the canyon. Most of them eventually found that guiding tourists into the canyon was more profitable than mining.

Several of the best trail hikes in the Canyon are featured in this section. These are historic trails that have been abandoned and receive only minimum maintenance. It is strongly suggested that hikers carry topographic maps on these hikes, as sections of trail may not be obvious. The Grand Canyon hikes are in Grand Canyon National Park, and overnight hikes require a free hiking permit that can be obtained from the backcountry office on the south rim. Hike reservations can be made in person at the backcountry office or in advance by mail. For information contact the National Park Service at the address listed under Public Agencies (p. 172). Campfires are not allowed in the park backcountry, so plan to cook on a backpacking stove.

# HIKE 1 *BOUCHER-HERMIT TRAILS*

**General description:** A three- to five-day backpack trip in the Grand Canyon.
**General location:** 8 miles west of Grand Canyon Village.
**Maps:** Grand Canyon 7.5-minute USGS.
**Difficulty:** Difficult.
**Length:** 18-mile loop.
**Elevation:** 6,700 to 2,800 feet.
**Special attractions:** Loop hike on historic trails.

*Hiking the Tonto Trail in the Grand Canyon.*

**Water:** Boucher Creek, Hermit Creek.
**Best season:** Fall through spring.
**Permit:** Required for overnight hikes.
**Information:** Grand Canyon National Park.
**Finding the trailhead:** From Grand Canyon Village drive west 4.5 miles to the end of the West Rim Drive. The signed trailhead for the Hermit Trail is west of the main parking area. During summer the road is closed to private vehicles, and access is via the free West Rim Shuttle bus. When you get your hiking permit from the park service also ask about the shuttle schedule. A hiker's special usually runs early in the morning.

**The hike:** In hot weather carry plenty of water as it is a long hike to the first water at Boucher Creek. Keep in mind that the temperature rises as you descend. One gallon per person is not excessive. In cool weather two quarts per person is sufficient.

Descend into the Canyon on the Hermit Trail, which is named in honor of Louis Boucher, a solitary prospector who constructed the nearby Boucher Trail to reach his mines at Boucher Creek. After a few switchbacks through the cliff-forming Kaibab limestone and the sloping Toroweap formation, the trail turns west and descends into Hermit Basin. Impressive trail construction was done in the Coconino sandstone, where the trail was paved with slabs of rock set on edge. Crossbedded layers of rock and sandblasting of the individual grains of sand prove that the Coconino sandstone

# HIKE 1  *BOUCHER-HERMIT TRAILS*

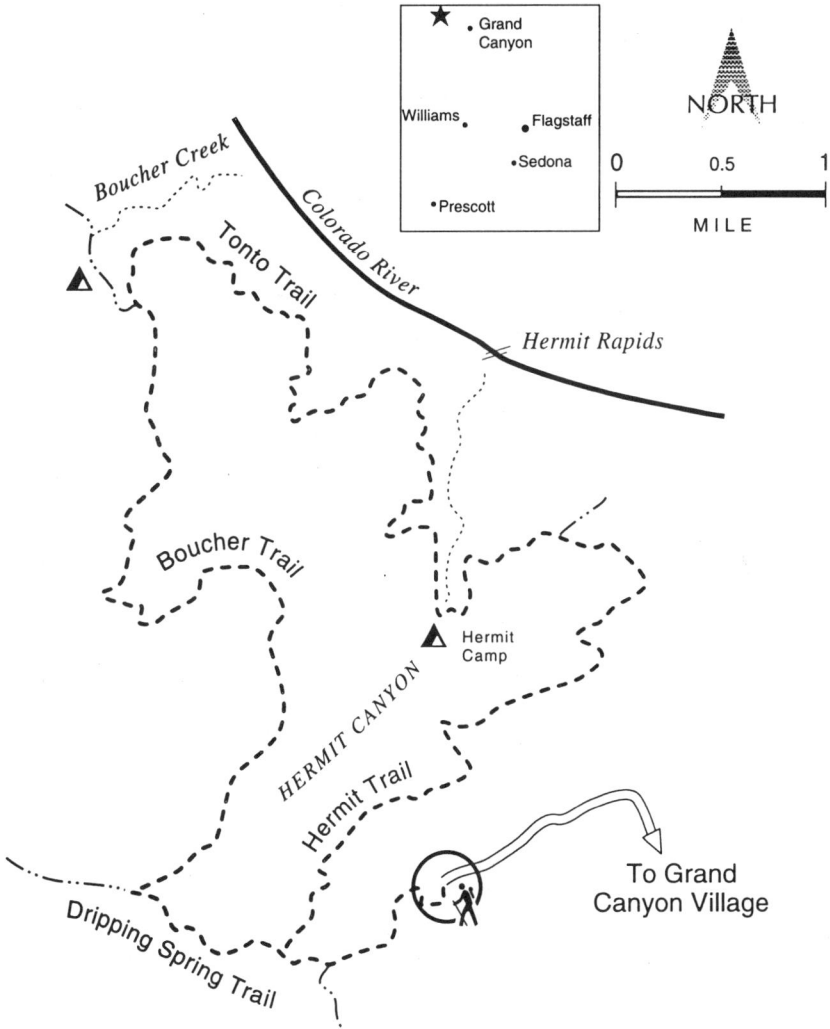

had its origin in a Sahara-like sand dune desert. Watch for fossil dinosaur tracks along this section of the trail as well.

In Hermit Basin, the trail passes the signed junction with the Waldron Trail, then meets the signed Dripping Spring Trail 1.2 miles from the rim. Turn left (west) and follow the Dripping Spring Trail as it contours around the head of Hermit Canyon. There are impressive views down this narrow gorge. After one mile, turn right (north) on the Boucher Trail, which continues to contour on the top of the red Esplanade sandstone. The trail stays on this level past Yuma Point, giving a view of the Hermit Trail and Hermit Canyon to the east. The soft, red Hermit shale forms this terrace, which the trail remains on until it takes advantage of a break in the cliffs below to descend. About 0.6 mile west of Yuma Point, the trail finds the break and descends abruptly through the layered, red Esplanade and Supai sandstones as it drops to the head of Travertine Canyon. After passing through the saddle south of Whites Butte, it descends the massive Redwall limestone cliff through a fault to the north. The Redwall limestone is actually a translucent gray rock composed entirely of the shells of millions of microscopic animals. These tiny ocean animals died and fell to the deep sea floor as a constant rain. The Redwall gets its name from the red stain that seeps down from the overlying red formations, coating the surface of the cliff.

As the slope moderates, the Boucher Trail descends through the greenish Muav limestone and ends at the junction with the Tonto Trail. Turn left (west) to descend to Boucher Creek, where there is water and campsites. If time allows, it is easy to walk cross-country about two miles to the Colorado River by descending Boucher Creek into the granite gorge. Boucher Rapid is small on the Grand Canyon scale but impressive nevertheless.

The loop hike continues on the Tonto Trail to the north and east. From the rim the Tonto Trail looks flat, but it constantly climbs and descends to avoid small drainages. It zigs into side canyons, and zags back out again. Allow plenty of time when hiking this section, especially since the occasional views of the Granite Gorge and the Colorado River are distracting. The trail follows the Tonto Plateau, formed from the greenish-purple Bright Angel shale, which is soft and erodes into slopes rather than cliffs. The trail skirts the head of Travertine Canyon, where huge deposits of travertine rock indicate the past presence of a large natural spring, now dry. After Travertine it swings into Hermit Canyon, to reach Hermit Camp after 4.4 miles.

There is always water in Hermit Creek and also a designated campsite. The cross-country side hike down Hermit Canyon is about 1.5 miles, and descends through the remaining rock formations to the Colorado River. The rim of lower Hermit Creek is formed by the Tapeats sandstone, a rock that was formed from beach sand. The somber dark gray rocks of the gorge are Vishnu schist, one of the oldest rocks on Earth. The hard, twisted schist is the roots of an ancient mountain range that has been entirely eroded away, leaving the nearly flat surface on which rests the Tapeats sandstone. The side canyon ends at Hermit Rapid, one of the largest in the Grand Canyon. For modern river craft, Hermit Rapid is fun but not challenging because the water is deep and free of rocks. At high water the waves reach heights of twenty feet or more. During the walk along Hermit Creek you'll see sections of trail construction from the tourist resort days. Up until about 1930, Hermit Camp on the Tonto Trail at Hermit Creek was the primary tourist resort in the Grand Canyon. A long aerial tram from Pima Point was used to ferry supplies to the camp. A Model T Ford was even sent down and used on a short network of roads. When the transcanyon Kaibab Trail was completed, the focus quickly switched to the Bright Angel Creek area, the present site of Phantom Ranch resort.

From Hermit Camp start the ascent out of the canyon by hiking northeast on the Tonto Trail. It is one mile to the junction with the Hermit Trail, where you turn right (east). At first the climb is gentle but the grade rapidly becomes steeper as the trail picks its way up the shale slopes. At the foot of the Redwall limestone, the trail begins a series of short switchbacks known as the Cathedral Stairs. At the top of the Redwall, the trail then swings southwest around Breezy Point and passes a section where the original horse trail was destroyed by a landslide. The trail climbs slowly until south of Breezy Point, where it takes advantage of a weakness in the Supai sandstone cliffs and abruptly climbs to the base of the Esplanade sandstone. (Breezy Point is an easy, short side hike with great views of Hermit Camp.) An old rest house marks Santa Maria Spring, which usually has water. Shortly after the spring, the Hermit Trail climbs through the Esplanade sandstone and passes the Dripping Spring Trail junction, 4.1 miles from the Tonto Trail. Turn left (east) and continue on the Hermit Trail 1.2 miles to the rim and the trailhead.

# HIKE 2 *HORSESHOE MESA*

**General description:** A day hike in the Grand Canyon.
**General location:** 11 miles east of Grand Canyon Village.
**Maps:** Grandview Point 7.5-minute, Cape Royal 7.5-minute USGS.
**Difficulty:** Moderate.
**Length:** 2 miles one way.
**Elevation:** 7,400 to 4,700 feet.
**Special attractions:** Historic mining district.
**Water:** None.
**Best season:** Fall and spring.
**Permit:** Required for overnight hikes.
**Information:** Grand Canyon National Park.
**Finding the trailhead:** From Grand Canyon Village drive south on the main park road then turn east on the East Rim Drive. Eleven miles from the Village, turn left (north) on the signed Grandview Point road and park in the signed trailhead parking.

**The hike:** Although this a strenuous hike, it should be no problem for experienced hikers. Keep in mind that the short distance is deceiving; the trail ascends 2,700 feet in 2 miles—an arduous climb by any standards—on the return trip. The Grandview Trail is well named, as it features an expansive view right from its start at the east side of the stone wall at the viewpoint. A series of switchbacks leads through the cliffs of the Kaibab limestone and out onto the steep slopes of the Toroweap Formation. Clever trail construction is used in sections through the Coconino sandstone. Parts of the trail are paved with blocks of sandstone fitted on edge, and in other places the trail is built up with log cribbing. These places can be exciting when a winter storm leaves two feet of snow on the trail.

After reaching the red slopes of the Hermit shale, the trail descends east, then north around the head of Cottonwood Creek, and finally comes out onto Horseshoe Mesa. When you reach the top of the Redwall limestone, it appears that you should be on the same level as Horseshoe Mesa, which is formed on the upper surface of the Redwall. But the trail descends yet another two hundred feet onto the mesa. This difference is caused by displacement along the Grandview Fault, which the trail crosses as it drops onto Horseshoe Mesa. The campground is near the abandoned Last Chance Mine, which is interesting to explore. The old copper mine was estab-

*The old Grandview Trail traverses the ledge midway in this photo.*

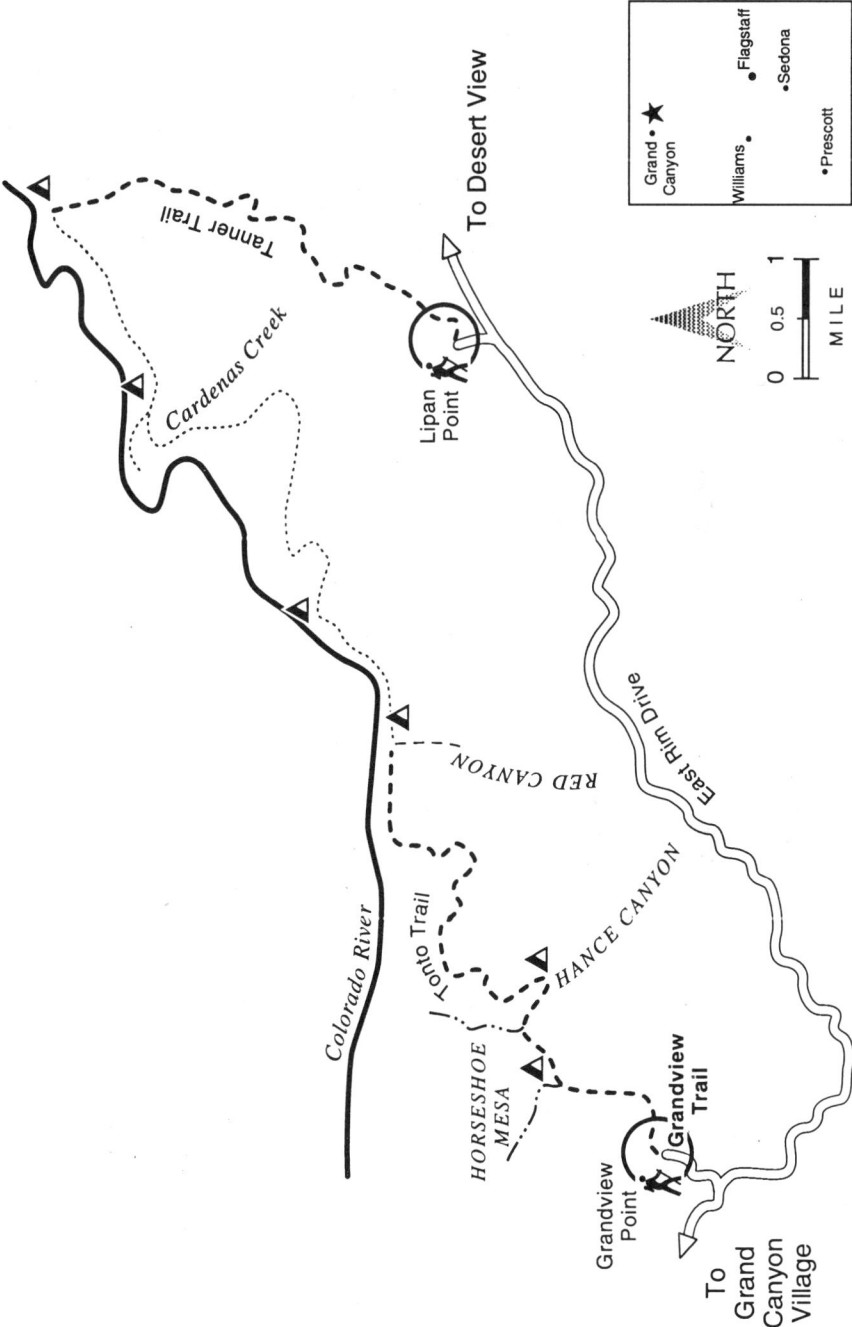

To Desert View

Tanner Trail

Cardenas Creek

Colorado River

Lipan Point

RED CANYON

East Rim Drive

Tonto Trail

HANCE CANYON

HORSESHOE MESA

Grandview Trail

Grandview Point

To Grand Canyon Village

NORTH

0    0.5    1

MILE

Grand Canyon ★

Williams •

• Flagstaff

• Sedona

• Prescott

lished by Pete Berry before the turn of the century, and the Grandview Trail was constructed to service the mine. The stone cookhouse still stands several hundred yards north of the campground. A vertical shaft on the mesa provided air to one of the mines, but the main access was via a horizontal shaft just below the rim to the southeast. Another shaft is located near the base of the Redwall limestone farther to the east. Water was obtained either from Miners Spring or a spring in Cottonwood Creek.

# HIKE 3 *TANNER-GRANDVIEW TRAILS*

**General description:** A four-day backpack trip on trail and cross country in the Grand Canyon.
**General location:** 16 miles east of Grand Canyon Village.
**Maps:** Desert View 7.5-minute, Cape Royal 7.5-minute, Grandview Point 7.5-minute USGS.
**Difficulty:** Difficult.
**Length:** 24.7 miles one way.
**Elevation:** 7,400 to 2,600 feet.
**Special attractions:** Interesting geology on two of the most scenic trails in the park.
**Water:** Colorado River, Hance Creek, Miners Spring.
**Best season:** Spring and fall.
**Permit:** Required for overnight hikes.
**Information:** Grand Canyon National Park.
**Finding the trailhead:** This one-way hike requires a car shuttle. To reach Grandview Point, the end of the hike, follow the directions under the Horseshoe Mesa Trail (Hike 2).

To reach the start of the hike, from Grand Canyon Village drive south on the main park road, then turn left (east) on the East Rim Drive. Continue fourteen miles, then turn left (north) at the signed Lipan Point turnoff and park in the parking lot.

**The hike:** The Tanner Trailhead is signed on the east side of the parking lot to the south of the viewpoint. A steep series of switchbacks descends rapidly through the rim formations to the saddle at the head of Seventyfive Mile Creek. After the confinement of the upper section of the trail, the sudden view to the west is startling. The trail now contours around Escalante and Cardenas Buttes on the gentle slopes of the red Supai sandstone. At the north end of Cardenas Butte, the trail drops abruptly through the Redwall limestone in a series of switchbacks, then works its way through the greenish Muav limestone and greenish-purple Bright Angel shale slopes. Massive fallen blocks of Tapeats sandstone mark the level of the rim of the Granite Gorge in the central Grand Canyon, but here the gorge is replaced by rolling hills. As the Tanner Trail descends the long ridge running north to the Colorado River, the reason for the change in the canyon's topography is apparent. In the central Canyon, the hard Vishnu schist is found at this level, and the resistant rock forms cliffs. Here, the softer shales of the Grand Canyon series replace the Vishnu schist, and these erode into relatively gentle slopes and valleys.

There are a few small campsites scattered around the mouth of Tanner Canyon

*Near the end of the Tanner Trail at the Colorado River.*

at the Colorado River. The route now turns south, and follows the bench just above the river. Although there has never been a formal trail between Tanner Canyon and Red Canyon, enough hikers have traveled the route in recent years to create a trail most of the way. Tanner Rapid, visible below, is shallow and rocky and creates more of a problem for river boats than some of the larger rapids. After skirting a narrow section where the river presses against its left bank, the trail moves inland and follows the foot of the shale slopes to the mouth of Cardenas Creek. Campsites are more plentiful here than back at the mouth of Tanner Canyon.

The trail crosses Cardenas Creek, but dead ends with a view of Unkar Rapid, which makes it a worthwhile side trip of about a mile round trip. Our route goes up the dry bed of Cardenas Creek about 0.2 mile, then leaves the bed to climb onto the ridge above the river. Walk to the west edge for a spectacular view of Unkar Creek Rapid, two hundred feet straight down. Now, turn south and climb the gentle red shale ridge directly toward Escalante Butte. Stay on the crest of the ridge to pick up the trail again as the ridge narrows. The trail turns west and skirts the head of the nameless canyon west of Cardenas Creek at about the 3,800 foot level. After rounding the west end of the point, it turns back to the east to descend into Escalante Creek. Walk down the bed of Escalante Creek, then leave the bed at about the 3,200 foot level (there is an impassable fall farther downstream) and climb through a low saddle to the south. Descend into the unnamed south fork of Escalante Creek and follow it to the Colorado River (a barrier fall has an obvious bypass on the left).

*Hance Rapid on the Colorado River at the lower end of Red Canyon, Grand Canyon National Park.*

Turn left along the river's left bank. Notice how a rising ramp of hard rock forms a cliff right into the river and forces our route to climb. The bench is Shinumo quartzite, a resistant layer of rock near the bottom of the Grand Canyon series. As the river rolls downstream through this section, the rocks at river level become harder and the gorge becomes more steeply walled and deeper. The contrast between this section and the river valley at the foot of the Tanner Trail is already impressive, but the narrowest section is still downstream. After about 0.5 mile, the route reaches the rim of Seventyfive Mile Canyon and turns east along the edge of the narrow, impassable gorge. About 0.4 mile up this side canyon, the route drops into the bed and follows it back to the river, passing almost directly underneath the trail two hundred feet above. At the river, turn left (downstream) again and walk about 0.6 mile along the easy beach to the mouth of Papago Creek. There are several good campsites here for small groups.

Just downstream from Papago Creek, a cliff falls directly into the river and appears to block the route. Go up Papago Creek a few yards and climb up a steep gully, which will require some scrambling. Work your way up easier ledges above to a point about three hundred feet above the river, then traverse east. If you are on the correct level you will be able to reach the head of a steep gully that can be used to descend to river level. The usual error is to traverse too low. If this happens retrace your steps until you can climb to a higher level. Once the river is reached a good trail follows the bank to the mouth of Red Canyon.

There is limited, sandy camping at Red Canyon. The Red Canyon Trail goes up the bed here and could be used for an early exit if necessary, but is steeper and harder to follow than the Grandview Trail. At this point start on the Tonto Trail, which climbs the slopes to the west. The view of mile-long Hance Rapid is great. Hance is one of the hardest Grand Canyon Rapids due to the numerous rocks. As you continue to climb above the river on the Tonto Trail, note the trail climbing the slope on the opposite side of the river. This trail goes to Asbestos Canyon and was used to reach the asbestos mines on the north side of the river.

About a mile from Red Canyon, the Tonto Trail turns south up Mineral Canyon. After crossing the dry canyon bed, the trail turns west again and climbs onto the greenish-gray shale slopes below Ayer Point. This terrace is called the Tonto Plateau and forms a prominent shelf about 1,200 feet above the Colorado River. The rim of the Tonto Plateau is formed from the hard Tapeats sandstone and overlooks the dark, narrow Granite Gorge, already impressive in this area. The Tonto Trail stays on the Tonto Plateau for about sixty miles. After Ayer Point, the Tonto Trail turns south into Hance Canyon along the Tapeats sandstone rim. Hance Creek may be dry where the trail crosses, but there is always water a short distance downstream. There is also camping below the impressive Tapeats narrows.

After crossing Hance Creek, the Tonto Trail continues northwest about 0.5 mile to a side canyon coming from the east side of Horseshoe Mesa. Turn west here, onto the East Grandview Trail. Miners Spring, reached from a spur trail about one mile from the Tonto Trail junction, is reliable. The final section of the trail climbs the high Redwall limestone cliff at the canyon head to reach Horseshoe Mesa and the junction with the main Grandview Trail. There is a backpacker's campground on Horseshoe Mesa, but water must be carried from Miners Spring.

The hike finishes on the Grandview Trail, ending on the rim at Grandview Point. For details, see Horseshoe Mesa (Hike 2).

# COCONINO PLATEAU

The Coconino Plateau is the southernmost portion of the Colorado Plateau and is the area surrounding the San Francisco Peaks north of the Mogollon Rim and south of the Grand Canyon. Several hundred cinder cones and old volcanoes dot the area, ranging in elevation from 8,000 to 12,633 feet. All of the hikes in this section (except for Meteor Crater) explore these old volcanic features. Kendrick Peak, the San Francisco Peaks, and Strawberry Crater are designated wilderness areas, while Meteor Crater is privately owned.

Although the Coconino Plateau was part of New Spain for three hundred years, the Spanish had little to do with it. American mountain men such as Bill Williams were the first to put the Coconino Plateau on the map. When most of Arizona was ceded to the United States in 1848, American exploration intensified. The area south of the San Francisco Peaks received attention because of several good springs that were a vital water source in an otherwise dry landscape. In 1851, a party under U.S. Army Captain Lorenzo Sitgreaves passed through the area south of the San Francisco Peaks, and in 1859 construction started on the Beale Wagon Road. Intended as an emigrant route to California, the Beale Road was used to reach Prescott after the discovery of gold there in 1863. In 1883, the transcontinental railroad line opened along the route of the Beale Road, and the tiny settlement of Flagstaff began to grow.

# HIKE 4 *CLOVER SPRING TRAIL*

**General description:** A day hike on Bill Williams Mountain.
**General location:** 1 mile west of Williams.
**Maps:** Bill Williams Mountain 15-minute USGS, Kaibab National Forest (Williams, Chalender, and Tusayan ranger districts).
**Difficulty:** Easy.
**Length:** 1.1 mile one way.
**Elevation:** 6,880 to 7,040 feet.

## HIKES 4 AND 5 *CLOVER SPRING TRAIL/BENHAM TRAIL*

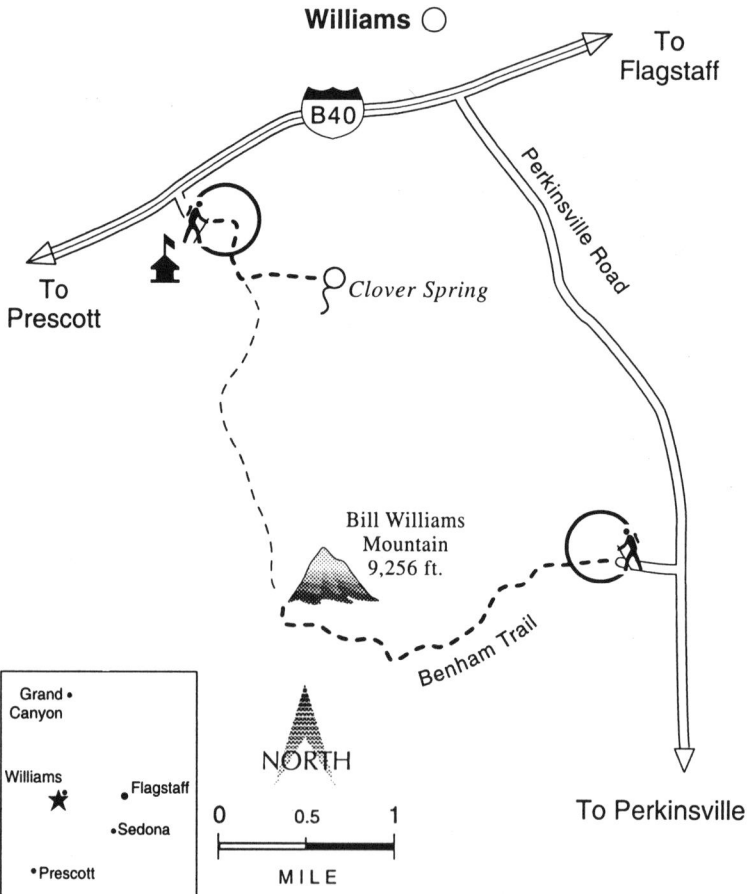

*Clover Spring at the end of the Clover Trail on Bill Williams Mountain.*

**Special attractions:** Pleasant, easy walk through pine-oak forest.
**Water:** Clover Spring.
**Best season:** Spring through fall.
**Information:** Williams Ranger District, Kaibab National Forest.
**Finding the trailhead:** From Williams drive west on Bill Williams Avenue (Business I-40), then just before the I-40 interchange west of town turn left (south) at the signed, paved turnoff for the Forest Service ranger station. Turn left again at the next signed turnoff for the ranger station, then follow the signs to the Bill Williams trailhead adjacent to the ranger station.

**The hike:** The trail is not shown on the topographic map. Follow the signed Bill Williams Trail as it leaves the parking area and crosses a meadow. Shortly the trail begins to climb moderately steeply in a series of switchbacks. The forest is especially fine in this area, with an interesting mixture of the ever-present ponderosa pine, Gambel oaks, alligator junipers, and even a few white fir.

White fir are much less common than Douglas-fir, and seem to favor cool drainage bottoms. Usually white fir can be distinguished from the Douglas-fir by their blue-green color. When white fir are growing next to Douglas-fir, the color difference is obvious; otherwise, you may have to look more closely. White fir cones grow upward from the branches, as do all true firs, while the Douglas-fir cones hang down. Some people also confuse white fir with blue spruce, but if you attempt to roll a few needles in your fingers you'll discover that they are flat. Spruce needles are square in cross section and easily roll in your fingers.

After the switchbacks end and the Bill Williams Trail levels out a bit, watch for an unmarked trail forking left (0.6 mile from the trailhead). Turn left here and follow the excellent trail as it traverses the hillside to the east. Clover Hill is visible ahead to the left through the trees. Another common plant grows along the trail here: the cliffrose. Usually a nondescript shrub that rarely reaches ten feet in height, in early summer it is often covered with a shower of small white flowers.

After a slightly downhill walk through the woods, the trail arrives at Clover Spring, 0.5 mile from the trail fork. Although the spring isn't much more than a slow trickle, it used to be an important water source in the early days of settlement. It supplied water for the ranger station for a time, and is an important water source for wildlife, as are all springs on this dry plateau.

# HIKE 5 *BENHAM TRAIL*

**General description:** A day hike on Bill Williams Mountain. (see map on p. 34).
**General location:** 5 miles south of Williams.
**Maps:** Bill Williams Mountain 15-minute USGS, Kaibab National Forest (Williams, Chalender, and Tusayan ranger districts).
**Difficulty:** Moderate.
**Length:** 8 miles one way.
**Elevation:** 7,240 to 9,256 feet.
**Special attractions:** Well-graded trail, beautiful forest, expansive views.

*The historic Benham Trail.*

**Water:** None.

**Best season:** Late spring through fall.

**Information:** Williams Ranger District, Kaibab National Forest.

**Finding the trailhead:** From Williams drive south on the Perkinsville Road (FR 173). Signs on Williams's main street identify this as the road to the Williams Ski Area. Continue 3.5 miles on this paved road, then turn right (west) on an unsigned dirt road. This dirt road is just before the signed left turn to Dogtown Reservoir. Continue 0.2 mile and turn right just before a gate with private property signs and park at the signed trailhead.

**The hike:** According to the Forest Service sign at the trailhead, the Benham Trail was originally constructed in 1920, then abandoned in 1951 when the present road was opened to the top of the mountain. The trail was reopened in 1976 as a recreation trail and named after H. L. Benham, the forest ranger on the Williams Ranger District from 1910 to 1911. It is not shown on the topographic map.

The Forest Service was created in 1903 to manage the national forest reserves that had been designated in the 1890s. Early forest rangers had their work cut out for them, as they were expected to enforce conservation laws over a vast area with little help.

From the trailhead, the Benham Trail is easy to follow as it wanders up the gentle slope to the west, through an open ponderosa pine and Gambel oak forest. Gambel oaks are deciduous and average only ten to twenty feet in height, with slender gray trunks. About 1.5 miles from the trailhead, the trail skirts the head of a gully then crosses through an ugly but short section of logged forest. Shortly afterward, the trail enters a dense section of Gambel oaks, where there are a few Douglas-firs. Among the Gambel oaks are a few much larger Emory and Arizona white oaks.

The trail begins to climb the southeast side of the mountain in a series of switchbacks, and the quality of the trail is evident in the massive amount of construction. This was probably the main supply trail for the fire lookout tower on the summit, as the slightly shorter Bill Williams Trail (see the *Hikers Guide to Arizona*) is blocked by snow later in the year than the Benham Trail. The trail crosses a switchback in the vehicle road and then reaches the south ridge of the mountain. Continuing to climb in switchbacks, the trail skirts another road switchback, where the Forest Service rerouted the trail. Above this point there is an interesting stand of Gambel oaks that are being crowded out by a young, dense stand of Douglas-fir. The trail crosses the road again, and shortly a small patch of quaking aspen indicates that the end of the trail is near. After a fourth road crossing, a few final switchbacks lead through a stand of small aspen. An unmarked trail to the left leads about fifty feet to the road and the head of the Bill Williams Trail. The Benham trail goes right and ends on the road in about one hundred yards. From here it is 0.5 mile to the summit along the road. The actual summit is crowded with radio buildings and towers.

There are excellent views of the western Coconino Plateau and the Mogollon Rim. Sycamore Canyon is visible to the south, as is Mingus Mountain. The Forest Service fire lookout is manned during high fire danger. Be sure to ask permission from the lookout before climbing the tower.

# HIKE 6 *KEYHOLE SINK TRAIL*

**General description:** A day hike near Sitgreaves Mountain.
**General location:** 11 miles east of Williams.
**Maps:** Williams 15-minute USGS, Kaibab National Forest (Williams, Chalender, and Tusayan ranger districts).
**Difficulty:** Easy.
**Length:** 1 mile one way.
**Elevation:** 7,100 to 6,960 feet.
**Special attractions:** Very easy trail to a petroglyph site.
**Water:** None.
**Best season:** Spring through fall.
**Information:** Chalender Ranger District, Kaibab National Forest.
**Finding the trailhead:** From Williams drive east on I-40 about 8 miles to the Pittman Valley Road exit. Cross the interstate to the north, then turn right (east) on old US 66. Continue 2 miles, then park on the right (south) in the Oak Hill Snowplay Area parking lot.

**The hike:** The signed trail (which is new and not shown on the topographic map) starts on the north side of the road at a gate. It descends very gradually through open ponderosa pine forest and small meadows, then turns northeast and passes a small

# HIKE 6  *KEYHOLE SINK TRAIL*

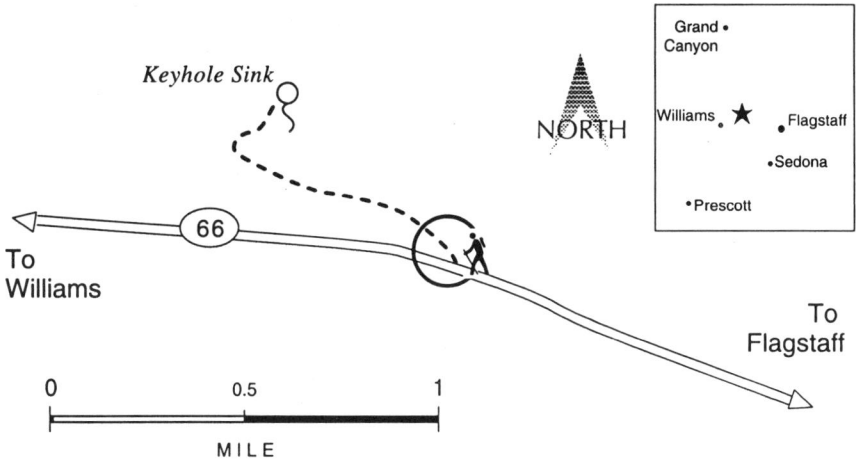

*Keyhole Sink*

66

To
Williams

To
Flagstaff

NORTH

Grand • Canyon

Williams • ★  • Flagstaff
  • Sedona
• Prescott

0        0.5        1

MILE

*Rock-climbers at Keyhole Sink near Sitgreaves Mountain.*

stand of aspen before ending in a box canyon. A rail fence, interpretive sign, and visitor's register mark the spot. The low, colorful volcanic cliffs, the aspens and pines, and the pool of water combine to make this a pleasant spot, especially in the late afternoon sun.

Look carefully to find a number of petroglyphs along the base of the wall. One of these clearly depicts a herd of deer entering the canyon. Usually the exact meaning of ancient rock art is more elusive. Please don't touch or otherwise disturb the petroglyphs; they are protected by federal law as a fragile link to the unwritten past. Such art work is one of the few signs of prehistoric human habitation in this section of the Coconino Plateau. While hunting parties probably passed through from time to time, there is little evidence of any permanent settlement. Probably the short growing season and the lack of water were discouraging.

# HIKE 7 *SYCAMORE RIM TRAIL*

**General description:** A trail and cross-country day hike on the rim of Sycamore Canyon.

**General location:** 28 miles southwest of Flagstaff.

**Maps:** Garland Prairie 7.5-minute USGS, Kaibab National Forest (Williams, Chalender, and Tusayan ranger districts).

**Difficulty:** Easy.

**Length:** 5.1-mile loop.

**Elevation:** 6,700 feet.

**Special attractions:** Easy walk along the rim of Sycamore Canyon and through a historic area.

**Water:** None.

**Best season:** Spring through fall.

**Information:** Chalender Ranger District, Kaibab National Forest.

**Finding the trailhead:** From Flagstaff drive about 16 miles west on I-40, then turn left (south) at the Parks exit onto the graded Garland Prairie Road (FR 141). Drive 12 miles, then turn left (south) on FR 56, a signed, graded road. Continue about 1.5 miles to the fenced, signed trailhead.

From Williams drive east on I-40 about 4 miles, then turn right (south) at the Garland Prairie Road exit (this is not the same exit for Garland Prairie mentioned above). Drive 8.5 miles to reach FR 56, then turn right (south) and continue 1.5 miles to the fenced, signed trailhead.

**The hike:** The Sycamore Rim Trail is a relatively new recreation trail and is not shown on the topographic map. It crosses the road at this trailhead. Follow the trail east, along the shallow valley that forms the head of Sycamore Canyon. After 0.5 mile the trail passes the remains of an old lumber mill. Not much is visible now except a few rotting timbers. Logging camps and mill sites in use around the turn of the century were temporary and were moved to follow the active logging. After the mill site the Rim trail crosses to the east rim and stays there. Gradually the drainage becomes a canyon, with seasonal water and aspen groves as well as beautiful old

# HIKE 7 *SYCAMORE RIM TRAIL*

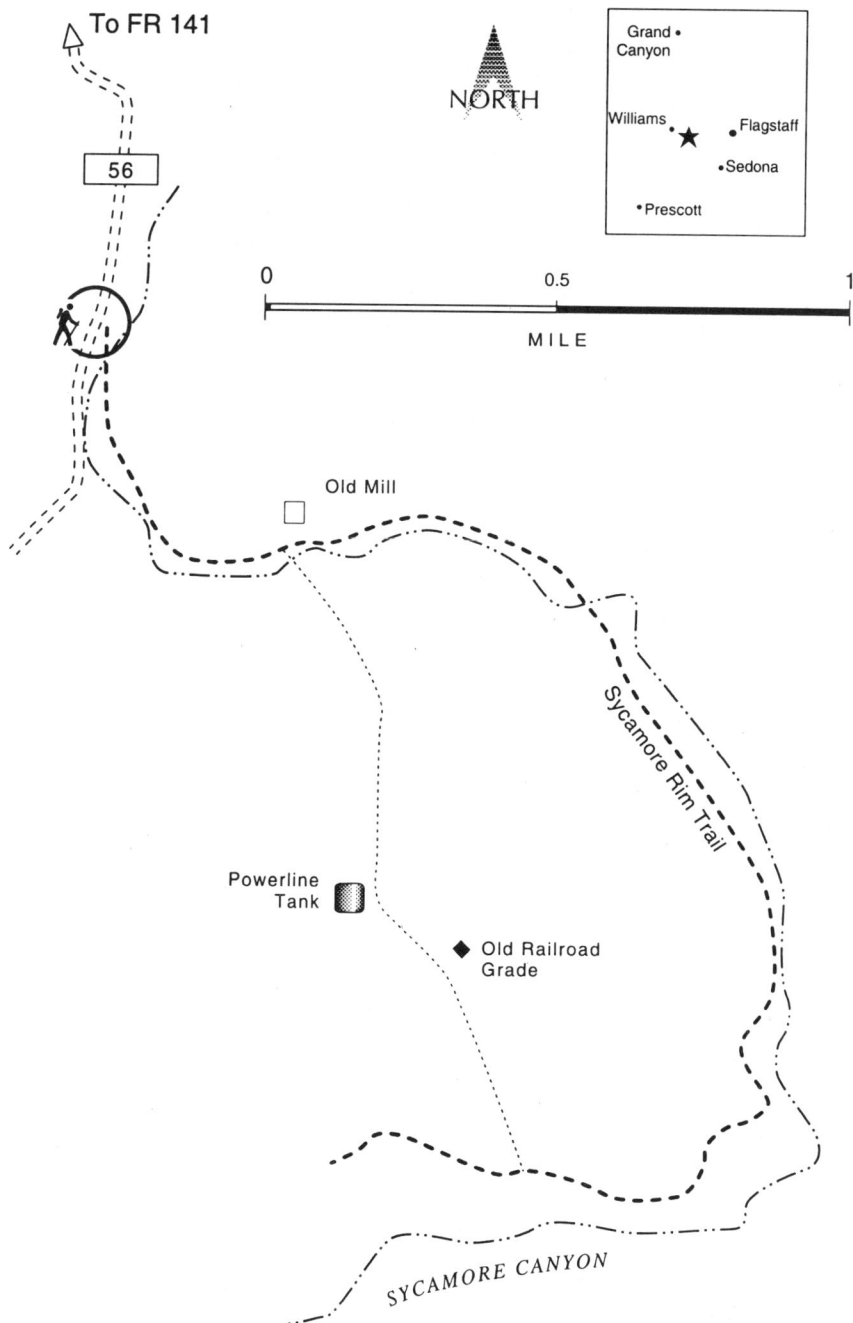

To FR 141

NORTH

Grand Canyon •

Williams •
★
• Flagstaff

• Sedona

• Prescott

56

0        0.5        1

M I L E

Old Mill

Sycamore Rim Trail

Powerline Tank

◆ Old Railroad Grade

*SYCAMORE CANYON*

*Hiking cross country on the return from the Sycamore Rim Trail, you may encounter this old railroad grade.*

pines. After about two miles of hiking, Sycamore Canyon starts to live up to its name. About 3.1 miles from the trailhead, the view opens out to the south, with a great view of Sycamore Canyon and Big Springs Canyon.

Leave the trail here and walk north cross-country into a large meadow. Watch for the remains of an old logging railroad grade that splits into two tracks. The rails are long gone and only the rows of ties mark the route. An unusual number of pines have grown up along the old railroad. Perhaps these came from seeds dropped from the log cars. After the transcontinental railroad reached the area in 1883, railroads were the most economical method of moving cut timber to the mills, as well as men and supplies into the forest. When logging was complete in an area (meaning that all the accessible large trees were cut), the rails would be removed and reused on another spur railroad. The road beds were built to the minimum standard necessary for their short-lived purpose. Today these old railroad grades can be traced for miles through the forest; some have been rebuilt into modern dirt roads.

Follow the old railroad grade to Powerline Tank, a stock tank, then head north across the meadow. At the far north end of the meadow, continue north a few dozen yards through the trees to the rim of Sycamore Canyon, at a point opposite the old mill site. Turn left (west) and walk up the bed of the shallow drainage or cross to the north side and intercept the Sycamore Rim Trail. It is about a mile back to the trailhead.

The cross-country hike from mile 3.1 can be avoided by retracing your steps on the Sycamore Rim Trail, which would make the total hike distance 6.2 miles.

# HIKE 8 *RED MOUNTAIN*

**General description:** A cross-country day hike on the Coconino Plateau.
**General location:** 32 miles northwest of Flagstaff.
**Maps:** Ebert Mtn 15-minute USGS, Coconino National Forest.
**Difficulty:** Easy.
**Length:** 0.5 mile one way.
**Elevation:** 6,900 to 7,050 feet.
**Special attractions:** Colorful, highly eroded volcanic mountain.
**Water:** None.
**Best season:** Spring through fall.
**Information:** Peaks Ranger District, Coconino National Forest.
**Finding the trailhead:** From Flagstaff drive 31 miles north on US 180, then turn left (west) on an unmaintained dirt road. The colorful face of Red Mountain is visible ahead. Continue 0.6 mile to the trailhead in a large clearing in the pinyon-juniper forest, and park.

**The hike:** From the clearing follow contour west around the hillside into the gully that drains the eroded area. Once in the bed of the drainage walk west into the heart of the reddish badlands. It is easy to imagine a volcanic explosion creating this area, but the crumbly spires and hoodoos are probably the result of water erosion of the

# HIKE 8  *RED MOUNTAIN*

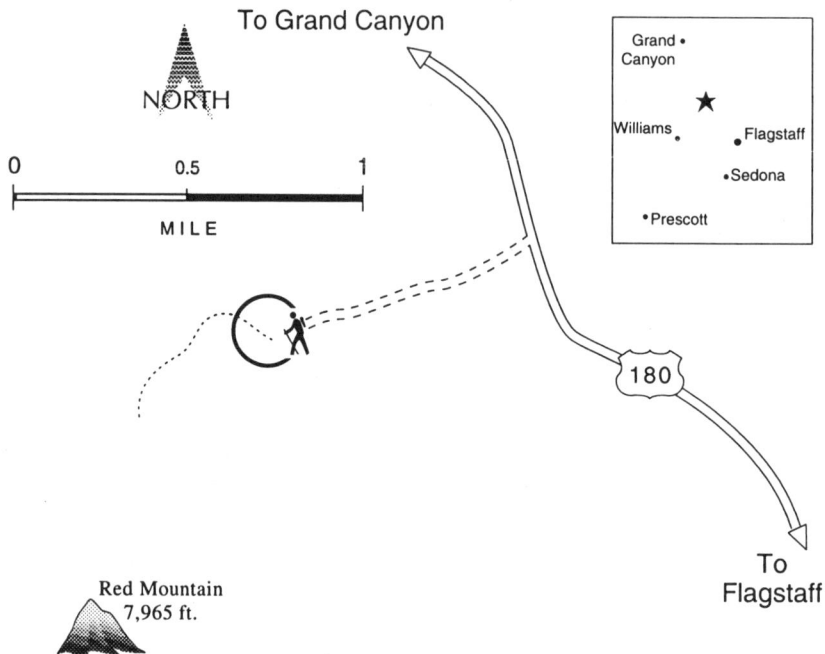

*Red Mountain in an aerial view. The hike follows the wash in the lower center of the photo into the eroded hoodoos on the northeast face of the mountain.*

old cinder cone. In fact, study of the topographic map shows Red Mountain as crescent shaped, with the crescent opening to the southwest. Probably the old crater was to the southwest as well, on the opposite side of the eroded area.

# HIKE 9  *KENDRICK PEAK TRAIL*

**General description:** A day hike on Kendrick Peak.
**General location:** 23 miles northwest of Flagstaff.
**Maps:** Kendrick Peak 7.5-minute USGS, Kaibab National Forest (Williams, Chalender, and Tusayan ranger districts).
**Difficulty:** Moderate.
**Length:** 4 miles one way.
**Elevation:** 8,000 to 10,418 feet.
**Special attractions:** Well-graded trail to the summit of the second highest mountain in northern Arizona.
**Water:** None.
**Best season:** Summer through fall.
**Information:** Chalender Ranger District, Kaibab National Forest.
**Finding the trailhead:** From Flagstaff drive north about seventeen miles on US 180, then turn left (west) on a graded dirt road (FS 193). Continue 3.2 miles, then turn right (northwest) on another graded dirt road (FS 171). Drive 1.6 miles, then turn

*Kendrick Lookout on the summit of 10,418 foot Kendrick Peak.*

## HIKES 9 AND 10 *KENDRICK PEAK TRAIL/ BULL BASIN-PUMPKIN TRAILS*

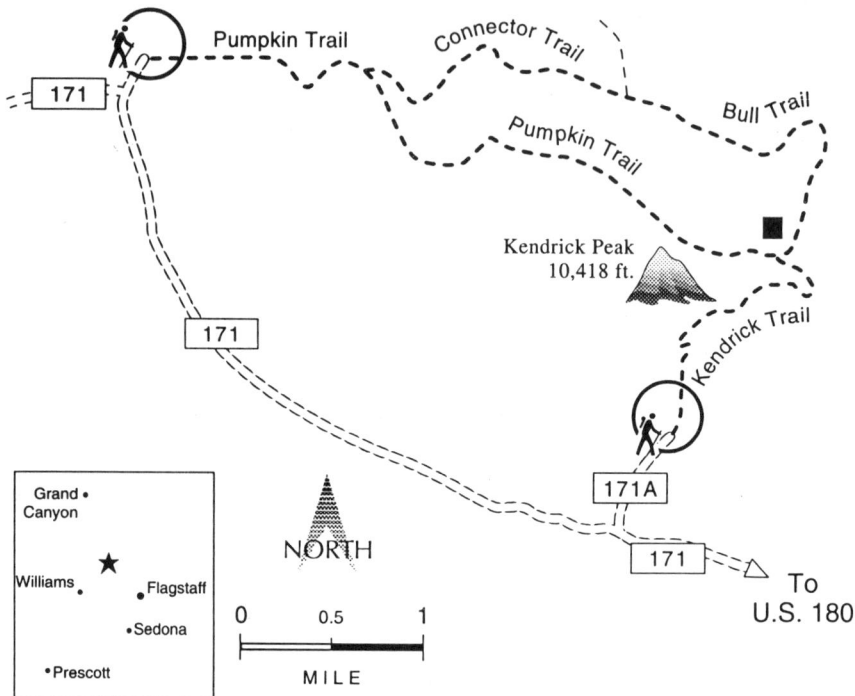

right (north) on another graded dirt road (FS 171A) and continue 0.6 mile to the signed trailhead.

**The hike:** The Kendrick Peak Trail is the easiest of the three trails to the summit of Kendrick Peak. Built for maintenance of the Forest Service fire lookout, it climbs the south side of the mountain in gradual switchbacks.

The first section of the trail was used as a road during a forest fire, and it climbs through a logged area with hundreds of tiny stumps. Fortunately this ugly area is quickly left behind, and most of the mountain is now protected in the Kendrick Peak Wilderness.

About 0.5 mile from the trailhead, the trail reaches a saddle and becomes much more scenic as it climbs through undisturbed forest. Aspens add to the charm of the ponderosa pine forest as the trail ascends through 9,000 feet. After two miles, the trail makes a major switchback to the northwest, and there are views of the summit with its squat lookout building. The trail enters a meadow on the east ridge of the peak and meets the Bull Basin Trail near an old cabin.

The cabin was built in the early part of the century by the fire lookout, who then lived in the cabin and rode his horse to the summit each day to watch for fires. The lookout obtained water from a spring to the south, which is unreliable today. In the early days of the Forest Service, fire lookouts often sat on the bare mountaintops to watch for fires. Amenities like lookout buildings and towers were constructed gradually as the permanent need for a fire watch became evident.

Continue on the Kendrick Peak Trail about 0.3 mile to the summit. The lookout welcomes visitors unless he or she is busy, but be sure to ask permission before climbing the stairs. From the catwalk or the ground, the views are stunning. The San Francisco Peaks to the east dominate the scenery, and you can also see many of the hundreds of old volcanoes and cinder cones that dot the area. A beautiful pine forest stretches in all directions, scarred here and there by old forest fire burns. To the north, the cliffs of the Grand Canyon's north rim are visible fifty miles away.

# HIKE 10  *BULL BASIN-PUMPKIN TRAILS*

**General description:** A day hike or overnight backpack on Kendrick Peak.
**General location:** 28 miles northwest of Flagstaff.
**Maps:** Kendrick Peak 7.5-minute, Moritz Ridge 7.5-minute USGS, Kaibab National Forest (Williams, Chalender, and Tusayan ranger districts).
**Difficulty:** Difficult.
**Length:** 10-mile loop.
**Elevation:** 7,300 to 10,418 feet.
**Special attractions:** Rugged, seldom-hiked loop, alpine forest, and excellent views.
**Water:** None.
**Best season:** Summer through fall.
**Information:** Chalender Ranger District, Kaibab National Forest.
**Finding the trailhead:** From Flagstaff drive north seventeen miles on US 180, then turn left (west) on a graded dirt road (FS 193). Continue 3.2 miles, then turn right (northwest) on another graded dirt road (FS 171). Drive 7.8 miles to the signed trailhead for the Pumpkin Center Trail, and park.

**The hike:** This is a strenuous hike on steep trails. There is no water, so hikers planning an overnight trip will have to carry water or do the hike in late spring when there are still snowdrifts near the summit. The rewards are worth the effort. None of the trails is shown on the topographic map, except for the short segment of the Kendrick Peak Trail used by this loop.

The Pumpkin Center Trail follows an old road east through the ponderosa pine forest and almost immediately starts climbing toward the west ridge of Kendrick Peak. After 1.6 miles, the trail climbs into a saddle and meets the Connector Trail. Turn left (east) here and continue as the Connector Trail contours the north slopes of the mountain along the wilderness boundary. The area has been logged right up to the boundary, but this section is soon left behind. After about a mile the trail passes through another saddle and crosses into Bull Basin. Two miles from the junction, the Connector Trail ends at the junction with the Bull Basin Trail.

Turn right (southeast) on the Bull Basin Trail. The first section of the trail climbs through a beautiful forest as it heads toward the north ridge of Kendrick Peak. The

*The coyote has successfully adapted to man's presence in the southwest and has actually increased its range.*

dense forest gives way to a series of alpine meadows just before the trail reaches the ridge crest. Here the trail turns south and climbs steeply to the 10,000-foot east shoulder of the mountain, about 1.8 miles from the Connector Trail junction. The trail climbs more gently now and ends near the old lookout cabin at the junction with the Kendrick Peak Trail. There are campsites along timberline at the north edge of the meadow. In early summer or late spring, lingering snowdrifts make it possible to camp without carrying water. The alpine meadow and splendid sunset and sunrise views south are worth the effort of carrying overnight gear up here. Building a campfire is not a good idea, by the way. Trees grow very slowly in this alpine environment and should not be burned. Carry a backpacking stove to melt snow and cook meals.

Turn right (west) on the Kendrick Peak Trail and follow it as it climbs about four hundred feet to the summit. Look on the west side of the lookout building for the beginning of the Pumpkin Trail, which begins descending immediately. The views are excellent from the upper part of the trail as it switchbacks though several meadows. As the trail enters deeper forest, it tends to follow the broad west ridge of the mountain. Watch for the junction with the Connector Trail as the forest becomes nearly pure ponderosa pine once again.

# HIKE 11 *CRATER LAKE*

**General description:** A day hike to a small lake near Kendrick Peak.
**General location:** 21 miles northwest of Flagstaff.
**Maps:** Kendrick Peak 7.5-minute USGS, Coconino National Forest.
**Difficulty:** Easy.
**Length:** 0.5 mile one way.
**Elevation:** 8,150 to 8,350 feet.
**Special attractions:** Lake within the crater of an extinct volcano.
**Water:** None.
**Best season:** Summer through fall.
**Information:** Peaks Ranger District, Coconino National Forest.
**Finding the trailhead:** From Flagstaff drive north seventeen miles on US 180, then turn left (west) on a small dirt road (FR 760). Continue one mile then turn right at a fork. After 0.2 mile continue straight ahead at the crossroads as you enter the northeast end of Crowley Park. The road crosses the meadow to the northwest and enters the forest. After another mile turn left at a fork. The road enters another meadow near Crater Spring Tank and becomes rough. You may want to park here; otherwise continue to a low saddle, one mile from the last fork, and park.

**The hike:** From the saddle walk up the old, closed road that heads east and climbs the south slope of the ancient cinder cone. After about 0.2 mile, the trail crosses through a saddle and descends into the crater. Crater Lake is a small pond ringed with aspens, and seems to hold water longer than the other two crater lakes in the area. It is a pleasant but optional walk around the pond or the crater rim.

## HIKE 11 *CRATER LAKE*

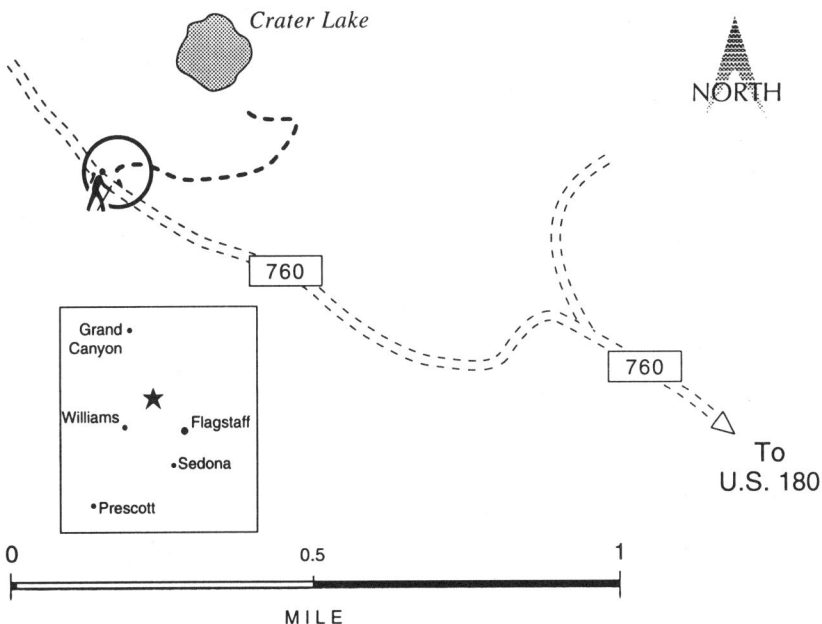

Crater Lake

NORTH

760

760

To
U.S. 180

Grand
Canyon

Williams

Flagstaff

Sedona

Prescott

0        0.5        1

MILE

# HIKE 12 *WALKER LAKE*

**General description:** A day hike to a cinder cone with a small lake near the San Francisco Peaks.

**General location:** 22 miles northwest of Flagstaff.

**Maps:** White Horse Hills 7.5-minute USGS, Coconino National Forest.

**Difficulty:** Easy.

**Length:** 0.5 mile one way.

**Elevation:** 8,170 to 8,270 feet.

**Special attractions:** Lake in a volcanic crater, views of the San Francisco Peaks.

**Water:** None.

**Best season:** Summer through fall.

**Information:** Peaks Ranger District, Coconino National Forest.

**Finding the trailhead:** From Flagstaff drive north twenty miles on US 180, then turn right (east) on the north Hart Prairie Road (FS 151). Continue on this graded dirt road 1.5 miles, then turn left (east) on another graded road (FS 418). Drive 0.2 mile, then turn left again (north) on an unmaintained road. Park at the end of the road, in another 0.2 mile.

**The hike:** The trail follows the old road, closed now, up the southwest slope of the cinder cone. It passes through a broad saddle after 0.2 mile and drops gently into

## HIKE 12 *WALKER LAKE*

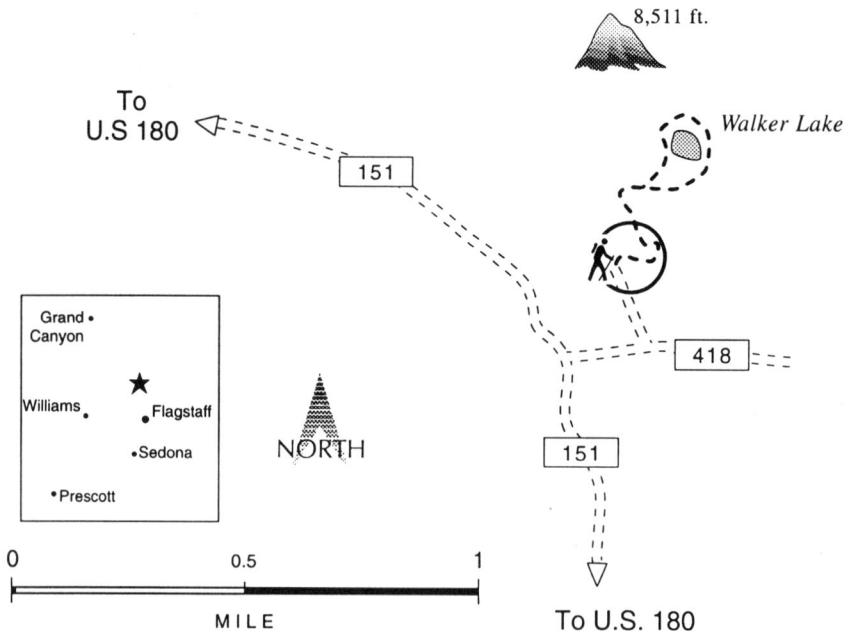

*Walker Lake is a shallow pond, which lies in the crater left by an old volcano.*

the volcanic crater. Walker Lake is fullest in late spring after a snowy winter. In late summer it is little more than a marsh. Considering how porous this volcanic area is, it's surprising that the runoff from the small watershed formed by the crater is enough to form even a small pond. Take a little extra time to walk around the lake. The north slope of the crater is barren due to a man-caused forest fire in the mid-1970s. The fire started near the lake, and high winds swept it up over the rim, where it traveled another five miles before being contained by fire fighters. The views of Humphreys Peak are great from the northwest side of the lake, and even better if you climb up the slope through the old burn.

# HIKE 13 *CRATER LAKE (HART PRAIRIE)*

**General description:** A cross-country day hike to the smallest of the three crater lakes near the San Francisco Peaks.
**General location:** 13 miles northwest of Flagstaff.
**Maps:** Wing Mountain 7.5-minute USGS, Coconino National Forest.
**Difficulty:** Easy.
**Length:** 0.5 mile one way.
**Elevation:** 7,900 to 8,200 feet.
**Special attractions:** Small lake in a volcanic cinder cone.
**Water:** None.
**Best season:** Summer through fall.

## HIKE 13 *CRATER LAKE (HART PRAIRIE)*

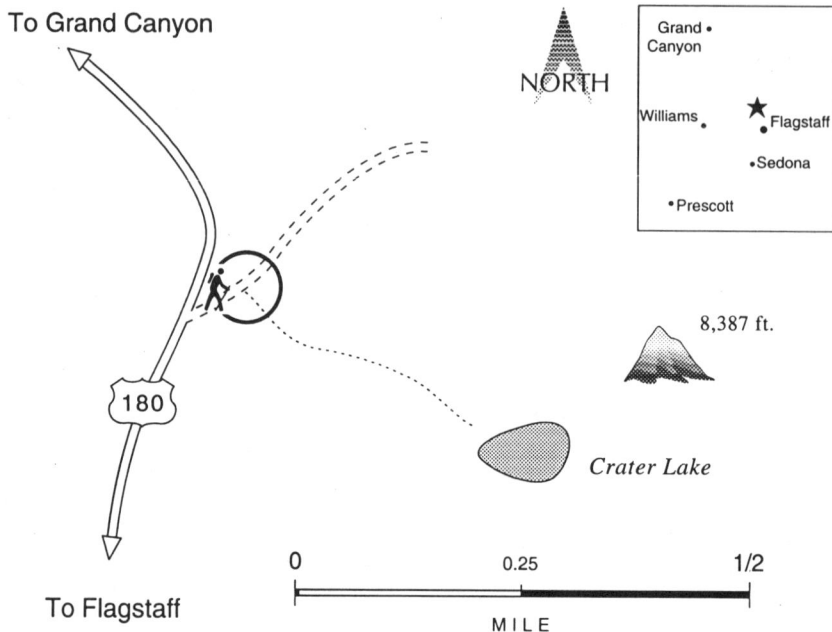

To Grand Canyon

NORTH

Grand •
Canyon

Williams •    ★ Flagstaff
              •
              • Sedona
• Prescott

8,387 ft.

180

Crater Lake

0          0.25        1/2
|————————————|————————————|
              M I L E

To Flagstaff

**Information:** Peaks Ranger District, Coconino National Forest.

**Finding the trailhead:** From Flagstaff drive north on US 180 ten miles to the south Hart Prairie Road (FS 151). Note your mileage here then continue on the highway 2.9 miles and park at a small dirt road on the right side of the highway. There will be a small meadow and the Little Horse water tank on the left side of the highway at this point.

**The hike:** Walk east through the gate, then turn southeast and walk cross country straight up the hill through the ponderosa pine and aspen forest. The grade becomes steeper as it climbs the west slope of the old volcanic cinder cone. The rim of the crater is about 0.2 mile from the highway. A small meadow and Crater Lake are straight ahead. This pond is the smallest of the three crater lakes in the area, and like the others is best in early summer after a snowy winter. The rim of the crater is heavily forested and doesn't offer much in the way of views.

# HIKE 14 *WING MOUNTAIN*

**General description:** A cross-country day hike on Wing Mountain.

**General location:** 10 miles northwest of Flagstaff.

**Maps:** Wing Mountain 7.5-minute USGS, Coconino National Forest.

**Difficulty:** Moderate.

**Length:** 2-mile loop.
**Elevation:** 7,600 to 8,578 feet.
**Special attractions:** Scenic alpine meadow.
**Water:** None.
**Best season:** Spring through fall.
**Information:** Peaks Ranger District, Coconino National Forest.
**Finding the trailhead:** From Flagstaff drive north on US 180 about seven miles, then turn left (west) on FS 222 (this turnoff is just past the Fort Valley Experimental Forest turnoff). Drive two miles, passing the junction of FS 519, then turn left into a small aspen-bordered meadow that is just past a large cinder pit. Park at the far west side of the meadow.

**The hike:** Walk southwest directly toward the summit through aspen and ponderosa pine. In a few places the young pines become almost too thick to walk through, but these patches are easy to avoid. The overcrowded trees are a result of heavy logging back at the turn of the century. The stumps of large pines are still visible, showing what the forest must have been like before it was logged. After you cross a fence, the forest becomes more open and shows less signs of logging. Douglas-fir appear and become more common during the climb. These trees are distinguished by their short, flat, single needles. Near the crater rim look for an occasional limber pine. Named for its flexible branches, which help the tree shed snow, it has medium length needles that grow five to a bunch. Go straight up to reach the rim, then turn right (northwest) to reach the summit, which is only a slight rise without much of a view.

*The view across the summit crater of Wing Mountain, looking toward Kendrick Peak.*

# HIKE 14  *WING MOUNTAIN*

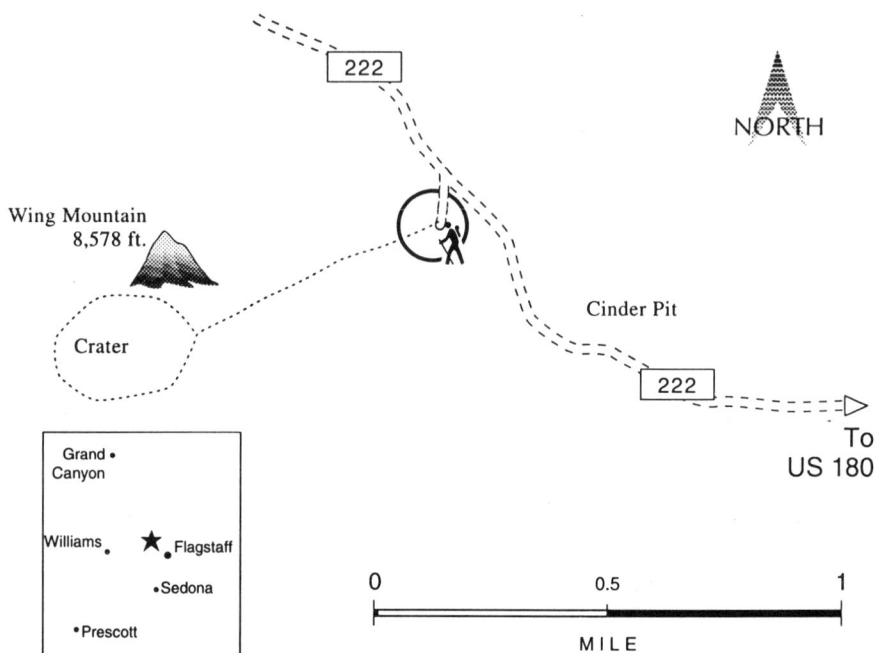

The walk around the crater rim is pleasant, dipping gradually to a low point on the west side. Along the way, there are views of Kendrick Peak to the northwest and an occasional glimpse of the meadow in the crater. From the southernmost point of the rim, there is an excellent view of Kendrick Peak rising above the grassy crater. Continue around the crater rim until you've completed the loop, then descend northeast to reach the meadow where you parked. The easiest way to do this is to head directly for distant Agassiz Peak, the closest of the San Francisco Peaks.

# HIKE 15  *S P CRATER*

**General description:** A cross-country day hike on the Coconino Plateau (see map on p. 56).

**General description:** A cross-country day hike on the Coconino Plateau (see map on p. 56).

**General location:** 37 miles northeast of Flagstaff.
**Maps:** S P Mountain 15-minute USGS.
**Difficulty:** Moderate.
**Length:** 1 mile one way.
**Elevation:** 6,240 to 7,000 feet.
**Special attractions:** Unusually symmetrical volcanic crater and a lava flow.
**Water:** None.
**Best season:** Spring through fall.

**Information:** Arizona State Land Department.

**Finding the trailhead:** From Flagstaff drive north on AZ 89 about thirty miles. Go one mile past the signed turnoff to Wupatki National Monument, then turn left (west) on an unsigned dirt road. This unmaintained road is passable to most vehicles except during or after wet weather. To the west, directly ahead, look for a cinder cone, S P Mountain, that is perfectly symmetrical (it's just to the right and beyond a closer hill). Continue five miles to the eastern base of S P Mountain, then turn left. After one mile, a four-wheel-drive road leads right (west) up a steep drainage on the south side of S P Mountain. Park here.

**The hike:** Follow the dirt road up the drainage to a saddle on the west side of S P Mountain. Now turn east and climb directly up the slope to the rim of S P Crater. It's a steep climb on a loose, cinder surface, but well worth the effort. In summer, this can be a hot hike, so carry water.

From the rim, S P Crater is four hundred feet deep, which is just half the height of the cinder cone itself. The volcano is so raw that it appears to have just stopped erupting. To the north, the five-mile length of the S P Lava Flow adds to the volcanic atmosphere of the place, and gives an idea what the Flagstaff area must have been like during periods of volcanic activity. S P Mountain is one of the northernmost cinder cones in the San Francisco volcanic field, but lava flows like this one cover much of the area to the north. The black rock lies like cake frosting on the gener-

*S P Lava Flow stretches five miles north from the base of S P Mountain.*

S P Lava Flow

S P Mountain
7,021 ft.

To
AZ 89

Grand •
Canyon

★

Williams •
•Flagstaff

•Sedona

•Prescott

NORTH

To
Colton Crater

0          0.5          1

M I L E

ally red sedimentary rock. Some of the lava flowed as far north as the Little Colorado River, a distance of twenty miles.

The initials, S P, are a cleaned up version of the original name of the cinder cone, which resembles a fixture common in pioneer bedrooms before the advent of indoor plumbing.

# HIKE 16 *COLTON CRATER*

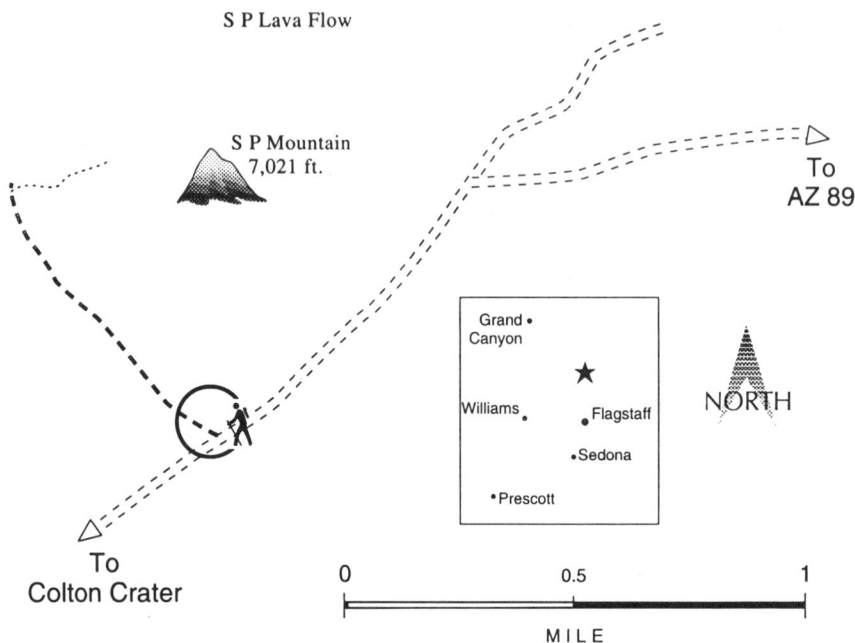

**General description:** A day hike on the Coconino Plateau.
**General location:** 39 miles northeast of Flagstaff.
**Maps:** S P Mountain 15-minute USGS.
**Difficulty:** Easy.
**Length:** 0.7 mile one way.
**Elevation:** 6,320 to 6,700 feet.
**Special attractions:** Unusually large volcanic crater.
**Water:** None.
**Best season:** Spring through fall.

**Information:** Arizona State Land Department.

**Finding the trailhead:** Follow the directions for S P Crater (Hike 15). From the trailhead, continue on the road another 1.2 miles southwest, then turn sharply left (east) onto a little used road that follows a fence line. Drive about 0.8 mile to a fainter road that goes right (south) through a wire gate, and park.

**The hike:** Follow the old road south through the gate, then 0.7 mile through the scattering of pinyon-juniper, and directly up the slope to the rim of Colton Crater. This large and colorful crater is more than 0.5 mile across. A small cinder cone actually rises from the floor of the crater. It must have formed after the more violent eruption that created Colton Crater.

Notice the scattered Utah juniper and Colorado pinyon pine. The pinyon pine may be identified by its short needles that grow in pairs. In good years, the pinyons produce a large crop of pine nuts, long a staple food of the Native Americans and still popular today. Looking back toward S P Crater, you'll notice that there are almost no pinyons or junipers there, but in the short distance to Colton Crater they are much more common. This is due to the increase in elevation, which draws more rain and snow and makes conditions more hospitable for the small trees.

*Colton Crater features a wide, deep crater with a small secondary cinder cone at the bottom.*

# HIKE 16  *COLTON CRATER*

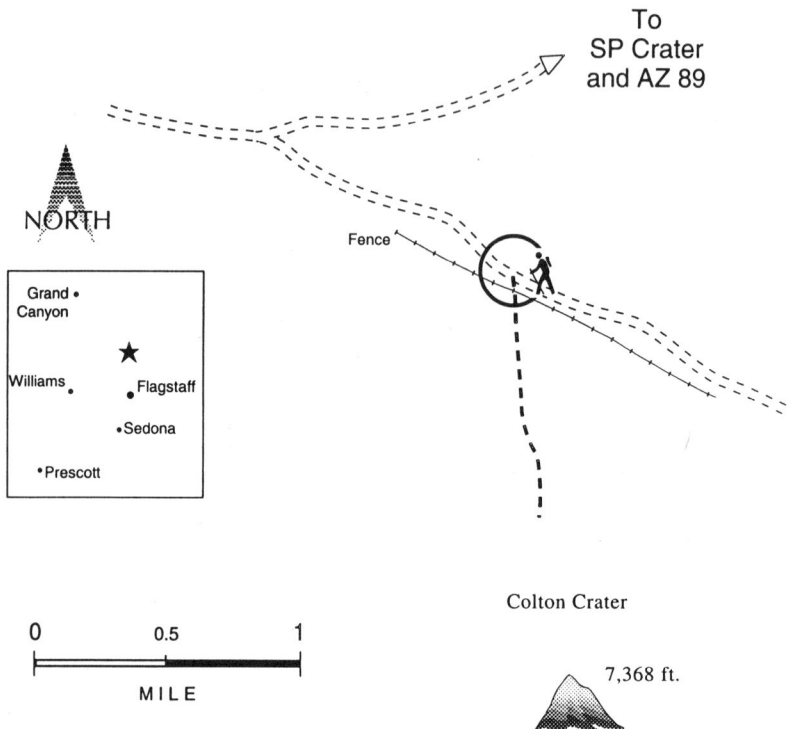

To
SP Crater
and AZ 89

NORTH

Fence

Grand •
Canyon

★

Williams •          • Flagstaff

• Sedona

• Prescott

Colton Crater

0          0.5          1

M I L E

7,368 ft.

---

# HIKE 17  *DONEY TRAIL*

**General description:** A day hike near Wupatki National Monument.
**General location:** 39 miles northeast of Flagstaff.
**Maps:** Wupatki SW 7.5-minute USGS.
**Difficulty:** Easy.
**Length:** 0.5 mile one way.
**Elevation:** 5,300 to 5,500 feet.
**Special attractions:** Cinder cone with extensive view of the Painted Desert.
**Water:** None.
**Best season:** All year.
**Information:** Peaks Ranger District, Coconino National Forest.
**Finding the trailhead:** From Flagstaff drive north about thirty miles on AZ 89, then turn right (east) at the signed turnoff for Wupatki National Monument. Follow this paved road east 9.2 miles, then turn right at the signed picnic area and park at the signed trailhead.

# HIKE 17 *DONEY TRAIL*

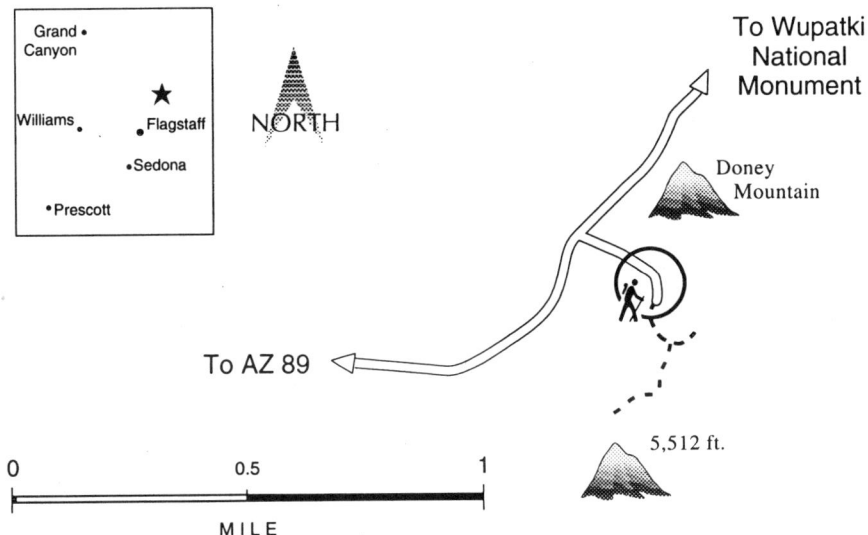

**The hike:** This broad, easy trail heads south toward the low saddle between two of the cinder cones. From the saddle, you can take a one-hundred-yard side hike to the north for a view from the lower cinder cone. Back on the main trail, continue south about 0.4 mile to the summit. The 360-degree vista includes a sweeping view of the Painted Desert, which got its name from the pastel-colored shale rocks that erode into soft, rounded shapes. Early or late in the day when the sun is low in the sky, the colors are intensified. During midday, the flat, intense sunlight washes out the colors.

# HIKE 18 *WUPATKI RUIN*

**General description:** A day hike in Wupatki National Monument.
**General location:** 44 miles northeast of Flagstaff.
**Maps:** Wupatki SE 7.5-minute USGS.
**Difficulty:** Easy.
**Length:** 0.5-mile loop.
**Elevation:** 4,800 feet.
**Special attractions:** Extensive and well-preserved Sinagua Indian ruin, very easy trail.
**Water:** At visitor center.
**Best season:** All year.
**Information:** Wupatki National Monument.
**Finding the trailhead:** From Flagstaff drive north about thirty miles on AZ 89, then turn right (east) at the signed turnoff for Wupatki National Monument. Follow this paved road east fourteen miles, and park at the visitor center.

NORTH

Grand Canyon

Williams  ★ Flagstaff

•Sedona

•Prescott

0    0.5    1

MILE

Wupatki Ruin

To AZ 89

To Sunset Crater

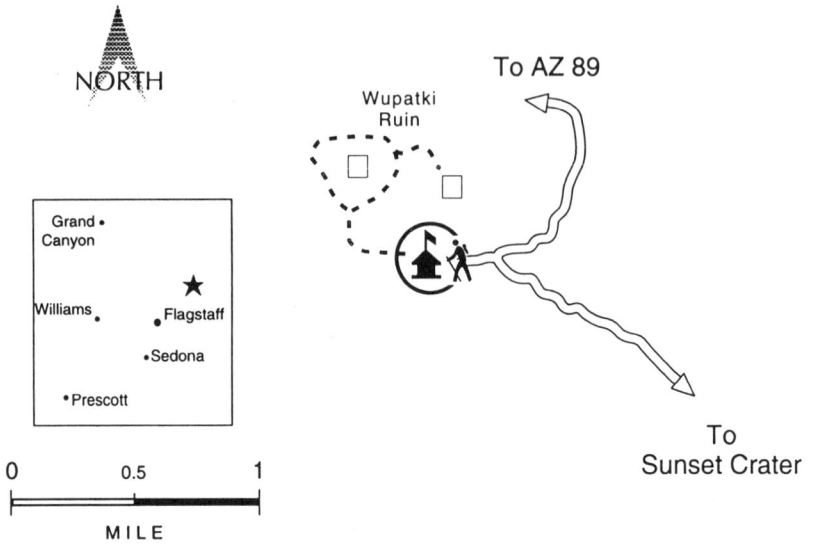

*Wukoki Ruin, backdropped by the San Francisco Peaks, in Wupatki National Monument.*

**The hike:** This paved trail may be reached either by walking through the visitor center or by walking around the right (north) side of the building. It is worthwhile spending time in the visitor center to learn about the Sinagua Indians who built Wupatki and many other structures in the area. The trail first passes an overlook with a good view of the ruin and its setting, then descends slightly to the ruin itself. The trail forms a loop around the hilltop, and there is a spur trail to an amphitheater.

After the initial eruption of Sunset Crater volcano in A.D. 1065 , the natives living in the Wupatki area were forced to abandon their homes and fields because of the rain of volcanic ash and cinders. A few years later, however, they discovered that the thin layer of ash acted as a mulch to retain soil moisture. This meant they could grow crops in many new areas. The result was a population explosion in the Wupatki area. Members of the Sinagua culture from the south, Anasazi from the northeast, and Cohonina from the west migrated to the area. The three cultures advanced rapidly due to the sharing of technology and the increased social interaction. But by the year 1225 the Wupatki area was mostly abandoned. A long drought that began in 1150 was probably a contributing factor.

# HIKE 19  *BONITO CRATER*

**General description:** A cross-country day hike near Sunset Crater.
**General location:** 16 miles northeast of Flagstaff.
**Maps:** O'Leary Peak 7.5-minute, Sunset Crater West 7.5-minute USGS.
**Difficulty:** Easy.
**Length:** 2.5-mile loop.
**Elevation:** 7,100 to 7,300 feet.
**Special attractions:** Lunar-like volcanic landscape.
**Water:** None.
**Best season:** Spring through fall.
**Information:** Sunset Crater National Monument.
**Finding the trailhead:** From Flagstaff drive north about twelve miles on AZ 89, then turn right (east) on the signed, paved road to Sunset Crater National Monument. Continue 4.5 miles and drive past the Sunset Crater parking area and along the north side of Sunset Crater. Park on the left just as the road starts into a cut. The parking is limited to two small pullouts that are not signed.

**The hike:** Note that Sunset Crater, on the south side of the road, is closed to hiking and climbing. The Park Service implemented this closure in 1976 to protect Sunset Crater from erosion. (Though the harsh volcanic landscape seems anything but fragile, the Cinder Hills area to the southeast of the National Monument shows what inappropriate use can do. Virtually every square foot of the Cinder Hills is marred by off-road vehicle tracks.) All of the National Monument except for Sunset Crater is open to hiking. Although this is a cross-country hike, the walking is easy on open, firm cinders.

Walk west along the highway a few yards until the road cut ends on the north side, then turn right (north). Contour north along the slopes of a small cinder hill

# HIKE 19 *BONITO CRATER*

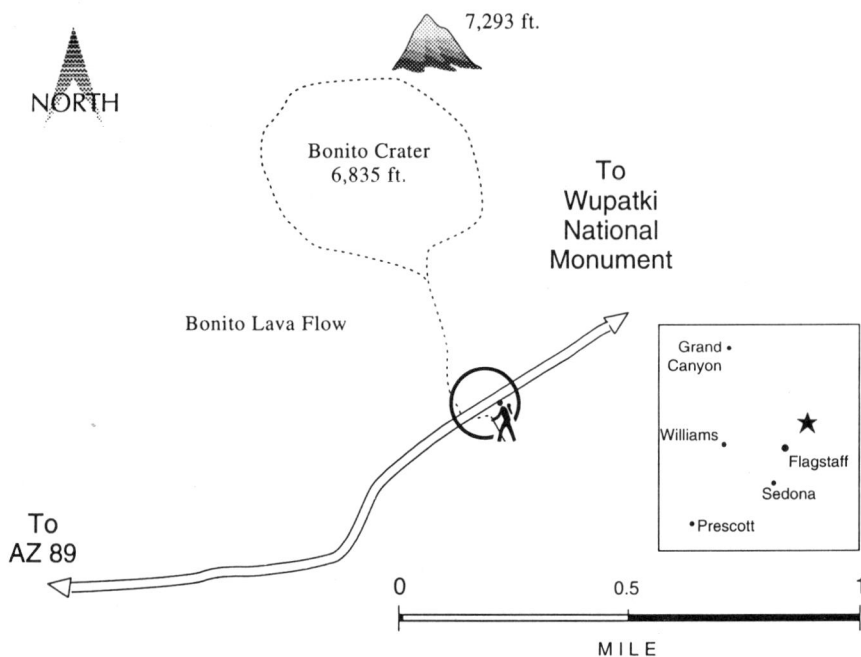

to your right, and head for a low saddle between this hill and the next, much larger one. On the left, look down at the jagged Bonito Lava Flow, which looks like it just poured out of the ground. In fact, the lava is more than seven hundred years old. Despite the crater's harsh appearance, life has found its way onto the shattered rock, as evidenced by the large pine trees.

After the saddle, continue north, staying at about the same level above the steeper slopes to the left. Soon the crater appears on the right as the slope turns into a definite rim. The rest of the hike follows the rim up and to the right, skirting the edge of the crater all the way back to the point where the rim was first encountered. The soil seems sterile, but in spring there will often be a few flowers and other plants. Along the highest part of the crater rim, a small community of ponderosa pine and sagebrush has established itself. The exposed ridge seems an unlikely place for this little patch of life, but on a windy day the explanation becomes clearer. The prevailing wind during snowstorms in this area is from the southwest, which piles snow into drifts on the lee side of ridges, providing just enough extra moisture for the pines.

As the crater rim turns south, there are good views of Sunset Crater across the road. The red cinders along its rim caused Major John Wesley Powell to give the ridge its name. In the clear air of the southwest in 1870, the Major was able to see Sunset Crater from the Grand Canyon country, sixty miles to the north. There are a few red cinders scattered along the route of this hike, possibly from Sunset Crater. Also, notice how the cinders are heaped into firm drifts, one to two feet high, along the sections of crater rim not protected by trees and sagebrush. Apparently the wind is strong enough at times to move the cinders, because the drifts seem to form only on exposed ridges. A final steep descent of the crater rim, heading southwest, completes the loop. Return by walking south to the road.

# HIKE 20 *WALNUT CANYON*

**General description:** A day hike in Walnut Canyon National Monument.
**General location:** 10 miles east of Flagstaff.
**Maps:** Flagstaff East 7.5-minute USGS.
**Difficulty:** Easy.
**Length:** 0.7-mile loop.
**Elevation:** 6,450 to 6,700 feet.
**Special attractions:** Walnut Canyon, ancient ruins.
**Water:** At visitor center.
**Best season:** All year.
**Information:** Walnut Canyon National Monument.
**Finding the trailhead:** From Flagstaff drive about ten miles east on I-40, then turn right (south) at the signed exit for Walnut Canyon National Monument. Continue three miles on the paved road to its end and the visitor center.

*The Sinagua people inhabited the cliffs of Walnut Canyon 800 years ago, and the ruins of their dwellings are preserved in Walnut Canyon National Monument southeast of Flagstaff.*

# HIKE 20  *WALNUT CANYON*

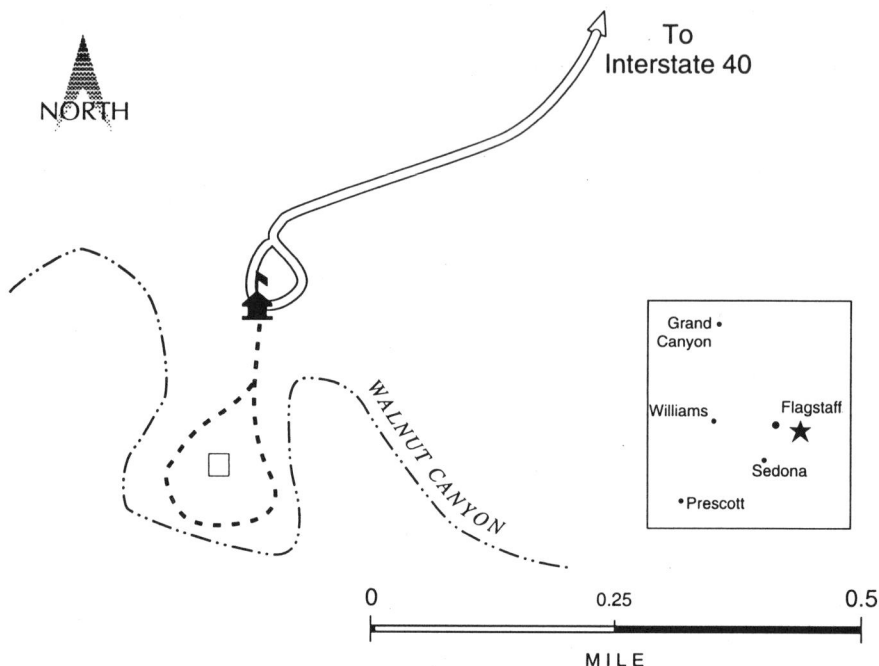

**The hike:** Take the time to look at the informative exhibits and books in the visitor center before exiting at the back to reach the trail. The trail descends about two hundred feet below the rim, then circles a small butte. Interpretive signs along the way explain the ruins as well as the plants and animals found in the area. Look for the many additional ruins at about the same level as the trail on the opposite walls of Walnut Canyon.

The Sinagua culture, which built the dwellings in the Walnut Canyon area, apparently arrived about A.D. 700 (*Sinagua* is a Spanish term meaning "without water.") Although the Sinagua depended on wild plants and animals for food, they also had developed agriculture, which required them to stay in one place. The cliff dwellings were built during the period of maximum occupation of Walnut Canyon, between 1125 and 1250. The Sinagua occupied sites from Wupatki, forty miles northeast of Flagstaff, to the Verde Valley fifty miles south. The cliff dwellings and other ruins clustered, with the ruins on the trail and on the rim near the visitor center being a good example. These clusters were probably occupied by related family groups. An extensive network of trails took advantage of natural routes along ledges and through breaks in the cliffs. Most of the farming took place on the canyon rim, where the Sinagua grew corn, beans, and squash. Artifacts have been found showing that the Sinagua traded with people from all over Arizona as well as southern California and northern Mexico. In fact, the Sinagua may have acted as middlemen because of their central location. In about 1250, the Sinagua abandoned Walnut

Canyon for unknown reasons, though the long drought that started in 1150 may have been a contributing cause. It is possible that their descendants live on in the Hopi villages to the north, which were founded in about 1200.

# HIKE 21 *METEOR CRATER RIM*

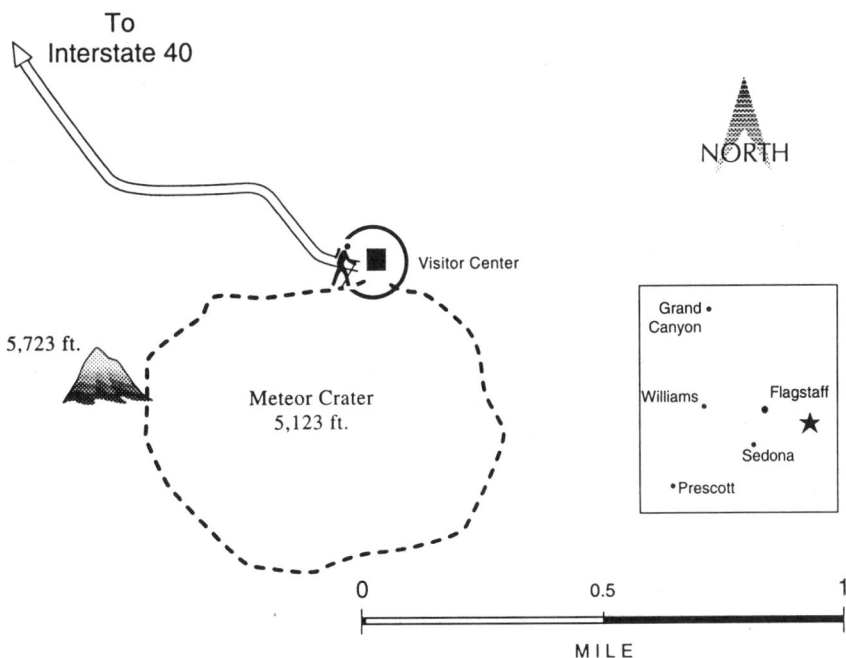

**General description:** A day hike at Meteor Crater.
**General location:** 46 miles east of Flagstaff.
**Maps:** Meteor Crater 7.5-minute USGS.
**Difficulty:** Easy.
**Length:** 2.2-mile loop.
**Elevation:** 5,620 to 5,723 feet.
**Special attractions:** Views of one of the most recent meteor strikes on the planet.
**Water:** At visitor center.
**Best season:** Fall through spring.
**Information:** Meteor Crater Enterprises.
**Finding the trailhead:** From Flagstaff drive east forty miles on I-40, then exit at the sign for Meteor Crater. Go south on this paved road six miles to its end at the visitor center.

**HIKE 21** *METEOR CRATER RIM*

To
Interstate 40

NORTH

Visitor Center

5,723 ft.

Meteor Crater
5,123 ft.

Grand
Canyon

Williams

Flagstaff
★

Sedona

Prescott

0          0.5          1

MILE

**The hike:** Ask at the visitor center for the latest hiking information and restrictions. Although open to the public, Meteor Crater is privately owned. After checking out the displays in the visitor center, begin the hike along the rim trail. You can go in either direction. The rim is nearly level, but the trail is always climbing or descending slightly. Because the force of the explosion piled the rim material higher than the surrounding plain, there are distant views of the Painted Desert and the San Francisco Peaks as well as the close view of the crater.

Meteor Crater was formed in a fraction of a second by a large meteor that exploded with the force of a nuclear weapon. The fireball wiped out all life within fifty miles and blasted out a crater six hundred feet deep and nearly a mile wide.

Unlike the moon, which is scarred with thousands of meteor craters, the earth has little evidence of meteor strikes. This is because the forces of erosion rapidly erase impact craters on Earth. Nevertheless, scientists are finding more evidence of past craters all the time, especially with the help of aerial and satellite imagery. Several ancient craters over sixty miles in diameter have been found, one in Canada and one in Europe, while off the coast of Yucatan the remains of a crater one hundred miles in diameter have been associated with the end of the dinosaurs. In this century, there have been several major meteor strikes. One occurred in Siberia in 1908, causing massive devastation to the forest in an uninhabited area, and another is suspected in the Indian Ocean in the 1970s.

# SAN FRANCISCO PEAKS

Culminating in 12,633-foot Humphreys Peak, the San Francisco Peaks are the highest mountains in Arizona. A horseshoe-shaped ring of peaks surrounds the 10,000-foot Interior Valley, which opens to the northeast. Like all the smaller mountains and hills on the Coconino Plateau, the Peaks are an ancient volcano. Some geologists believe that the mountain was once 16,000 feet high or higher before the summit exploded much like the recent explosion of Mount St. Helens. As recently as ten thousand years ago, glaciers were present in the Interior Valley and in the northeast canyons. Glacial features can be seen on several of the hikes. Most of the San Francisco Peaks are protected in the Kachina Peaks Wilderness.

In 1889, C. Hart Merriam, a biologist with the U.S. Biological Survey, camped at Little Spring on the northwest slopes of the San Francisco Peaks near the new settlement of Flagstaff. He came to study the great variety of plant life that grew on the mountain and its surrounding plateau. He soon noticed that plants tended to grow in associations determined by the climate. The climate grows cooler and wetter as the elevation increases because the high terrain extracts more rain and snow from storm clouds. Merriam determined that a one thousand-foot elevation gain is approximately equivalent to six hundred miles of northward travel. Groups of plants grow at elevations where the climate is to their liking. Animals dependent on certain plants for food are also associated with these plant communities. Merriam coined the term "life zone" to describe plant and animal communities and described the characteristic life zones of Northern Arizona. Although later studies have complicated the simple life zone concept, it's still a useful way to understand the plant and animal communities. From the Colorado River at the bottom of the Grand Canyon to the top of the San Francisco Peaks is an elevation gain of more than 10,000 feet in fifty-two miles, a climate change equivalent to a journey from northern Mexico to northern Canada.

Hiking on the mountain is somewhat restricted. The Interior Valley forms part of a watershed for the City of Flagstaff and is closed to overnight camping. Day hiking is allowed. All of the mountain above 11,400 feet (approximate timberline) is closed to cross country hiking; hikers must stay on trails. This closure is to protect an endangered plant that grows only on the San Francisco Peaks. For more information on these closures, contact the Coconino National Forest, Peaks Ranger District, at the address and phone listed under Resources at the end of the book.

# HIKE 22 *AUBINEAU TRAIL-NORTH RIDGE HUMPHREYS PEAK*

**General description:** A day hike on the San Francisco Peaks.
**General location:** 23 miles north of Flagstaff.
**Maps:** White Horse Hills 7.5-minute, Humphreys Peak 7.5-minute USGS, Coconino National Forest.
**Difficulty:** Difficult.
**Length:** 6-mile loop.
**Elevation:** 8,000 to 11,400 feet.
**Special attractions:** Remote glacial canyon and scenic alpine ridge. This is an excellent hike for the hot days of June.
**Water:** None.
**Best season:** Summer through fall.
**Information:** Peaks Ranger District, Coconino National Forest.
**Finding the trailhead:** From Flagstaff drive north on US 180 for about eighteen miles, then turn right (east) on the north Hart Prairie Road (FS 151), a maintained dirt road. Continue 1.6 miles, then turn left on the Hostetter Tank Road (FS 418), also maintained dirt. Drive 3.7 miles to the signed Aubineau Trail trailhead, and park on the right.

**The hike:** The walk begins in Aubineau Canyon, which at this point appears to be a minor drainage. A good foot trail (not shown on the topographic map) follows the dry creek bed uphill through an open ponderosa pine forest. After about 0.7 mile, the old Aubineau trail joins from the left (east). Our trail continues up the creek bed. The canyon becomes much deeper, and the open ponderosa pine forest gradually gives way to a denser forest of Douglas-fir, quaking aspen, and limber pine. About three miles from the trailhead, the forest opens up, with a view of upper Aubineau Canyon and the northeast slopes of Humphreys Peak. In June, snow still lingers on the mountainsides. The Aubineau Trail ends at the Aubineau Canyon Road after another hundred yards.

The lack of trees in the valley is due to numerous snow avalanches that roar down the northeast slopes of Humphreys Peak. Some of these slides reach the bottom of the canyon with such power that they continue below the road, crossing back and forth several times before the snow finally loses its momentum. Such a large ava-

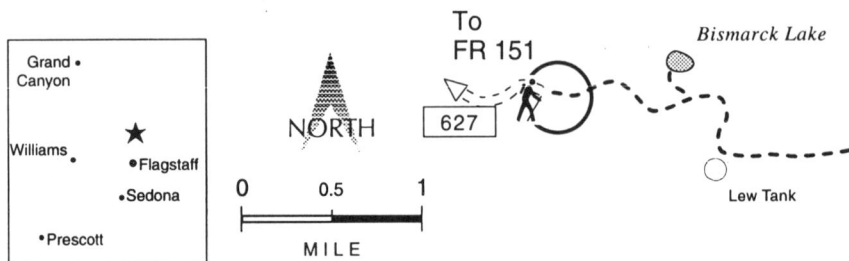

lanche will destroy any small trees attempting to grow in the avalanche path.

Hikers desiring a moderate hike can turn around at this point, and return to the trailhead via the Aubineau Trail. To continue on the loop hike, cross the valley to the west and ascend the avalanche path directly across from the end of the trail. By staying along the tree line, it is possible to avoid the worst of the loose scree and rock. You will reach the ridge at or below the 11,400-foot level, which is approximately timberline. Now turn right (north) and descend the ridge. The ridge forks in several places; stay to the east and remain on the ridge directly above Aubineau Canyon. The gnarled and twisted bristlecone pines and Englemann spruce near timberline attest to the difficulty of life in this alpine environment. Near the 8,800-foot elevation, Aubineau Canyon turns sharply to the northeast. Again, stay on the ridge just above the canyon. Below 8,400 feet, Aubineau Canyon becomes much shallower. Turn right and descend into the canyon bottom, rejoin the Aubineau Trail, and return to the trailhead.

# HIKE 23 *LEW TANK MEADOW*

**General description:** A day hike on the San Francisco Peaks.
**General location:** 15 miles north of Flagstaff.
**Maps:** Humphreys Peak 7.5-minute USGS, Coconino National Forest.
**Difficulty:** Easy.
**Length:** 2.5 miles one way.
**Elevation:** 8,600 to 9,600 feet.
**Special attractions:** Alpine meadows, wildlife.
**Water:** None.
**Best season:** Summer through fall.
**Information:** Peaks Ranger District, Coconino National Forest.
**Finding the trailhead:** From Flagstaff drive north on US 180 about ten miles, then turn right (east) on the south Hart Prairie Road (FS 151). Continue 5.6 miles on this graded dirt road, then turn right (east) on the unsigned but graded Bismarck Lake

road (FS 627). Park at the end of the road, about one mile from the turnoff.

**The hike:** This area is closed to motor vehicles to protect wildlife habitat. The closure seems to be having an effect; I have seen more wildlife, including black bear and Merriam's elk, since the old road was closed by the Forest Service.

The trail follows the old road through ponderosa pine forest. After about 0.2 mile, the trail enters a meadow and skirts a stock tank. This is a good place to see elk, especially during twilight. At the east end of the meadow, the trail climbs a short distance through the forest, then enters a much larger meadow with an excellent view of the northwest slopes of Humphreys Peak with its many ridges and canyons.

About a mile from the trailhead, a spur trail branches left (north) to Bismarck Lake. Only a muddy pond most of the year, Bismarck Lake has been expanded with an earthen dam and is also a good place to view wildlife, as the bear claw marks on the aspens attest. This is also the boundary of the Kachina Peaks Wilderness Area.

The main trail continues east up the meadow, then turns south and contours through a short section of forest. The trail passes Lew Tank, another stock tank, about 1.5 miles from the trailhead, then turns left and continues into another alpine meadow. The trail fades out at the east end of the meadow at about the 9,600-foot level, where there is a sweeping view to the west.

*Hiking the meadow on the way to Lew Tank.*

# HIKE 24  *HUMPHREYS PEAK TRAIL*

**General description:** A day hike on the San Francisco Peaks (see map on p. 72).
**General location:** 14 miles northwest of Flagstaff.
**Maps:** Humphreys Peak 7.5-minute USGS, Coconino National Forest.
**Difficulty:** Moderate.
**Length:** 4 miles one way.
**Elevation:** 9,300 to 12,633 feet.
**Special attractions:** Scenic alpine ridge, 100-mile views.
**Water:** None.
**Best season:** Summer through fall.
**Information:** Peaks Ranger District, Coconino National Forest.
**Finding the trailhead:** From Flagstaff drive northwest on US 180 about seven miles, then turn right (north) on the paved and signed Arizona Snowbowl Road. Continue 6.5 miles to the ski area lodge, and turn left into the parking lot below the lodge. Park at the north end by the signed trailhead.

**The hike:** Note that cross-country hiking is prohibited by the Forest Service above 11,400 feet on the San Francisco Peaks. This trail was completed in 1985 and is not shown on the topographic map.

The trail starts by following the chairlift uphill along upper Hart Prairie but soon veers left into the trees on the far side of the meadow. The trail ascends in a series of long switchbacks through the dense ponderosa pine, Douglas-fir, and quaking aspen forest associated with the Canadian life zone. These give way to limber pine and Englemann spruce in the higher sections of the forest. Near timberline, the forest is mostly subalpine fir, Arizona corkbark fir, and bristlecone pine, representing the classic subalpine life zone. At timberline, the trail crosses the west-facing ridge and climbs up to Agassiz Saddle at 11,800 feet. The few trees in this area show the effect of the harsh climate. They grow in low mats to conserve heat and protect themselves from wind. In winter, snow collects around the dense foliage, forming drifts that further protect the trees. The climate in this life zone is similar to that in the Arctic regions of northern Canada and Alaska.

From Agassiz Saddle, the Weatherford Trail branches south along the ridge (see the Humphreys-Kachina Trail Loop, Hike 25). The Humphreys Peak Trail turns north and skirts the west side of the ridge. The next mile of the trail is above timberline with no shelter and should not be attempted if thunderstorms, high wind, or snowstorms threaten. After about 0.2 mile the last struggling trees are left behind as the trail continues to climb along the ridge toward the invisible summit. Several false summits are passed, each one appearing to be the final summit. There are choice views of the Interior Valley to the east along the way, making it tempting to stop to catch one's breath in the thin air.

The summit is marked by low stone shelter walls, and one of the finest views in Arizona. If the air is clear, 10,300-foot Navajo Mountain can be seen to the north-northeast, in Utah, and the 11,400-foot White Mountains can be seen in east central Arizona near the New Mexico border. The Mogollon Rim and some of its canyons can be seen to the south, as well as the mountain ranges beyond.

*Starting near the Arizona Snowbowl Ski Area, the Humphreys Peak Trail climbs the beautiful west slopes of the San Francisco Peaks to the highest summit in Arizona.*

## HIKES 24 AND 25 *HUMPHREYS PEAK TRAIL/ HUMPHREYS-KACHINA TRAILS*

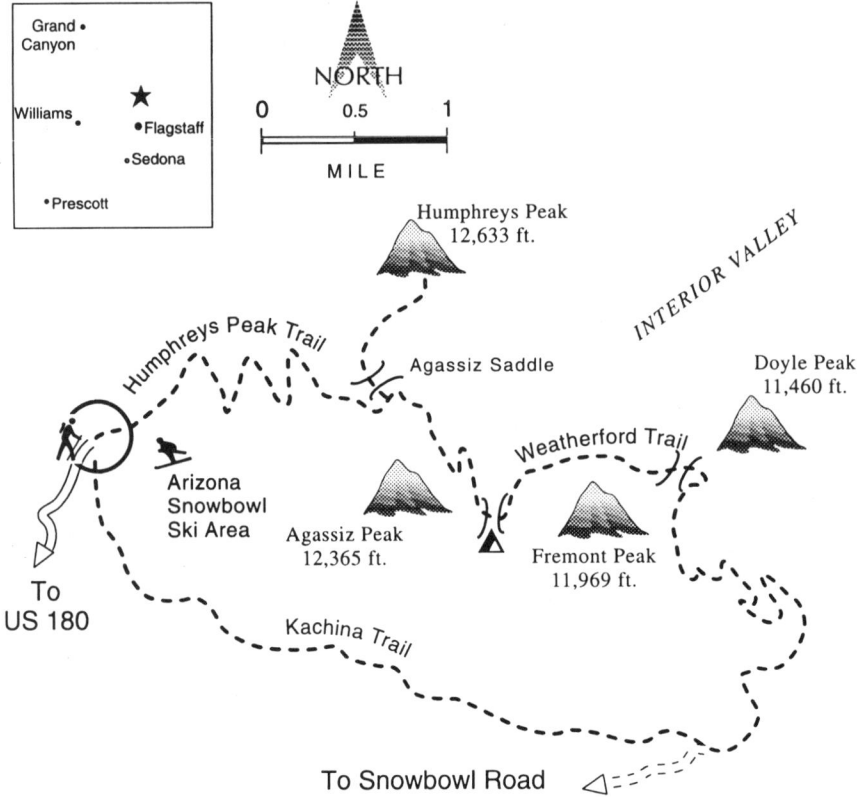

---

# HIKE 25 *HUMPHREYS-KACHINA TRAILS*

**General description:** A day hike or overnight backpack trip on the San Francisco Peaks.

**General location:** 14 miles northwest of Flagstaff.

**Maps:** Humphreys Peak 7.5-minute USGS, Coconino National Forest.

**Difficulty:** Difficult.

**Length:** 15-mile loop.

**Elevation:** 8,600 to 12,040 feet.

**Special attractions:** Rugged alpine terrain viewed from a good trail.

**Water:** Snow in early summer, otherwise none.

**Best season:** Summer through fall.

**Information:** Peaks Ranger District, Coconino National Forest.

**Finding the trailhead:** From Flagstaff drive northwest on US 180 about seven miles, then turn right (north) on the paved and signed Arizona Snowbowl Road. Continue 6.5 miles to the ski area lodge, and turn right into the first parking lot. Drive to the far end of the parking lot and park at the signed trailhead for the Kachina Trail.

**The hike:** For those who prefer to do this long, high-altitude loop as a backpack trip, note that there is no water along the trail. It is most practical to do this loop in early summer when a few patches of snow still linger on the north slopes. With a good backpacking stove, it's then easy to melt the dense spring snow for water. If there is no snow, then water will have to be carried. It may be easier to do the loop as a long day hike under those conditions.

Walk the parking lot back to the ski lodge. At the north end of the parking lot below the lodge, locate the signed Humphreys Peak Trailhead. Follow this trail under the ski lift and across Hart Prairie into the forest. (See the Humphreys Peak Trail for a detailed description.) Please note that the Forest Service requires hikers to stay on trails on the San Francisco Peaks above the 11,400-foot level.

At Agassiz Saddle, the Humphreys Peak Trail meets the Weatherford Trail at a signed junction. Follow the Weatherford Trail as it climbs the ridge to the south about 0.2 mile to a flat spot on the ridge crest. This scenic spot at over 12,000-feet in elevation was the parking area for the Weatherford Road, a scenic drive built in the 1920s and abandoned a few years later. The present Weatherford Trail follows the old road as it switchbacks down the east face of Agassiz Peak. The trail enters an open forest of Englemann spruce and bristlecone pine as it drops to Fremont Saddle, at 11,200 feet between Agassiz and Fremont Peaks. (This saddle is named correctly on the Coconino National Forest map, but incorrectly on the Humphreys Peak quad.) There is good camping for small groups in the saddle, which is somewhat protected from high wind by the trees. Campfires should not be built in this alpine area where trees grow very slowly. (You may be burning bristlecone pine, which are the oldest living things on earth.) There are still a few boards lying around, all that remains of Doyle's Camp. Doyle was an early settler and a guide, and his name marks Doyle Saddle as well as Doyle Peak, the fourth highest of the San Francisco Peaks.

The trail descends the northeast slopes below the saddle in a series of broad switchbacks, then leaves the thicker part of the forest behind as it traverses east onto the rugged north slopes of Fremont Peak. This very alpine section offers expansive views of the Interior Valley in the foreground and the Painted Desert in the far distance. The old road crosses several major avalanche paths before reaching Doyle Saddle at 10,800 feet, two miles from Fremont Saddle. These avalanche paths are very active during the winter, which is why there are few or no trees. The saddle is open and windswept, the result of a wild fire which burned the saddle and part of the valley to the north around the turn of the century. Camping is not good here due to the lack of protection from wind, but a few passable sites are located in the trees at the start of the ridge to the west.

Below Doyle Saddle, the trail widens as it descends the southeast slopes of Fremont Peak. Three more avalanche paths are crossed before the trail starts down a series of switchbacks into Weatherford Canyon. Four miles from Doyle Saddle, the trail passes the signed wilderness boundary and comes out into a broad, gentle meadow on the south slopes of Fremont Peak. Here the present Weatherford Trail

*Fremont Peak from the upper Weatherford Trail.*

turns left and descends to the southeast, but our route continues on the old road that crosses the meadow to the southwest. At the west edge of this meadow, you'll see the signed Kachina Trail on the right. Follow it to the west.

The Kachina Trail was one of several trails built during the mid-1980s as part of a new recreational trail system on the Peaks and is not shown on the topographic map. It climbs gently westward across the slopes of Fremont Peak, traversing several beautiful, aspen-lined meadows. Watch for elk; at times there are more elk tracks than human tracks on the trail. About two miles from the start of the Kachina Trail it crosses the upper part of Friedlein Prairie, the largest meadow on the south side of the Peaks. The meadow is much larger than shown on the topographic map, extending all the way down to the Friedlein Prairie Road. The trail crosses the canyon that comes down from Fremont Saddle, then continues across the lower slopes of Agassiz Peak. In another two miles it crosses a fairly deep, rocky canyon, then comes out onto a gentle slope. The forest here is primarily aspen, Douglas-fir, and limber pine. Several small meadows are encountered, then the trail passes under a powerline at the wilderness boundary. Soon the paved Snowbowl Road is visible through the trees to the left, and the trailhead is reached in another 0.2 mile.

# HIKE 26 *WEATHERFORD CANYON*

**General description:** A trail and cross-country day hike on the San Francisco Peaks.
**General location:** 8 miles north of Flagstaff.
**Maps:** Humphreys Peak 7.5-minute USGS, Coconino National Forest.
**Difficulty:** Moderate.
**Length:** 6-mile loop.
**Elevation:** 8,024 to 9,500 feet.
**Special attractions:** Scenic alpine canyon.
**Water:** None.
**Best season:** Summer through fall.
**Information:** Peaks Ranger District, Coconino National Forest.
**Finding the trailhead:** From Flagstaff drive northwest about three miles on US 180, then turn right (north) on the Schultz Pass road (FR 420). Continue past the end of the pavement on a maintained dirt road to the signed Weatherford Trail at Schultz Pass, about 5.5 miles from US 180. Park on the right (south) in the fenced parking area next to Schultz Tank.

**The hike:** The walk begins across the road from the east end of the parking area and follows the Weatherford Trail, an old road. The trail crosses a cleared pipeline corridor and continues to climb gradually north on a ponderosa pine-covered slope. Stay on the well-used trail for 0.7 mile, then turn right at an unsigned fork onto the Aspen Spring trail, another old road. The trail descends slightly into Weatherford Canyon and continues up the canyon through a dense stand of young aspen. The old road forms a tunnel through the thick trees for about 0.5 mile, then the forest becomes more open. About 0.8 mile from the Weatherford Trail, look for an open grassy slope on the right. The Aspen Spring trail continues up the canyon to the northwest, while Weatherford Canyon, the main canyon, turns northeast. Leave the trail here and go northeast along the foot of this slope, staying on the left (north) side of Weatherford Canyon. (If you miss this turnoff and continue on the Aspen Spring trail, you will rejoin the Weatherford Trail in about 0.2 mile. You can turn left and join the return portion of the hike, described below.)

Although there is no official trail, faint elk trails exist and the walking is easy through the open meadow. There are views of forested Schultz Peak to the east. After about 0.5 mile of open terrain, the meadow ends and there is a short section of deadfall to negotiate. Many of the fallen trees were killed by the exceptionally heavy, wet snowfall of 1992-93. Stay to the left side of the canyon as it turns northwest and the forest opens up again. Here there are glimpses of the bald summit of Fremont Peak and several of its avalanche paths, which follow gullies down into upper Weatherford Canyon. At this point turn left and climb directly up the west slope of the canyon to the Weatherford Trail, a distance of about one hundred yards. The old road is impossible to miss, unless you continue too far up Weatherford Canyon. In this case you will still intercept the trail, but at the 10,600-foot level! 

Turn left on the Weatherford Trail and follow it south along the slopes of Fremont Peak. There are views down into Weatherford Canyon at several points. One mile

## HIKES 26 AND 27 *WEATHERFORD CANYON/SCHULTZ PEAK*

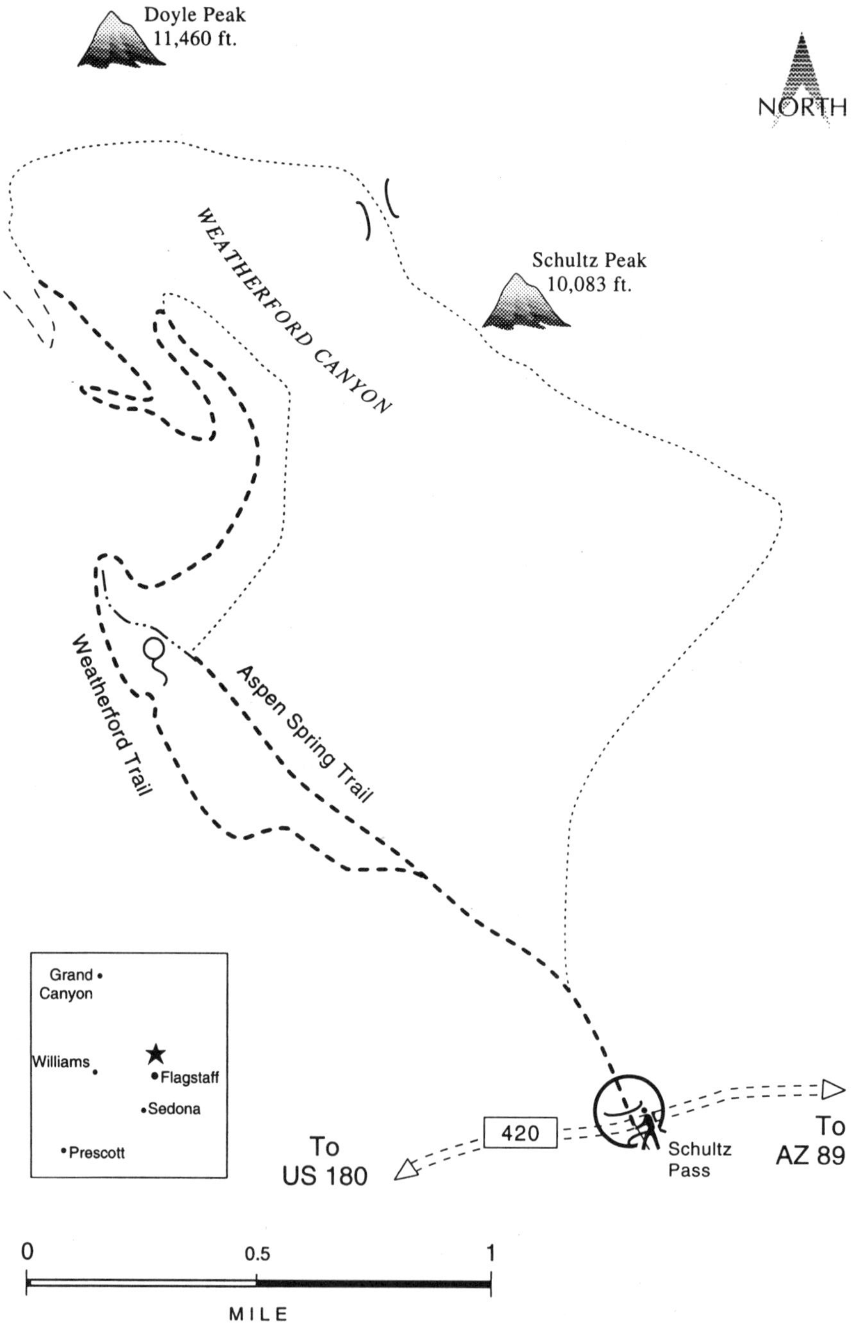
Doyle Peak
11,460 ft.
NORTH
WEATHERFORD CANYON
Schultz Peak
10,083 ft.
Weatherford Trail
Aspen Spring Trail
Grand Canyon
Williams
Flagstaff
Sedona
Prescott
420
To US 180
Schultz Pass
To AZ 89
0
0.5
1
MILE

from the point at which you intercepted the trail, it turns sharply right around a ridge, then enters a meadow. An unmarked trail where the Weatherford Trail leaves the meadow is the Aspen Spring trail. (It is possible to turn left here and follow the Aspen Spring trail about 0.2 mile to the point where you left it, and continue back to the trailhead. But staying on the Weatherford Trail affords different scenery.)

The Weatherford Trail enters the forest again, but emerges into a much larger meadow in 0.3 mile. The old road drops through the meadow in several badly eroded switchbacks, then descends gradually into Weatherford Canyon. The lower Aspen Spring Trail junction is about 1.2 miles from the upper end. Continue on the Weatherford Trail 0.7 mile to the trailhead.

# HIKE 27 *SCHULTZ PEAK*

**General description:** A cross-country day hike on the San Francisco Peaks.
**General location:** 8 miles north of Flagstaff.
**Maps:** Humphreys Peak 7.5-minute, Sunset Crater West 7.5-minute USGS, Coconino National Forest.
**Difficulty:** Moderate.
**Length:** 9-mile loop.
**Elevation:** 8,024 to 10,200 feet.
**Special attractions:** Cross-country walk along a fine alpine ridge.
**Water:** None.
**Best season:** Summer through fall.
**Information:** Peaks Ranger District, Coconino National Forest.
**Finding the trailhead:** From Flagstaff drive northwest about three miles on US 180, then turn right (north) on the Schultz Pass road (FR 420). Continue past the end of the pavement on a maintained dirt road to the signed Weatherford Trail at Schultz Pass, about 5.5 miles from US 180. Park on the right (south) in the fenced parking area next to Schultz Tank.

**The hike:** The walk begins across the road from the east end of the parking area and follows the Weatherford Trail, an old road, for about 0.4 mile. Leave the road and go cross country northeast, directly up the gentle slope. About 0.5 mile from the Weatherford Trail, the slope becomes much steeper as it ascends Schultz Peak. About two miles from the trailhead, the ridge levels out at Peak 9,822, which is the southernmost point along the Schultz Peak ridge. Now turn northwest and walk the gentle ridge 1.2 miles to Schultz Peak. This is probably one of the least climbed peaks in the area, yet the views of the San Francisco Peaks and the Dry Lake Hills are excellent. The beautiful alpine meadows, lined with aspen, limber pine, and ponderosa pine are a pleasure to walk through.

From Schultz Peak continue northwest a couple of hundred yards to a shallow saddle. Contour left along the slopes of Doyle Peak, and maintain the same elevation around to the west to intercept the Weatherford Trail in about 1.5 miles. As you cross several avalanche paths look for the trail crossing high above. It is possible to climb up to meet it, but it is much easier to contour. Holding a steady contour will bring you to the old road at one of its switchbacks. Turn left and proceed downhill.

Stay on the Weatherford Trail 4.1 miles to the trailhead. For more details on the Weatherford Trail, see the Weatherford Canyon Loop (Hike 26), and the Humphreys-Kachina Trails (Hike 25).

# HIKE 28 *LOCKETT MEADOW-PIPELINE LOOP*

**General description:** A day hike on the San Francisco Peaks.
**General location:** 22 miles northeast of Flagstaff.
**Maps:** Sunset Crater West 7.5-minute, Humphreys Peak 7.5-minute USGS, Coconino National Forest.
**Difficulty:** Moderate.
**Length:** 4-mile loop.
**Elevation:** 8,600 to 9,400 feet.
**Special attractions:** Glacial valley, alpine meadows.
**Water:** Watershed cabins during the summer only.
**Best season:** Summer through fall.
**Information:** Peaks Ranger District, Coconino National Forest.
**Finding the trailhead:** From Flagstaff drive north on AZ 89, the main street through town, and continue eighteen miles to the Lockett Meadow road (FR 522), and turn left (west). This graded dirt road is 0.8 mile north of the signed Sunset Crater National Monument turnoff. About 1.1 miles from AZ 89, the Lockett Meadow road turns sharply right and begins climbing. (The road straight ahead dead ends at a private cinder pit.) Continue 2.8 miles to its end at the southwest side of Lockett Meadow. In years of heavy snowfall, the road will be blocked by snowdrifts until late spring.

**The hike:** The area of this hike, the Interior Valley of the San Francisco Peaks, is closed to all overnight camping to protect the Flagstaff city watershed. For details on this closure contact the Forest Service. Maps of the closure area are normally posted at the trailhead.

The trail (not shown on the topographic map) climbs gradually southwest through fine stands of quaking aspen, ponderosa pine, and the occasional limber pine. The valley floor is broad and fairly flat, though cut by numerous small gullies. If you take the time to walk to either side of the valley, you'll notice that the bordering slopes are very steep. This is characteristic of valleys carved by glaciers. The moving ice shapes the entire valley into a broad U-shape. Valleys carved entirely by water have a V-shaped cross section. Another glacial characteristic is the unsorted debris composing the valley floor. Rocks and boulders of all sizes are randomly scattered around, instead of being sorted by size as they are when carried and deposited by running water. As a glacier moves down hill, it scours rock from its bed. More rock falls from the slopes above and is carried by the glacier. When the ice melts, the sand, gravel, rocks, and boulders are dropped in an unsorted heap, called "till."

After 1.5 miles, the trail reaches a small group of cabins at the junction of several roads. During the summer, untreated spring water is available at a tap by the largest cabin. Turn onto the leftmost road, FR 146. The main cabin serves as an

# HIKES 28 AND 29 *LOCKETT MEADOW-PIPELINE LOOP/ FLAGSTAFF SPRING*

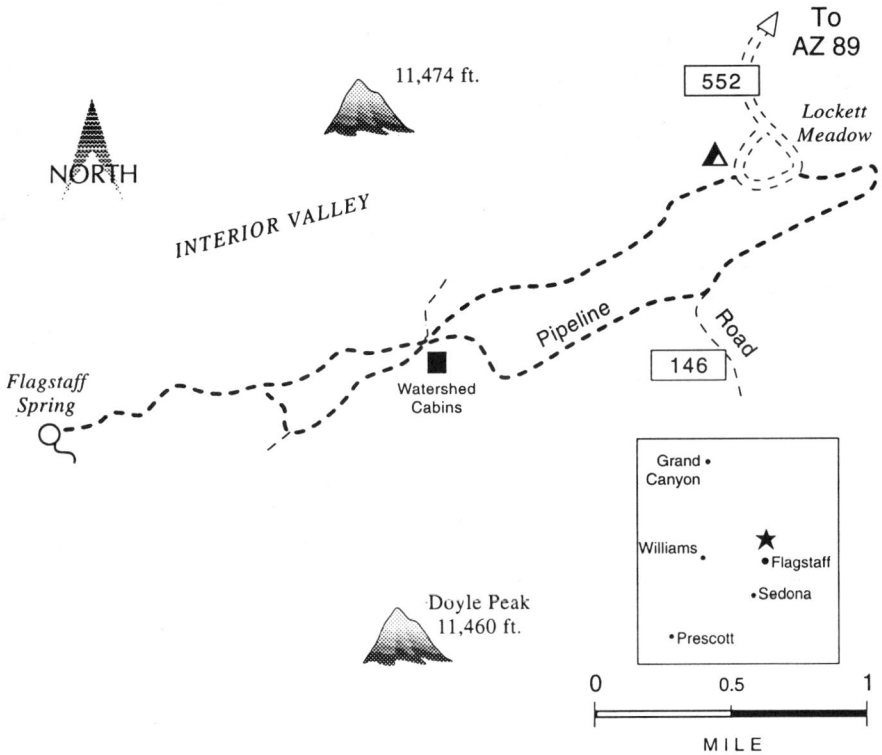

emergency shelter for snow surveyors from the U.S. Soil Conservation Service. Snow surveys are conducted throughout the mountains of the West in order to predict the amount of snow runoff that will occur in the spring. Because much of the drinking and irrigation water used in the West comes from mountain watersheds, such predictions are important. The smaller cabins protect the pipelines that collect water from springs and wells higher in the Interior Valley. The pipelines merge into one pipe that follows the road we are about to hike.

The pipeline road (FR 146) contours through a beautiful aspen stand as it heads east-northeast along the lower slopes of Doyle Peak. Used for access to the watershed project in the Interior Valley, the road is closed to all motor vehicles except those on official business. Generally the only traffic is on weekdays when an occasional maintenance truck passes by, so this road makes a very pleasant and cool hike. Hikers may also encounter mountain bikes and horses. Mountain bikes are allowed on the San Francisco Peaks except in the Kachina Peaks Wilderness, and horses are allowed everywhere except in the watershed above the cabins.

After 1.2 miles, the road passes through a gate and turns sharply right as it crosses the east ridge of Doyle Peak. Leave the road to the east-northeast and follow an old, closed road (not shown on the topographic map) down the ridge. The forest becomes much more open as it is mostly ponderosa pines. About one mile after leaving the pipeline road, the old road turns left (northwest) into a saddle next to Sugarloaf, the large cinder cone blocking the lower end of the Interior Valley. Lockett Meadow is visible below to the northwest. Follow the old road through the saddle and west another 0.2 mile into Lockett Meadow, then follow the Lockett Meadow loop road west to the trailhead. As you descend into the meadow, there are excellent views of the Interior Valley.

# HIKE 29 *FLAGSTAFF SPRING*

**General description:** A day hike on the San Francisco Peaks.
**General location:** 22 miles northeast of Flagstaff. (see map on p. 79)
**Maps:** Sunset Crater West 7.5-minute, Humphreys Peak 7.5-minute USGS, Coconino National Forest.
**Difficulty:** Moderate.
**Length:** 6.5-mile loop.
**Elevation:** 8,600 to 10,600 feet.
**Special attractions:** Alpine valley, avalanche path.
**Water:** Watershed cabins during the summer only.
**Best season:** Summer through fall.
**Information:** Peaks Ranger District, Coconino National Forest.
**Finding the trailhead:** Follow the directions for the Lockett Meadow-Pipeline Loop to reach the Lockett Meadow trailhead.

**The hike:** The first 1.5 miles of this hike follow the trail to the watershed cabins described under the Lockett Meadow-Pipeline Loop (Hike 28). See that description for more information. There is untreated spring water at a tap near the largest cabin.

From the cabins take the road continuing west-southwest up the Interior Valley. It is usually signed for Bear Paw Spring and Raspberry Spring. This road is open only to official vehicles, so you will probably not encounter any traffic. One hundred yards beyond the cabins, the road forks. Take the unsigned right fork, which goes to Bear Paw Spring. This road climbs steadily through the dense alpine forest, which sometimes opens up for glimpses of the high peaks. Along the way is evidence of bygone construction during the watershed project.

Flagstaff has outgrown its water supply many times. In the early part of the century, only a couple of decades after the city's founding, someone had an idea: tap the springs in the Interior Valley of the San Francisco Peaks. In an area with very few springs, this water was worth considerable effort to reach. A pipeline was built up Schultz Creek, west of the Dry Lake Hills, to Schultz Pass, then around the east slopes of Doyle Peak and into the Interior Valley. From the present site of the watershed cabins, branch pipelines were built to all of the springs in the valley. An attempt was even made to tap a spring in Aubineau Canyon on the northeast side of Humphreys Peak.

In the 1950s, in an attempt to find more water, the city drilled a number of exploratory wells in the Interior Valley. Some were successful, so diesel-powered pumps were installed. Most of the old roads dating from the exploration period are overgrown now,

*One of several wells belonging to the city of Flagstaff in the Interior Valley of the San Francisco Peaks.*

but the valley doesn't have a wilderness feeling. Until the mid 1970s, the entire watershed was closed to all public access, including hiking and cross-country skiing. Increasing public interest in the inner valley finally caused the Forest Service to open the area to day hiking and skiing. Today the springs are protected by cement and locked steel hatches. There is no access to any of the springs shown on the maps.

About 0.7 mile from the watershed cabins, a road forks left. This will be the return loop, but for now continue on the main road (right), which ends in another 0.8 mile below Flagstaff Spring. The most notable feature here is the incredible swath of destruction in the two-hundred-year-old fir and spruce. The winter of 1972-73 was an unusually snowy one, and sometime during that winter a large avalanche came down the southeast face of Humphreys Peak and destroyed the trees.

An optional cross-country side hike to Humphreys Cirque is worth doing. Continue up the forested slope, proceeding southwest from Flagstaff Spring, to reach the rim of the cirque at 11,200 feet. The rim is near timberline, and there are excellent views of the stark alpine ridges above. Return to Flagstaff Spring the way you came.

To continue on the main hike, retrace your steps east down the road 0.8 mile to the junction mentioned above, then turn right. This road goes south about 0.5 mile to the south branch of the Interior Valley, passing through some fine aspen stands before reaching a broad open meadow just west of one of the city well sites with its noisy diesel pump. This meadow has the best views in the Interior Valley. From left to right the summits are Doyle Peak, Fremont Peak, Agassiz Peak, and when visible, Humphreys Peak. From this vantage point Fremont Peak is the most striking, with its pyramidal northeast face.

Turn left at the road junction in the meadow, and descend to the east northeast, following the road back to the watershed cabins. Then return to the trailhead via the Lockett Meadow trail, the way you came.

# HIKE 30 *SUNSET-BROOKBANK TRAILS*

**General description:** A day hike in the Dry Lake Hills.

**General location:** 8 miles northwest of Flagstaff.

**Maps:** Humphreys Peak 7.5-minute, Sunset Crater West 7.5-minute USGS, Coconino National Forest.

**Difficulty:** Moderate.

**Length:** 5.3-mile loop.

**Elevation:** 7,900 to 8,800 feet.

**Special attractions:** Easy access, beautiful alpine forest and meadows.

**Water:** None.

**Best season:** Summer through fall.

**Information:** Peaks Ranger District, Coconino National Forest.

**Finding the trailhead:** From Flagstaff drive northwest about three miles on US 180, then turn right (north) on the Schultz Pass road (FR 420). Continue past the end of

*The San Francisco Peaks from the Brookbank Trail.*

# HIKES 30, 31 AND 32 *SUNSET-BROOKBANK TRAILS/ SUNSET TRAIL/ROCKY RIDGE TRAIL*

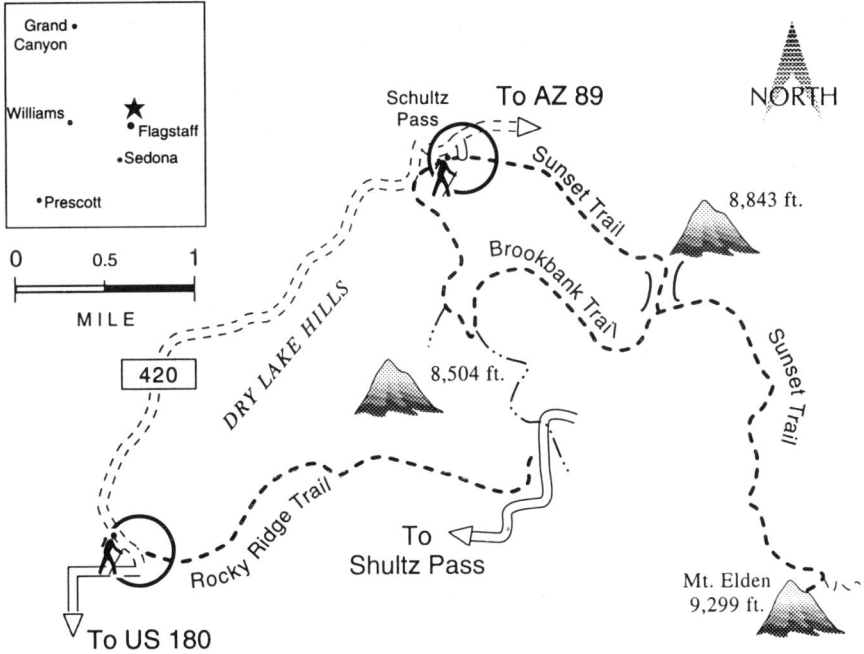

the pavement on a maintained dirt road to the signed Sunset Trail turnoff at Schultz Pass, about 5.3 miles from US 180. Park on the right (south) at the signed trailhead, about one hundred yards from the main road.

**The hike:** For details on the first 1.9 miles of this hike, see the Sunset Trail (Hike 31). Neither of the trails on this hike are shown on the topographic maps.

From the junction of the Sunset Trail and the Brookbank Trail continue straight ahead on the Brookbank trail as it contours across the slope westward. Here the forest is a lush mixture of ponderosa pine, Douglas-fir, and aspen. Less than 0.2 mile from the junction with the Sunset Trail, the Brookbank Trail crosses a gentle saddle and turns north. It descends though a small meadow then contours around a hill to the northwest. The forest is so dense here that there are very few views. After 1.9 miles the trail reaches an unmarked junction. The main trail turns left, but our loop goes right, uphill. In about 0.1 mile, the trail enters a large meadow with a seasonal lake, the largest in the Dry Lake Hills.

The trail turns into an old road as it crosses the meadow. Watch for a trail branching right (north) before the road crosses the meadow. Take this trail directly toward the San Francisco Peaks, skirting a small stock tank on the east, and then join an old road just west of the stock tank.

Follow the road downhill to the north for 1.1 miles to the Schultz Creek Trail where there is a locked gate. Turn right (east) and follow the Schultz Creek Trail 0.4 mile to the trailhead.

# HIKE 31 *SUNSET TRAIL*

**General description:** A day hike on the Dry Lake Hills and Mount Elden.
**General location:** 8 miles northwest of Flagstaff. (see map on p. 83)
**Maps:** Humphreys Peak 7.5-minute, Sunset Crater West 7.5-minute, Flagstaff East 7.5-minute USGS, Coconino National Forest.
**Difficulty:** Moderate.
**Length:** 4.7 miles one way.
**Elevation:** 8,000 to 9,299 feet.
**Special attractions:** Views of Flagstaff, natural fire recovery.
**Water:** None.
**Best season:** Summer through fall.
**Information:** Peaks Ranger District, Coconino National Forest.
**Finding the trailhead:** From Flagstaff drive northwest about three miles on US 180, then turn right (north) on the Schultz Pass road (FR 420). Continue past the end of the pavement on a maintained dirt road to the signed Sunset Trail turnoff at Schultz Pass, about 5.3 miles from US 180. Park on the right (south) at the signed trailhead, about one hundred yards from the main road.

**The hike:** The Sunset Trail, which is not shown on the topographic map, crosses the gentle slope above Schultz Tank through beautiful ponderosa pine and aspen forest, then enters a small drainage and turns uphill. Climbing steadily but at a moderate grade, the well-used trail stays on the right side of the drainage for more than a mile. It then crosses a road and veers out of the drainage to the left and enters a more open forest. The openness is due to the fact that the area was once logged. Selective logging was practiced here, meaning that most trees were left uncut. Contrast this older style of logging to clear cutting, where all of the trees are removed. Locally the trend is toward shelterwood cutting, a misleading term since most of the trees are removed in this style of logging.

The trail reaches the ridge crest, where there are good views of the San Francisco Peaks to the north, then descends west on the south side of the ridge to meet the Brookbank Trail 1.9 miles from the trailhead. The Sunset Trail turns sharply left and gradually descends the lush forested slopes to reach the broad saddle and beautiful meadow between the Dry Lake Hills and Mount Elden. It then climbs gradually to the north ridge of Mount Elden. The devastated east slopes of the mountain suddenly come into view, contrasting sharply with the fine forest you've just hiked. This man-caused forest fire started at the base of the mountain in June 1977. High winds and hot weather fanned the fire into an inferno that rapidly climbed the south face, threatening the radio equipment on the summit, as well as the beautiful pine and fir forest. Heavy application of aerial retardant saved most of the radio equipment,

*The Radio Burn viewed from the upper Sunset Trail on Mount Elden.*

but the forest on the summit and northeast slopes of Mount Elden was totally consumed in an intense crown fire. The fire was finally contained along the ridge now traversed by the Sunset Trail, and along AZ 89, several miles east of the foot of the mountain. Small aspen trees are growing in the burn, the first step toward a new fir forest that will appear several hundred years from now.

After it first reaches the ridge, the trail traverses just below the crest on the east for about 0.5 mile, then goes through another saddle. The Mount Elden Road is visible one hundred yards to the west, and a short spur trail goes down to the road. Now, the trail stays on the ridge and close to the road. The last stretch traverses the north slope just below the summit of Mount Elden, and the trail ends at a ridge as it meets the Mount Elden Trail. It is a short climb to the summit on this trail. A Forest Service fire tower stands on the highest point amid the steel forest of radio towers; visitors are usually welcome, but be sure to ask permission from the lookout before climbing the stairs. Even from the ground, the view of Flagstaff is impressive 2,000 feet below. The Mogollon Rim and the rugged mountains beyond can be seen fifty to one hundred miles to the south. East and northeast lie the Cinder Hills in the foreground and the Painted Desert in the background. The San Francisco Peaks rise dramatically to the northwest, and the upper part of the Sunset Trail is visible in the old burn.

# HIKE 32 *ROCKY RIDGE TRAIL*

**General description:** A day hike in the Dry Lake Hills. (see map on p. 83)
**General location:** 4 miles northwest of Flagstaff.
**Maps:** Flagstaff West 7.5-minute, Humphreys Peak 7.5-minute, Sunset Crater West 7.5-minute USGS, Coconino National Forest.
**Difficulty:** Easy.
**Length:** 2.8 miles one way.
**Elevation:** 7,200 to 7,600 feet.
**Special attractions:** Easy access, moderate grade, sunny south exposure.
**Water:** None.
**Best season:** Spring through fall.
**Information:** Peaks Ranger District, Coconino National Forest.
**Finding the trailhead:** From Flagstaff, drive northwest about three miles on US 180, then turn right (north) on the Schultz Pass road (FR 420). Continue 0.8 mile to the end of the pavement and park near the gate. (The gate may be closed in spring to protect the Schultz Pass Road from erosion when it is wet from snowmelt.)

**The hike:** Walk through the gate, then down an unmaintained dirt road to the right (northeast) about 0.1 mile to the signed trailhead. The Schultz Creek Trail follows the old road beyond its closure; the Rocky Ridge Trail goes right (east) and climbs up a gentle slope, staying below the steep south slope of the Dry Lake Hills. (It is not shown on the topographic map.) It climbs gradually through open ponderosa pine and oak forest, and eventually turns more to the north as it enters the canyon between the Dry Lake Hills and Mount Elden. About 1.6 miles from the trailhead, an

*A hiker on the Rocky Ridge Trail on the Dry Lake Hills.*

unmarked spur trail turns right, descends to the Mount Elden road and connects to the Oldham Trail. The main trail stays above the road for another 1.2 miles, then descends to end at the road and the junction with the Oldham Trail. See that trail description (Hike 34) for the possibility of continuing on either the Oldham or Brookbank Trails.

This trail can be hiked earlier in the spring than the other trails in the Dry Lake Hills and on Mount Elden thanks to its southern exposure—the winter snowpack melts here more quickly. It can sometimes be hiked in mid-winter during dry periods.

# FLAGSTAFF

In 1876, a party of emigrants camped a few miles southeast of the San Francisco Peaks. They celebrated the one hundredth anniversary of the signing of the Declaration of Independence by stripping a large ponderosa pine to use as a flagstaff, which gave the tiny settlement its name. When the railroad was completed in 1883, Flagstaff began to grow, primarily as a lumbering and ranching town.

# HIKE 33 *BUFFALO PARK*

**General description:** A day hike on Switzer Mesa (see map on p. 90).
**General location:** In Flagstaff.
**Maps:** Flagstaff West 7.5-minute USGS.
**Difficulty:** Easy.
**Length:** 2-mile loop.
**Elevation:** 7,100 feet.
**Special attractions:** Scenic mesa with easy access from Flagstaff.
**Water:** At entrance during the summer.
**Best season:** Spring through fall.
**Information:** Flagstaff Parks and Recreation Department.
**Finding the trailhead:** This hike is located in the north-central section of the city, adjacent to the Coconino National Forest. From the junction of US 180 and Business I-40 (Route 66) drive east one block to Beaver Street, then turn left (north). Continue one mile then turn right (east) on Forest Avenue, which becomes Cedar Avenue. Cedar will curve left; turn left at the signed turnoff for Buffalo park and the U.S. Geological Survey. Drive past the Survey complex to the end of the road and park in the large dirt parking lot.

**The hike:** Walk through the entrance gate then continue north on the old road. After about 0.1 mile turn right on the old road branching right (northeast). Stay on the outer loop road as it does a two-mile loop around the park. There are several left turns offering shortcuts, if desired. The park but not the trail is shown on the topographic map.

Buffalo Park was originally developed to hold a small herd of bison. The high

*The loop trail through Buffalo Park follows old roads that were originally laid out to allow tourists to view the buffalo from the safety of their cars.*

fences, roads, and entrance station were built so that people could drive through the park and see the bison. In the late 1960s, the herd was moved to a state bison range, and the facilities were abandoned. Since then, the park has become popular with hikers, walkers, mountain bikers, and runners. In the late 1980s it narrowly escaped having a major road built through it, but that proposal was soundly rejected by a citizens' initiative. It appears the people of Flagstaff appreciate the remarkable views and serenity of this elevated mesa within the city more than they desire a shortcut to the Grand Canyon.

# HIKE 34 *OLDHAM TRAIL*

**General description:** A day hike on Mount Elden.
**General location:** On the north side of Flagstaff.
**Maps:** Flagstaff West 7.5-minute, Humphreys Peak 7.5-minute USGS, Coconino National Forest.
**Difficulty:** Moderate.
**Length:** 4.5 miles one way.
**Elevation:** 7,000 to 8,200 feet.
**Special attractions:** Access to the Mount Elden-Dry Lake Hills trail system from Flagstaff.

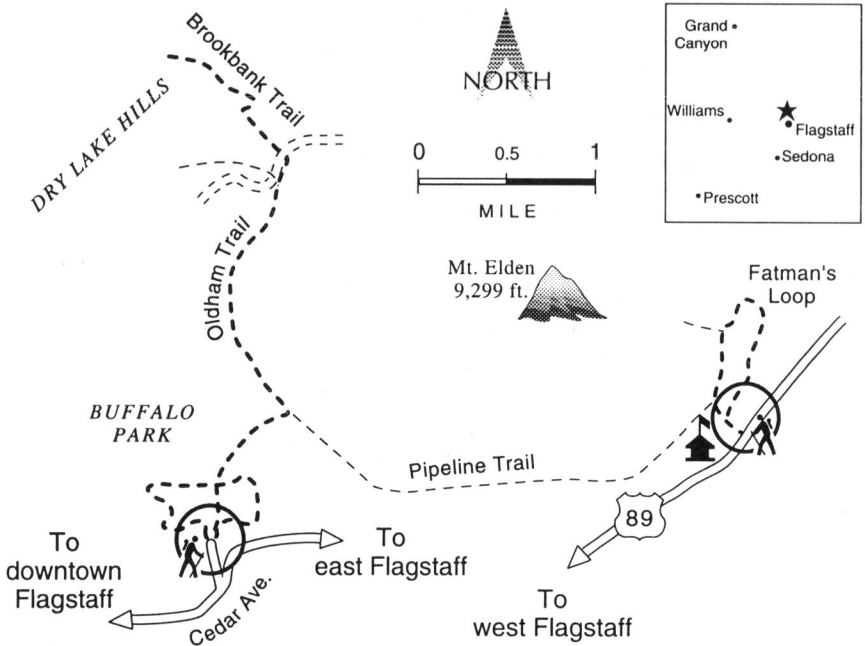

**Water:** None.
**Best season:** Summer and fall.
**Information:** Peaks Ranger District, Coconino National Forest.
**Finding the trailhead:** Follow the directions for Buffalo Park (Hike 33).

**The hike:** Go through the old gate into Buffalo Park, then continue north on the straight road that goes to the gas pipeline station at the north side of the park. The signed Oldham Trail starts just to the right (east) of the buildings, at a gap in the fence. Follow the trail off the northeast side of the mesa. Numerous false trails go left and right in this area; don't take any turns until the main trail crosses a broad pipeline cut. At this point the signed Pipeline Trail turns right (east) along the pipeline, and the Oldham Trail (our trail) turns left (northwest) along the foot of Mount Elden. After about two miles, the canyon narrows and the Mount Elden road is visible to the left. A one-hundred-foot-high basalt cliff to the right is very popular with rock climbers. This is the junction with the Rocky Ridge Trail, which is across the road to the west. The Oldham Trail becomes less distinct along the foot of the cliff, but continue to the point where the nearby road takes a turn to the right. (You will have passed the climbing area by this time.) Cross the road to reach the start of the Brookbank Trail, an old wagon road that switchbacks up a drainage. Just before reaching an open meadow,

*The Fatman's Loop on the southeast slopes of Mount Elden is an easy hike with fine views from the rugged boulder-covered terrain.*

the Brookbank Trail turns right (east) at an unsigned junction. (See the Sunset-Brookbank trails on page 82 for details.) Stay left on the main trail and continue a few hundred yards to the meadow, where there is a fine view of the San Francisco Peaks.

# HIKE 35  *FATMAN'S LOOP*

**General description:** A day hike on Mount Elden. (see map on p. 90)
**General location:** At the northeast edge of Flagstaff.
**Maps:** Flagstaff East 7.5-minute USGS, Coconino National Forest.
**Difficulty:** Easy.
**Length:** 2-mile loop.
**Elevation:** 6,900 to 7,200 feet.
**Special attractions:** Access to the Mount Elden-Dry Lake Hills trail system.
**Water:** None.
**Best season:** Spring through fall.
**Information:** Peaks Ranger District, Coconino National Forest.
**Finding the trailhead:** In Flagstaff, drive to the east side of town on Route 66, the main street. Just past the junction with I-40, you'll pass the Flagstaff Mall on the right. The four lane road, now AZ 89, curves left; turn left at the signed Mount Elden Trailhead

**The hike:** Although the sound of traffic on nearby AZ 89 removes any wilderness feeling this trail once had, it is still an enjoyable walk with some nice views. Follow the trail past the information sign. After a few hundred yards, turn right at an unsigned junction. This is the start of the Fatman's Loop; you'll return on the left fork. The trail wanders through a thick pine-oak forest at the east base of Mount Elden for about 0.5 mile to an unsigned fork. Stay left here as the right fork goes down to AZ 89. The trail begins to climb as it passes through a jumble of large boulders. There are views of the rugged slopes of Mount Elden, a view made more wild by the scarring left from the Radio Fire. The trail turns left and begins to contour to the south, meeting the signed junction with the Mount Elden Trail about one mile from the trailhead.

The Fatman's Loop continues south and begins to descend as it works its way down through the boulders. About 0.4 mile from the Mount Elden Trail junction, a sign marks the Pipeline Trail on the right; stay left and continue another 0.4 mile to the unmarked junction where you started the loop. The trailhead is a few hundred yards ahead.

# HIKE 36  *OBSERVATORY MESA TRAIL*

**General description:** A day hike in west Flagstaff.
**General location:** In west Flagstaff.
**Maps:** West Flagstaff 7.5-minute USGS.
**Difficulty:** Easy.

**Length:** 1.6 miles one way.

**Elevation:** 7,000 to 7,400 feet.

**Special attractions:** Urban trail leading into the Coconino National Forest.

**Water:** None.

**Best season:** Summer through fall.

**Information:** Flagstaff Planning Division.

**Finding the trailhead:** From the intersection of Business I-40 (Route 66) and US 180 (Humphreys Street), drive west on Route 66. Continue straight; do not turn left at the underpass. Continue several blocks, then turn right on Thorpe Road. You'll pass the Adult Center building on the left; watch for the ball park on the right. The best parking for the trail is the ball park parking lot.

**The hike:** The trail actually crosses through the ball park area from the east, but this hike picks up the trail on the west side of Thorpe Road, where a sign marks the Urban Trail system. There is also a map of the trail system. The Observatory Mesa Trail goes west through the city park and then follows a gully west about 0.4 mile. Watch for bicycles, especially on the steep downhill sections. The trail turns left and climbs steeply out of the gully to reach the top of Observatory Mesa in another 0.2 mile. From here the trail turns west again through the pine forest. It ends at a gate and a junction with several forest roads. It is possible to use these roads for an extended hike.

Observatory Mesa is named for Lowell Observatory located on its southeast edge.

*The snowcapped San Francisco Peaks viewed from near the beginning of the Observatory Mesa Trail, part of the new Flagstaff Urban Trail System.*

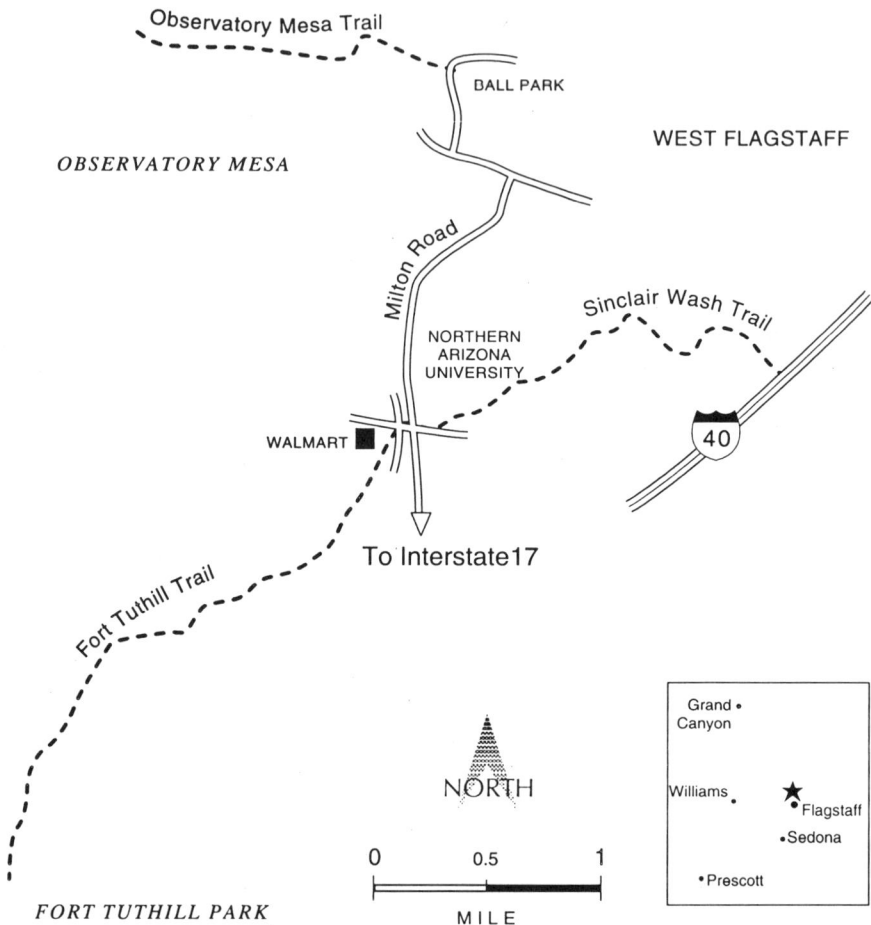

The observatory was established in 1894, just a few years after the settlement of Flagstaff. An influx of astronomers and other researchers began, forever changing the character of the small logging town.

# HIKE 37 *FORT TUTHILL TRAIL*

**General description:** A day hike in Flagstaff.
**General location:** In southwest Flagstaff.
**Maps:** Flagstaff West 7.5-minute USGS.
**Difficulty:** Easy.
**Length:** 3.3 miles one way.

**Elevation:** 6,900 to 7,000 feet.
**Special attractions:** Urban trail with easy access to Coconino National Forest.
**Water:** None.
**Best season:** Spring through fall.
**Information:** Flagstaff Planning Division.
**Finding the trailhead:** Go south on Milton Road in west Flagstaff, then turn right (west) on Woodlands Village Drive. Go one block to Beulah Street. The trail starts here and follows the west side of Beulah Street. There is no specific parking for the trail as it is part of the Flagstaff Urban Trail System. There is public parking on several side streets nearby.

**The hike:** The Flagstaff Urban Trail System is intended for use by pedestrians and cyclists, and is closed to all motor vehicles. These trails are most useful for those living or staying in Flagstaff, and is especially useful for those who do not have a car. Three of the trails offer access to the Coconino National Forest surrounding the city. Eventually the urban trail system will provide multiple access points to the Forest Service trail system on the city's boundaries.

The Fort Tuthill Trail skirts the east edge of the Walmart parking lot, below street level, as it follows Sinclair Wash to the south. It then joins an old logging railroad grade as it continues south under I-40. After passing the University Heights development, there is more open, undeveloped forest. About two miles from the trailhead, the Fort Tuthill Trail crosses AZ 89A then skirts the west edge of Mountain Dell subdivision. Beyond this the trail is in undeveloped forest. It passes through several meadows with views of the San Francisco Peaks to the north, and finally ends at Fort Tuthill County Park. Eventually, another segment of trail will be built east of I-17 making it possible to do a loop back to Flagstaff. Check with the city planning division for the current status of the trail system.

Milton Road, in southwest Flagstaff, was originally called Milltown Road because it connected Flagstaff to Milltown. Old Flagstaff was located in the present downtown area, and Milltown was to the southwest along the foot of Observatory Mesa. As the name implies, Milltown was the site of a lumber mill, in this case owned by Tim Riordan. After reading Milton's *Paradise Lost*, Riordan decided to rename the street leading to his mill in honor of one of his favorite authors.

# HIKE 38 *SINCLAIR WASH TRAIL*

**General description:** A day hike in Flagstaff. (see map on p. 94)
**General location:** In southwest Flagstaff near Northern Arizona University.
**Maps:** Flagstaff West 7.5-minute USGS.
**Difficulty:** Easy.
**Length:** 2.1 miles one way.
**Elevation:** 6,900 to 6,800 feet.

*A small bridge crosses Sinclair Wash on the Fort Tuthill Trail.*

**Special attractions:** Easy access for hikers in Flagstaff without a vehicle.
**Water:** None.
**Best season:** Spring through fall.
**Information:** Flagstaff Planning Division.
**Finding the trailhead:** Go south on Milton Road in west Flagstaff, then turn right (west) on Woodlands Village Drive. Go one block to Beulah Street. The trail starts here and follows the north side of Woodlands Village Drive. There is no specific parking for the trail as it is part of the Flagstaff Urban Trail System, but there is public parking on several side streets nearby.

**The hike:** This is another trail in the Flagstaff Urban Trail System. The trail crosses Milton Road then stays on the north side of McConnell Circle as it follows Sinclair Wash downstream onto the university campus. After a couple of blocks the street dead ends in a parking lot, and the urban trail becomes more enjoyable for hiking as it winds in and out of small drainages. After crossing south San Francisco Street it continues down Sinclair Wash around a subdivision. The Lonetree Road crossing is somewhat confusing; just remember that the trail follows the wash. A few yards downstream, Sinclair Wash ends as it joins the Rio de Flag. The trail continues another mile downstream before ending at the I-40 overpass. This is the least urban portion of the trail. Another trail is being planned that will connect this point to Lake Mary Road to the southwest and to the Foxglenn-Continental area to the northeast. Meanwhile, the hiker without a car can use the Sinclair Wash Trail to reach undeveloped forest south of I-40.

*The Sinclair Wash Trail follows the Rio de Flag on the south side of Flagstaff.*

# LAKE COUNTRY

Most of Coconino Plateau lacks surface water, despite the 100 inches of snow-fall each year because of porous limestone and volcanic bedrocks. But the area south-east of Flagstaff is the exception and is known as the Lake Country because of the numerous small lakes. Most lakes there are shallow, but some have been augmented with dams. The lakes are remnants of the wet period at the end of the last ice age, about 10,000 years ago. Many of the natural meadows that occur throughout the forest are dry lake beds, some of which still hold water after wet winters. These meadows have dense soil, formed from silt deposited in the former lake, which makes it difficult for ponderosa pines to take root. The forest slowly reclaims the meadows, spreading inward from the edges.

Three of the hikes in this section are near Mormon Lake, the largest natural lake in Arizona and a haven for wildlife.

# HIKE 39 *SANDYS CANYON TRAIL*

**General description:** A day hike near Lower Lake Mary.
**General location:** 7 miles southeast of Flagstaff.
**Maps:** Flagstaff East 7.5-minute USGS, Coconino National Forest.
**Difficulty:** Easy.
**Length:** 1.1 miles one way.
**Elevation:** 6,620 to 6,820 feet.
**Special attractions:** Interesting geology and views.
**Water:** None.
**Best season:** Spring through fall.
**Information:** Mormon Lake Ranger District, Coconino National Forest.
**Finding the trailhead:** From Flagstaff drive about 7.6 miles southeast on Lake Mary Road (FH 3), then turn left (east) just after crossing a cattleguard. The unsigned gravel road leads into a campground; bear left and continue to the signed trailhead at the northeast corner of the campground.

**The hike:** The first section of this trail follows an old road directly toward the rim of Walnut Canyon, visible ahead. (The trail is not shown on the topographic map.) At the rim it turns left (north) and skirts the edge for about 0.4 mile. The ponderosa pine forest here is open and spacious, and views of Walnut Canyon are only a few steps to the east. At one point there is an outcrop of volcanic rock on the rim, with a massive boulder field below formed from the old lava. On the opposite wall of the canyon, the horizontal strata of the Kaibab limestone form white cliffs. The Kaibab limestone forms much of the surface of the Coconino Plateau but is covered with lava flows in the Flagstaff area.

The trail crosses a shallow drainage then turns sharply right (east) and descends Sandys Canyon. A sign marks this spot. A few aspen trees, wild grape vines, and

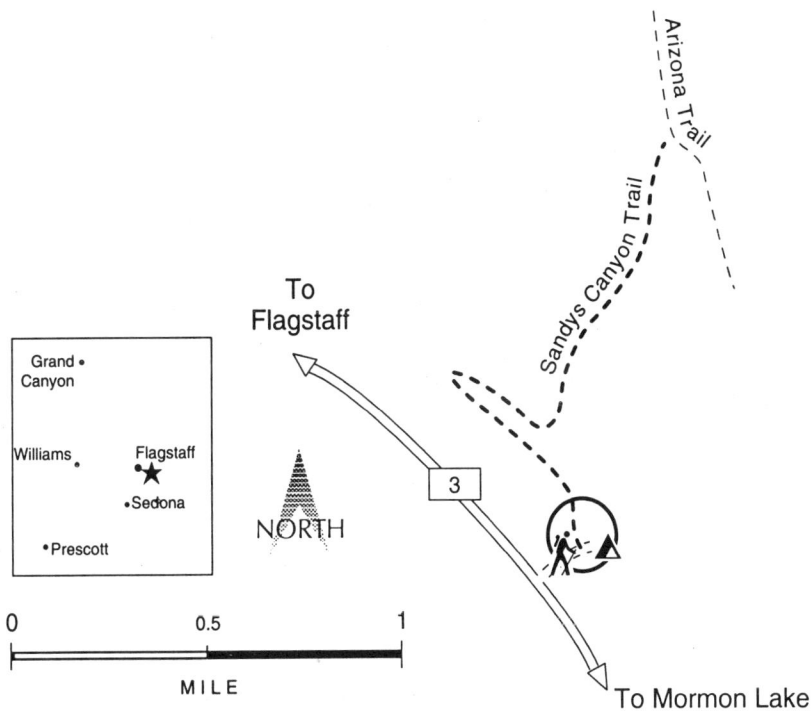

poison ivy can be found during this short descent to the floor of Walnut Canyon. The grapevines here are a tangled mass of low growing vines and leaves, and the poison ivy ("leaves of three, let it be") grows as single plants.

After the trail crosses the (normally dry) bed of Walnut Creek it turns left (north) and follows a former jeep road up the canyon bottom. The canyon is broad and has an open feeling. After about 0.5 mile the trail emerges into a meadow and ends at the signed junction with the Arizona Trail. It is worth turning right (south) and walking a few steps to another fine meadow and an impressive cliff of Coconino sandstone. Also found in the Grand Canyon, the Coconino was formed from wind drifted sand dunes, and the cross-bedded layers of sand are still visible in the rock today.

# HIKE 40  *OLD MORMON LAKE HIGHWAY*

**General description:** A day hike at the edge of Mormon Lake.
**General location:** 27 miles southeast of Flagstaff.
**Maps:** Mormon Lake 7.5-minute USGS, Coconino National Forest.
**Difficulty:** Easy.
**Length:** 1 mile one way.
**Elevation:** 7,150 feet.
**Special attractions:** Arizona's largest natural lake, great wildlife viewing.

**Water:** None.

**Best season:** Spring through fall.

**Information:** Mormon Lake Ranger District, Coconino National Forest.

**Finding the trailhead:** From Flagstaff drive twenty-seven miles southeast on Lake Mary Road (FH 3). The highway skirts the east side of Mormon Lake then descends through a cut. Watch for the turnoff to Kinnikinick Lake on the left, then turn right (east) onto an unmarked, unmaintained dirt road which descends toward the lake then turns right. Go through the gate (low clearance cars should be parked here) and drive a short distance to a fork; turn right, uphill, and drive a few yards to a second gate and park. This gate is normally locked to protect the area's wildlife.

**The hike:** This walk follows the old road along the shore of the lake. (The topographic map shows only the old road, not the current highway.) It is nearly level and is about twenty feet higher than the lake so there is a good view. This hike is best done at sunrise or sunset, the best times for wildlife viewing. The first mile is the most interesting, although the road can be followed more than three miles along the eastern shore. Cottonwood and aspen trees grow in an unusual association. Most of the year, Mormon Lake is more a marsh than a lake. After the spring snowmelt, it sometimes becomes much larger. It is the largest "natural" lake in Arizona when it is full. Although there is no dam (in contrast with Upper and Lower Lake Mary), man still has had a hand in it. The Mormon Lake area was first settled by Mormons who started dairy farming in the area. In the pioneer days the lake area was never more than a marsh, so the settlers ran cattle on the rich forage. Eventually, the hooves of

*Quaking aspen frames the view of Mormon Lake and the San Francisco Peaks along the old Morman Lake Highway.*

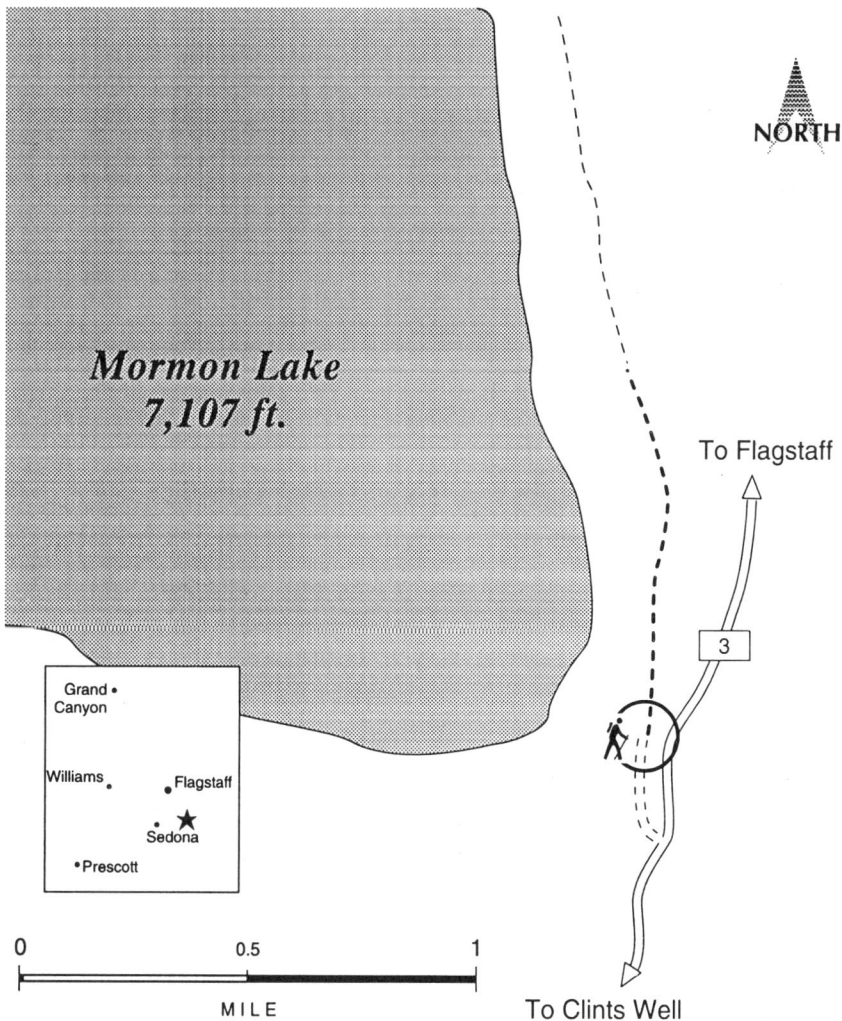

NORTH

*Mormon Lake*
*7,107 ft.*

To Flagstaff

3

Grand •
Canyon

Williams •    • Flagstaff

• ★
Sedona

• Prescott

To Clints Well

0                    0.5                    1

M I L E

the cattle compacted the soil and made it less porous, so that the marsh became a lake in wet years. Today, the lake and its marshes are important for wildlife.

# HIKE 41 *LAKE VIEW TRAIL*

**General description:** A day hike near Mormon Lake.
**General location:** 28 miles southeast of Flagstaff.
**Maps:** Mormon Lake 7.5-minute, Mormon Mountain 7.5-minute USGS, Coconino National Forest.
**Difficulty:** Easy.
**Length:** 1.4 miles one way.
**Elevation:** 7,160 to 7,600 feet.

**101**

**Special attractions:** Pleasant walk through pine-oak forest and expansive views of Mormon Lake and forest.

**Water:** None.

**Best season:** Spring through fall.

**Information:** Mormon Lake Ranger District, Coconino National Forest.

**Finding the trailhead:** From Flagstaff drive about twenty-seven miles south on Lake Mary Road (FH 3), then turn right (west) on the Mormon Lake Road (FR 90). Continue five miles, then turn right (west) into Double Spring Campground. The trailhead is signed and is on the left at the south side of the campground.

**The hike:** The Lake View Trail (not shown on the topographic map) climbs gradually along a shallow drainage through pine-oak forest for about a mile, then switchbacks up a hill to the rim of a rock outcrop. It works its way along the outcrop about 0.2 mile to a point with a commanding view of the forest and the south end of Mormon Lake. The lake is about a mile away so the view is not as intimate as the view from the Ledges Trail (Hike 42).

*The Lake View Trail is well named, as it features a panoramic view of Mormon Lake from a rock outcrop.*

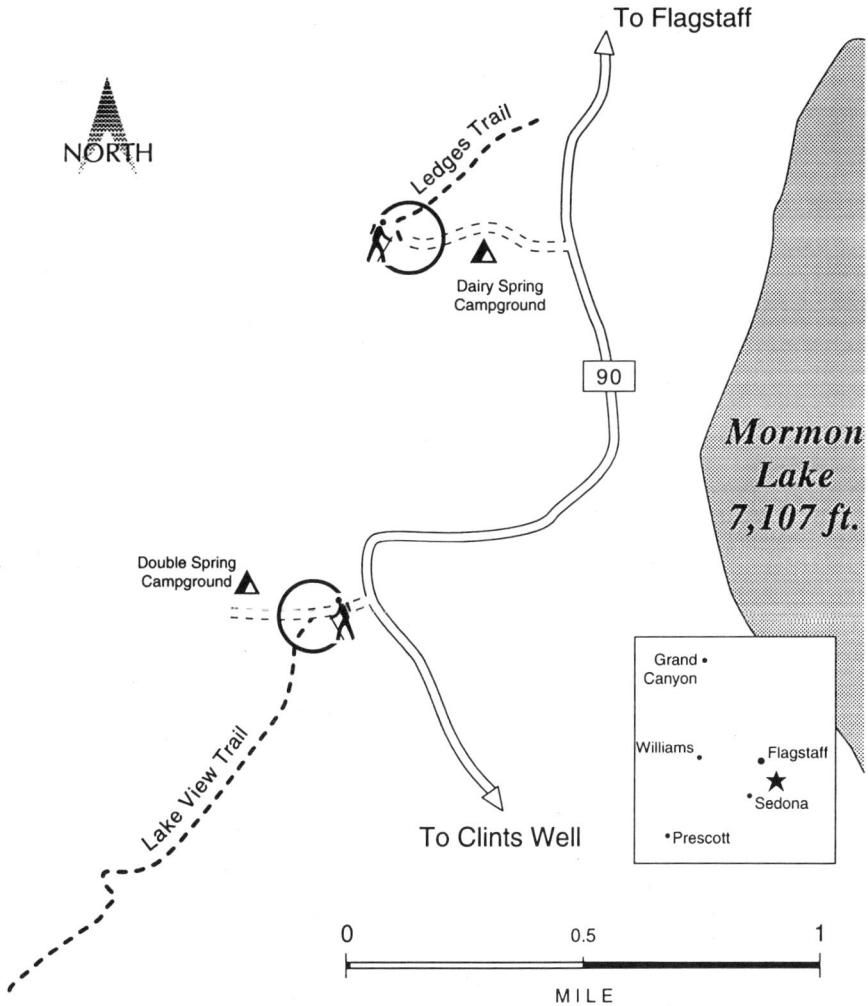

To Flagstaff

NORTH

Ledges Trail

Dairy Spring
Campground

90

*Mormon
Lake
7,107 ft.*

Double Spring
Campground

Lake View Trail

To Clints Well

Grand •
Canyon

Williams •

• Flagstaff
★
• Sedona

• Prescott

| 0 | 0.5 | 1 |

M I L E

# HIKE 42 *LEDGES TRAIL*

**General description:** A day hike near Mormon Lake.
**General location:** 22 miles southeast of Flagstaff.
**Maps:** Mormon Lake 7.5-minute USGS, Coconino National Forest.
**Difficulty:** Easy.
**Length:** 0.6 mile one way.
**Elevation:** 7,250 to 7,350 feet.
**Special attractions:** Wildlife viewing, excellent vantage point near Mormon Lake.
**Water:** None.
**Best season:** Spring through fall.

**Information:** Mormon Lake Ranger District, Coconino National Forest.

**Finding the trailhead:** From Flagstaff drive about twenty-seven miles south on Lake Mary Road (FH 3), then turn right (west) on the Mormon Lake Road (FR 90). Continue 3.6 miles, then turn right (west) into Dairy Spring Campground. Drive through the campground to site 26 and the signed trailhead.

**The hike:** This well-defined trail traverses the hillside above a row of summer homes, climbing gradually for about 0.5 mile. It then descends to a small ledge with a close view of the north end of Mormon Lake. Although the paved Mormon Lake Road is only about 0.2 mile away, the road is nicely hidden in the trees, and the view of the lake from this vantage point is nearly unspoiled. This is a great place to watch wildlife, as the ledge is about one hundred feet above the lake. Bring binoculars, and plan to arrive around sunrise or before sunset for the best viewing. The trail continues to a private camp; it's best to return the way you came.

# SECRET CANYONS

Along the Mogollon Rim a series of deep canyons cut deep into the Coconino Plateau. Sycamore Canyon is the westernmost of these. Protected in the Sycamore Canyon Wilderness, the forty-mile-long canyon offers some outstanding hiking and backpacking. To the east of Sycamore Canyon, a series of sandstone canyons and cliff-bound mesas are protected in the Red Rock-Secret Mountain Wilderness. There are a large number of short trails in the area, offering excellent day hiking and easy overnight hiking.

# HIKE 43  *KELSEY-DORSEY LOOP*

**General description:** A day hike in the Sycamore Canyon Wilderness (see map on p. 106).
**General location:** 21 miles southwest of Flagstaff.
**Maps:** Sycamore Point 7.5-minute USGS, Coconino National Forest.
**Difficulty:** Moderate.
**Length:** 7-mile loop.
**Elevation:** 5,900 to 7,000 feet.
**Special attractions:** Rugged, remote canyon.
**Water:** Kelsey, Babes Hole and Dorsey Springs.
**Best season:** Spring through fall.
**Information:** Peaks Ranger District, Coconino National Forest.
**Finding the trailhead:** From Flagstaff drive west on West US 66 (Business I-40) about two miles, then turn left (south) on the Woody Mountain Road (FR 231). This road starts out as paved but soon becomes graded dirt. Continue 13.7 miles, then turn right (west) at Phone Booth Tank onto a narrower, graded dirt road (FS 538). Continue on the main road 5.3 miles, then turn right (northwest) onto an unmaintained road (FS 538G). Continue 1.9 miles to the end of the road at the Kelsey trailhead.

**The hike:** The Kelsey Trail immediately descends west through ponderosa pine forest and drops over the upper rim of Sycamore Canyon. After less than 0.5 mile it passes

Kelsey Spring, then turns south to cross a drainage. The trail follows this drainage northwest to Babes Hole Spring. The main trail continues to descend, but our trail goes south at a junction near the spring. There are good views of rugged Sycamore Canyon to the west as the trail contours above the inner rim. At Dorsey Spring, 1.5 miles from Babes Hole Spring, turn left (east) onto the Dorsey Spring Trail. The trail climbs over a low ridge and drops into a drainage, which it follows nearly to the outer rim before swinging north. The trail goes through a low saddle in the forest before turning east again and climbing gradually to the trailhead, 1.5 miles from Dorsey Spring.

Continue along the seldom-traveled dirt road 0.6 mile, then turn left (northeast) at the junction. Go another 0.5 mile to reach Kelsey Spring Road (FS 538G). Turn left (north) and walk 1.3 miles to the end of the road and your car. It is possible to do a car shuttle to avoid the hike on the road, but there is almost no traffic on these roads, and they form a pleasant loop hike.

# HIKE 44 *WINTER CABIN-KELSEY LOOP*

**General description:** A trail and cross-country overnight backpack trip in the Sycamore Canyon Wilderness.
**General location:** 21 miles southwest of Flagstaff.
**Maps:** Sycamore Point 7.5-minute USGS, Coconino National Forest.
**Difficulty:** Difficult.
**Length:** 14-mile loop.
**Elevation:** 4,600 to 6,650 to feet.
**Special attractions:** Remote, rugged canyon.
**Water:** Kelsey, Babes Hole, Dorsey, Winter Cabin, and Geronimo springs, and seasonally in Sycamore Canyon.
**Best season:** Spring through fall.
**Information:** Peaks Ranger District, Coconino National Forest.
**Finding the trailhead:** Follow the directions for the Kelsey-Dorsey Loop (Hike 43), and drive to the Kelsey trailhead.

**The hike:** Follow the Kelsey Trail as it drops over the upper rim of Sycamore Canyon. After less than 0.5 mile it passes Kelsey Spring, then turns south to cross a drainage. The trail follows this drainage to the northwest to Babes Hole Spring. Turn left (south) on the trail to Dorsey Spring (the Kelsey Trail continues to descend—it will be our return route.) There are occasional good views of rugged Sycamore Canyon to the west as the trail contours above the canyon's inner rim, passing through pine groves and crossing brushy chaparral areas. About 1.5 miles from Babes Hole Spring, the trail reaches Dorsey Spring where the Dorsey Trail goes east to the rim; continue south. The trail continues to contour, then after about a mile it climbs through a saddle and turns more to the east as the outer canyon widens. Note the change in vegetation as the trail passes onto this drier, south-facing slope. The trail swings around a broad basin and then ends at Winter Cabin, 2.3 miles from Dorsey Spring. Winter Cabin Spring is in the drainage next to the ruin.

The Hog Hill Trail comes from the northeast, and the Winter Cabin Trail joins

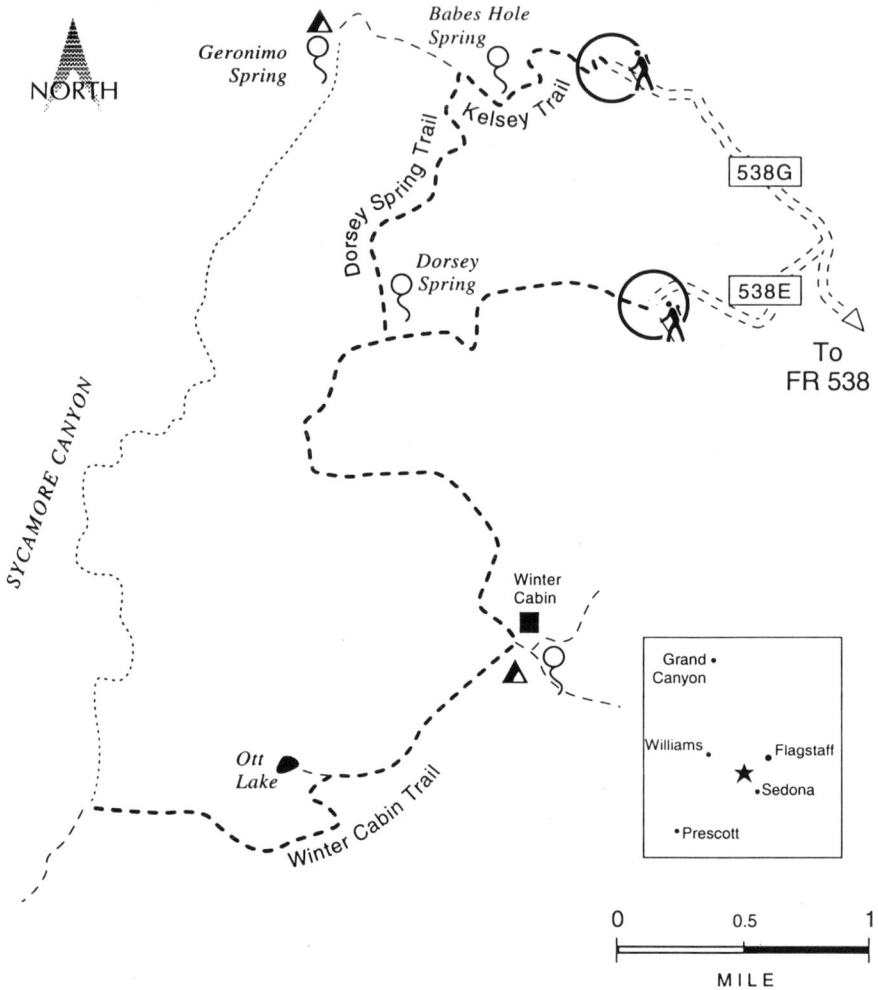

from the southeast. Our route turns right (west) onto the Winter Cabin Trail and follows it as it descends a gentle slope. The trail crosses through a saddle and the view becomes more open as the pine forest is left behind for pinyon-juniper woodland. An unsigned spur trail leads to Ott Lake, which is dry most of the time. Now the trail turns more to the south and works its way into a drainage, which it follows to the bed of Sycamore Canyon.

Turn right (north) and hike cross country up Sycamore Canyon. The going is normally easy up the broad and open streambed. But Sycamore Canyon is a major drainage and it can have a lot of water flowing down it, especially after a wet storm or during the early spring snowmelt. Even after the creek has stopped running, large

*Overlooking Sycamore Canyon from the Mogollon Rim.*

pools can make progress difficult. The best time to do this hike is when the pools are nearly dried up, but not totally. Otherwise the only water source is Geronimo Spring. Plan to carry enough water for an overnight camp. If you reach Sycamore Canyon and there is too much water for safe hiking, retrace your steps.

After about 2.7 miles you'll pass through a short but interesting narrows carved through the Coconino sandstone. Then it is another mile to Little LO Canyon, a side canyon entering from the right (east). Walk a few yards up Little LO Canyon to reach Geronimo Spring. Exit the canyon on the Kelsey Trail, which climbs steeply up the southeast slope just northeast of the spring. After about 0.5 mile the grade becomes easier. Babes Hole Spring is on the left about one mile from Geronimo Spring. Continue on the Kelsey Trail another mile to the rim and the trailhead.

# HIKE 45 *PARSONS TRAIL*

**General description:** A two or three day cross-country and trail backpack trip in the Sycamore Canyon Wilderness.
**General location:** 10 miles north of Cottonwood.
**Maps:** Clarkdale 7.5-minute, Sycamore Basin 7.5-minute USGS, Coconino National Forest.
**Difficulty:** Difficult.
**Length:** 17.6-mile loop.

**Elevation:** 3,600 to 4,900 feet.

**Special attractions:** Remote red rock canyon wilderness, permanent stream.

**Water:** Sycamore Creek; permanent creek downstream from Parsons Spring; seasonal pools upstream.

**Best season:** Spring and fall

**Information:** Sedona Ranger District, Coconino National Forest; Chino Valley Ranger District, Prescott National Forest.

**Finding the trailhead:** From Cottonwood drive to the north end of town on AZ 89A, then turn right (east) on the paved, signed road to Tuzigoot National Monument. After 0.2 mile, turn left (north) on FR 131, a graded dirt road. Drive ten miles to the end of the road at the Sycamore Canyon trailhead.

**The hike:** Sycamore Creek is normally dry above Parsons Spring. During spring, seasonal pools above this point make it possible to do this loop without carrying water. During drier seasons, such as fall or late spring, water will have to be picked up at Parsons Spring and carried to camp. The catch is that during early spring, Sycamore Creek may be flooding from snow melt in the high country, and this loop trip may be impossible. If the creek is running muddy at the trailhead, content yourself with a short day hike to Summers Spring, about 1.5 miles from the trailhead. Do not attempt to cross the creek when it is flooding. In summer, this loop is recommended only for hikers experienced in dry camping in hot weather.

From the trailhead follow the good trail 0.2 mile north into Sycamore Creek. On the left, the Packard Trail crosses the creek; this is our return trail. Continue following Sycamore Creek on the broad, easy trail along the east bank. Sycamore Creek flows year round and supports a rich variety of riparian trees, including the Arizona sycamore for which the canyon is named. About 1.5 miles from the trailhead, the canyon swings sharply left, then right, and the trail becomes less traveled. Above Parsons Spring, the source for Sycamore Creek, the creek bed dries up and the trail ends. Continue up Sycamore Creek by boulder hopping along the broad, dry wash. You may see seasonal pools of water in the bends of the creek. Also, watch for petroglyphs along the rock walls of the canyon. Although strenuous, progress up the creek bed is relatively fast because the periodic floods keep the bed clear of brush. The gorge becomes shallower after about six miles. At 7.6 miles, leave the canyon to the left (west) on the Sycamore Pass Trail, which crosses the Canyon and joins the Taylor Cabin Trail above the west bank. Turn left (south) on the Taylor Cabin Trail. There are several good campsites for small groups on the bluffs overlooking the creek to the east. There is no water unless there are pools in Sycamore Creek.

After the confines of Sycamore Creek and the rugged boulder hopping, it is a pleasure to walk the easy Taylor Cabin Trail southwest through the open pinyon-juniper forest. About 0.6 mile from Sycamore Creek, the trail crosses Cedar Creek. (This creek is usually dry at the crossing, but water can sometimes be found upstream about a mile.) The trail climbs gradually for another mile and passes through a broad saddle to enter Sycamore Basin. The walking is very easy through this open basin with fine views of the surrounding red rock formations. The trail crosses Cow Flat then skirts the head of a side canyon and climbs gently to another pass.

Walk a few hundred yards southwest on FR 181, an unmaintained dirt road, then

# HIKE 45 PARSONS TRAIL

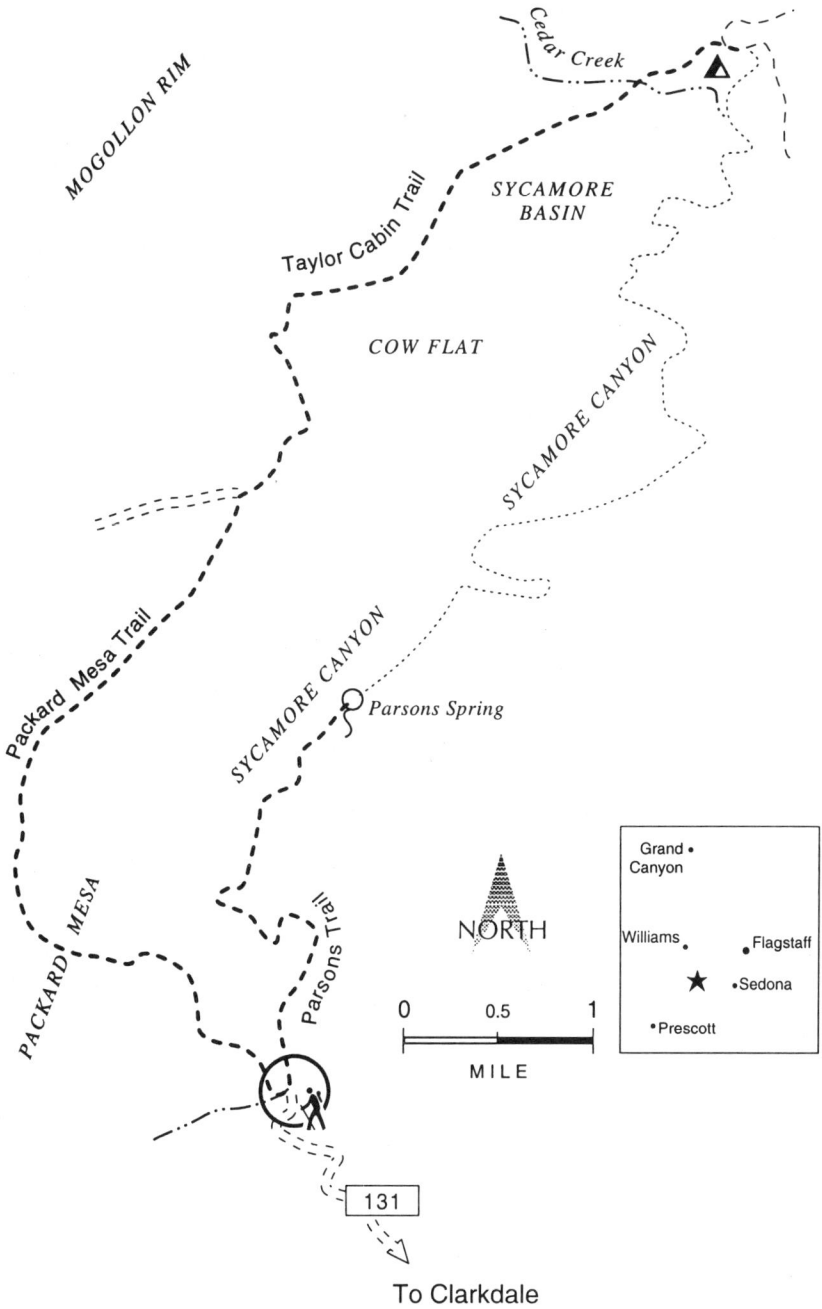

*Cedar Creek*

MOGOLLON RIM

SYCAMORE BASIN

Taylor Cabin Trail

COW FLAT

SYCAMORE CANYON

Packard Mesa Trail

SYCAMORE CANYON

Parsons Spring

PACKARD MESA

Parsons Trail

NORTH

| 0 | 0.5 | 1 |
MILE

Grand Canyon •
Williams •    • Flagstaff
★    • Sedona
• Prescott

131

To Clarkdale

turn left (south) on the Packard Mesa Trail. Packard Mesa forms the west rim of lower Sycamore Canyon, and the trail generally stays near the crest as it works its way south. About four miles from FR 181, the trail turns east and descends into Sycamore Canyon. It crosses the creek and meets the trail to Parsons Spring about 6.2 miles from FR 181. Walk up the Parsons Trail to the trailhead.

# HIKE 46 *TAYLOR CABIN TRAIL*

**General description:** A two or three day backpack trip in the Sycamore Canyon Wilderness.
**General location:** 19 miles west of Sedona.
**Maps:** Sycamore Point 7.5-minute, Sycamore Basin 7.5-minute, Loy Butte 7.5-minute USGS, Coconino National Forest.
**Difficulty:** Difficult.
**Length:** 19.1 miles.
**Elevation:** 4,200 to 6,800 feet.
**Special attractions:** Remote canyon wilderness.
**Water:** Seasonal in Sycamore Creek.
**Best season:** Spring through fall.
**Information:** Sedona Ranger District, Coconino National Forest.
**Finding the trailhead:** From Sedona drive west about eight miles on AZ 89A, then turn right (northwest) on the signed FR 525, a graded dirt road. Go 2.2 miles, then turn left (west) at a sign for FR 525C. Stay on FR 525C 8.8 miles to its end at Sycamore Pass. The last mile or two frequently washes out and may be very rough, but the rest is passable to ordinary cars. The Casner Mountain Trail, the return for this loop hike, meets FR 525C one mile east of Sycamore Pass, and this is a good place to leave your vehicle.

The hike: The Sycamore Pass Trail descends gradually to the west, then turns north after about one mile. The trail is distinct and easy to follow through the pinyon-juniper forest, though it is not shown on the Sycamore Basin topographic map. The inner gorge of Sycamore Canyon is visible to the west, and the cliffs of Casner Mountain rise on the east. The trail turns north and contours the lower slopes of Casner Mountain, gradually getting closer to Sycamore Canyon. Finally, 4.8 miles from the trailhead, it descends to Sycamore Creek and crosses it to join the Taylor Cabin Trail on the west bank. There are several campsites for small groups on the bluff just to the south. There may be water in Sycamore Creek during the spring, but it is dry later in the year. Enough water should be carried for a dry camp if the creek is dry. (In an emergency, there may be water in Cedar Creek about two miles away. Go south on the Taylor Cabin Trail about 0.6 mile, then walk cross country up Cedar Creek for a little over one mile.) During heavy rain or periods of snow melt, it may be impossible to safely cross the creek.

Turn right (northeast) on the Taylor Cabin Trail, which stays on the bench to the west of Sycamore Creek. After about two miles, the trail descends to the creek and becomes much harder to find. Watch for Taylor Cabin on the west bank; the trail passes

# HIKE 46  TAYLOR CABIN TRAIL

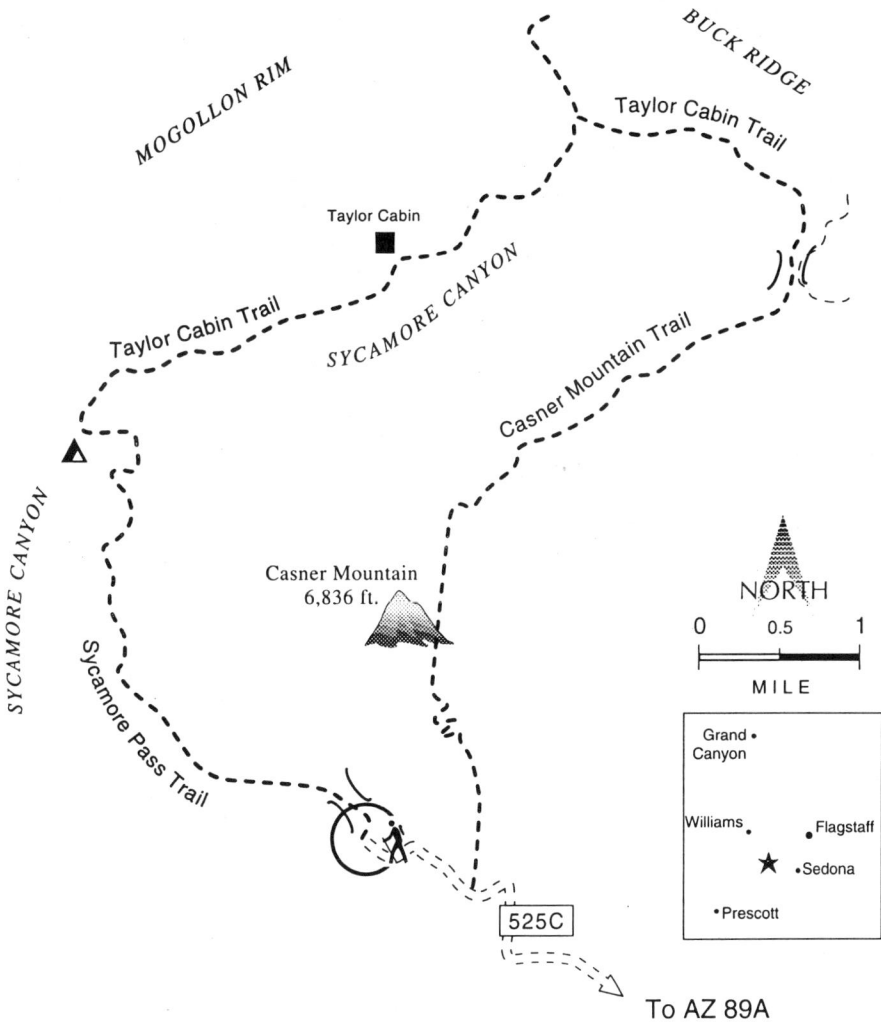

right by this old rancher's line cabin. The trail stays on the west side of the creek after Taylor Cabin. If the trail is lost then boulder-hop directly up the creek bed.

About 4.8 miles from the Sycamore Pass Trail, the Taylor Cabin Trail turns right (east) and climbs out of Sycamore Canyon. Watch carefully for the turnoff, which is usually marked by cairns. The topographic maps are essential for finding this trail. Most of the trail follows the major drainage south of Buck Ridge, often staying right in the bed of this very pretty canyon. Near the top the trail turns more to the south and climbs steeply through a fine stand of ponderosa pine and Douglas-fir. A single switchback leads to the top of the ridge, where there are excellent views of Sycamore

*An aerial view of Sycamore Canyon looking toward Casner Mountain and the Taylor Cabin Trail.*

Canyon and Taylor Basin. The trail reaches a pass and the junction with the Casner Mountain and Mooney Trails, 2.3 miles after leaving Sycamore Creek.

Turn right (southwest) on the Casner Mountain Trail, which is an old road built during power line construction. The road is now closed to vehicles and makes a scenic finish to this loop hike. Follow the trail southwest along the narrow ridge leading to Casner Mountain. There are views of Sycamore Canyon on the west and Mooney Canyon on the east. After about three miles the trail climbs onto Casner Mountain, a broad plateau capped with dark volcanic rocks. A gradual descent leads to the south edge of the plateau, where the trail descends rapidly in a series of switchbacks. Near the bottom of the descent the trail is shown as ending on the topographic map; if you lose it just follow the power line down to FR 525C. Unless you parked your vehicle at this point on FR 525C, turn right (west) and walk one mile up the road to the Sycamore Pass trailhead.

# HIKE 47  ROBBERS ROOST

**General description:** A day hike near the Sycamore Canyon Wilderness.
**General location:** 19 miles west of Sedona.
**Maps:** Loy Butte 7.5-minute USGS, Coconino National Forest.
**Difficulty:** Easy.

**Length:** 0.3 mile one way.

**Elevation:** 5,100 feet.

**Special attractions:** Old outlaw hideout, exceptional view of the red rock country.

**Water:** None.

**Best season:** All year.

**Information:** Sedona Ranger District, Coconino National Forest.

**Finding the trailhead:** From Sedona drive west about eight miles on AZ 89A, then turn right (northwest) on the signed FR 525, a graded dirt road. Go 2.2 miles, then turn left (west) at a sign for FR 525C. Stay on FR 525C for 7.5 miles, then turn right (north) on an unmaintained road that climbs up a ridge toward the east side of Casner Mountain. (Casner Mountain can be identified by the power line running down its south slopes.) Go 1.1 miles up this road until you are directly west of Robbers Roost, a low red rock mesa across the gully to the east. The trailhead and trail are unmarked.

**The hike:** Follow an unmarked trail across the shallow gully and up to the north side of Robbers Roost. Then, traverse a red sandstone ledge around to a cave on the east side of the rock, just below the rim. Inside the cave, a small wall was supposedly built by the robbers for defense. The main attraction, however, is the picture window view of Secret Mountain, Bear Mountain, and the Sedona area from within the cave. A hole though a small fin provides a smaller window. It is also interesting to explore the top of this small mesa. After a rain, temporary water pockets reflect the sky and the red rocks.

## HIKE 47  ROBBERS ROOST

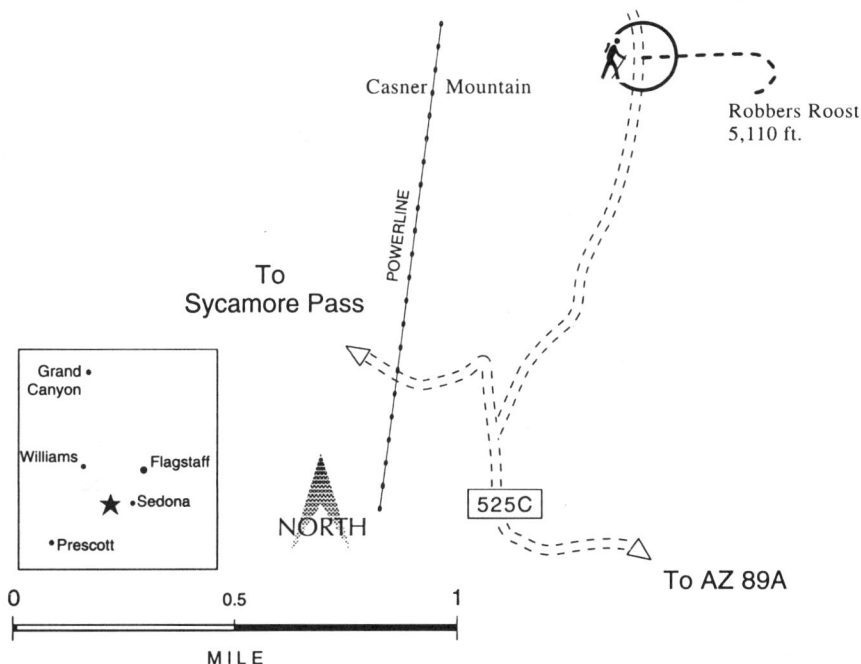

# HIKE 48 *SECRET MOUNTAIN TRAIL*

**General description:** A day hike or overnight backpack trip in the Secret Mountain-Red Rock Wilderness.

**General location:** 20 miles southwest of Flagstaff.

**Maps:** Loy Butte 7.5-minute, Wilson Mountain 7.5-minute USGS, Coconino National Forest.

**Difficulty:** Moderate.

**Length:** 4.7 miles one way.

**Elevation:** 6,300 to 6,600 feet.

**Special attractions:** Historic cabin, varied vistas of the Red Rock-Secret Mountain Wilderness.

**Water:** None.

**Best season:** Spring through fall.

**Information:** Sedona Ranger District, Coconino National Forest.

**Finding the trailhead:** From Flagstaff drive west on West Route 66 (Business I-40) about two miles, then turn left (south) on the Woody Mountain Road (FS 231). This road starts out as paved but soon becomes graded dirt. Continue 13.7 miles, then turn right (west) at Phone Booth Tank onto a narrower, graded dirt road (FS 538). Continue on this road 6.8 miles, passing the turnoff to Turkey Butte Lookout. The road is unmaintained after this point but is passable to low clearance vehicles, with care, when it is dry. After a storm or during snow melt, the mud will be impassable. In another 1.5 miles the road passes just west of a power line, then passes a stock tank. About 8.9 miles from Phone Booth Tank, FR 238 turns left (southeast) at the junction with FR 538B and crosses under the power line. Continue 2.7 miles to the end of the road.

**The hike:** The trailhead is on the edge of the Mogollon Rim, but the view is mostly blocked by the bulk of Secret Mountain rising to the south. Start by following the Secret Mountain Trail along the ridge to the southeast. It drops down to the saddle between the rim and Secret Mountain, meeting the Loy Canyon Trail. (This trail is an alternative way to reach Secret Mountain; see Hike 49 for more information).

The Secret Mountain Trail climbs about two hundred feet onto Secret Mountain, where there is an unmarked trail junction. These two side trails lead east to view points overlooking Secret Canyon. The main trail continues south about one mile across the gentle pine and oak forested terrain to the ruins of Secret Cabin. This was a Forest Service fire guard station, used in the days before roads were built. Water can sometimes be found in the drainage east of the ruin.

From the cabin continue south as the trail reaches a point on the west rim of Secret Mountain with views to the southwest toward the Verde Valley and Mingus Mountain. The trail now heads generally southeast and skirts the southwest rim of Secret Mountain. It ends about 3.2 miles from Secret Cabin, at the eastern tip of Secret Mountain. The view is down Long Canyon, with the mass of Maroon Mountain to the east dividing Long and Secret canyons.

There is nearly unlimited camping along the trail, so it makes a pleasant, easy overnight backpack trip if you are willing to carry water for a dry camp.

*Lightning fires are a common late summer occurrence in Northern Arizona.*

To Flagstaff

538

Loy Canyon Trail

Secret Cabin

SECRET MOUNTAIN

LOY CANYON

Secret Mountain Trail

6,615 ft.

Hancock
Ranch

525

To AZ 89A

NORTH

0          0.5          1

M I L E

Grand •
Canyon

Williams •          •

★ •Sedona

• Prescott

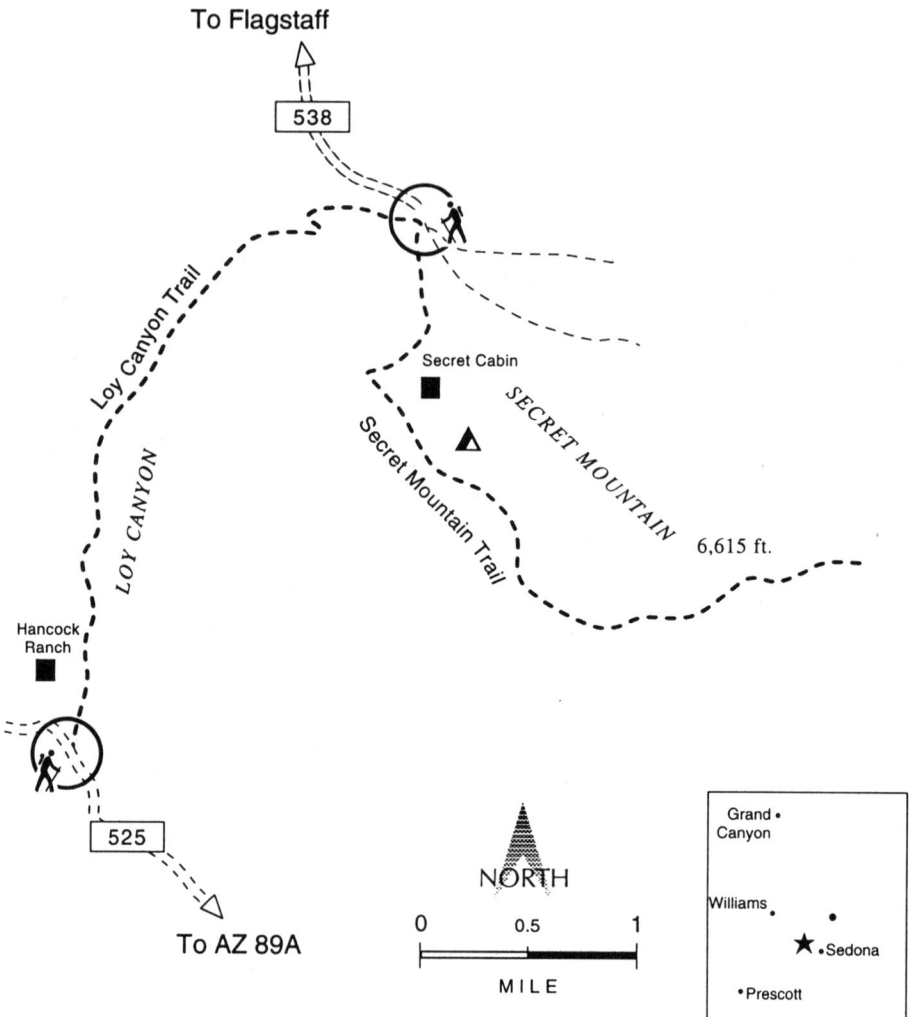

# HIKE 49 *LOY CANYON TRAIL*

**General description:** A day hike or overnight backpack trip in the Red Rock-Secret Mountain Wilderness.

**General location:** 12 miles northwest of Sedona.

**Maps:** Loy Butte 7.5-minute USGS, Coconino National Forest.

**Difficulty:** Moderate.

**Length:** 4.3 miles one way.

**Elevation:** 4,700 to 6,400 feet.

**Special attractions:** Less visited red rock canyon.

**Water:** None.

**Best season:** All year.

**Information:** Sedona Ranger District, Coconino National Forest.

**Finding the trailhead:** From Sedona drive to the west end of town on AZ 89A, then turn right (north) on the paved Dry Creek Road (FR 152C). After 2.8 miles turn left (southwest) at a signed junction, remaining on FR 152C. Continue 1.6 miles, then turn left (southwest) again. FR 152C becomes graded dirt after the second junction. After three miles, turn right (north) onto graded FR 525. Stay on FR 525 for 3.7 miles to the signed trailhead for Loy Canyon. (If you go too far you will see the Hancock Ranch to the right.)

**The hike:** Loy Canyon faces directly south and so is drier than most of the canyon hikes in the Red Rock-Secret Mountain Wilderness. This, coupled with its length, makes it less crowded than the canyons in the Dry Creek Basin to the east. However, it is a fine hike, well worth doing, and it is one of the few trails to the Mogollon Rim.

Initially the trail skirts the Hancock Ranch along its east boundary, then joins the dry creek bed which it follows northward through the open pinyon-juniper forest. Conical Loy Butte looms to the west, and the cliffs of Secret Mountain bound Loy Canyon on the east. After about two miles, the canyon becomes narrower, and the trail turns slightly toward the northeast. In another mile the trail and the canyon turn toward the east and become steeper. The buff-colored Coconino sandstone cliffs of the Mogollon Rim tower above the trail to the north, and matching cliffs form the north end of Secret Mountain. Watch carefully for the point where the trail leaves the canyon bottom and begins climbing the north side of the canyon in a series of switchbacks. Though it is a steep climb, the reward is an expanding view of Loy Canyon. Notice the contrast between the brushy vegetation on this dry south-facing slope and the cool, moist pine and fir forest across the canyon to the south.

The Loy Canyon Trail ends where it joins the Secret Mountain Trail in the saddle between Secret Mountain and the Mogollon Rim. It is possible to turn left (north) to reach the Mogollon Rim, or right (south) and hike out onto Secret Mountain. A trip combining the Loy Canyon Trail with the Secret Mountain Trail would make a good overnight backpack trip. See the Secret Mountain Trail description (Hike 48) for details.

# HIKE 50 *DOE MOUNTAIN*

**General description:** A trail and cross-country day hike near the Red Rock-Secret Mountain Wilderness. (see map on p. 121)

**General location:** 5 miles northwest of Sedona.

**Maps:** Wilson Mountain 7.5-minute USGS, Coconino National Forest.

**Difficulty:** Easy.

**Length:** 2.8-mile loop.

**Elevation:** 4,600 to 5,000 feet.

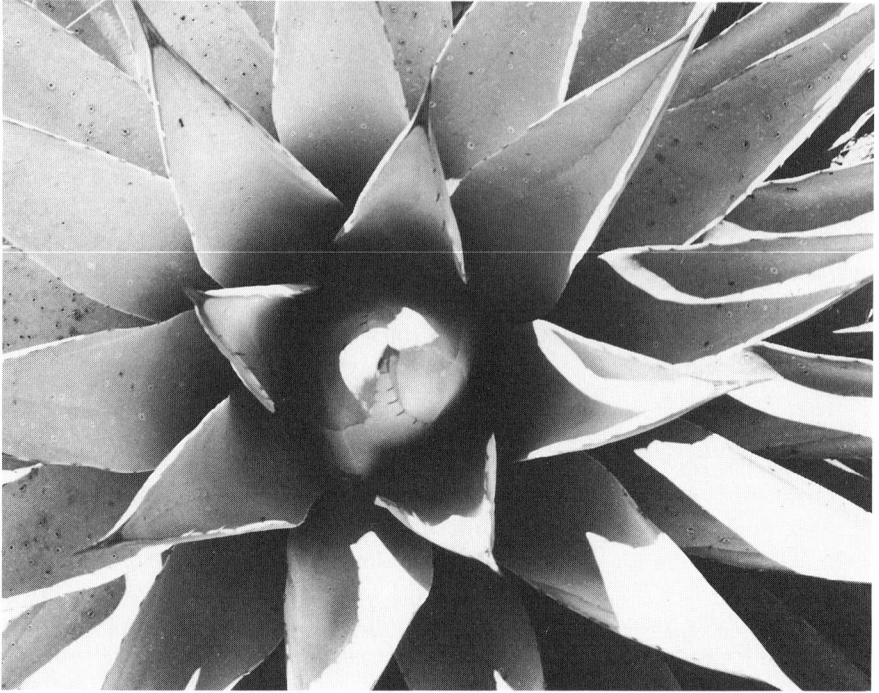

*Agave, or century plant, is a desert-dwelling relative of the lily.*

**Special attractions:** Views of Bear Mountain and the Red Rock-Secret Mountain Wilderness.

**Water:** None.

**Best season:** All year.

**Information:** Sedona Ranger District, Coconino National Forest.

**Finding the trailhead:** From Sedona drive to the west end of town on AZ 89A, then turn right (north) on the paved Dry Creek Road (FR 152C). After 2.8 miles, turn left (southwest), remaining on FR 152C. After another 1.6 miles, turn left (southwest) again, remaining on FR 152C, which becomes graded dirt. After 1.3 miles, park on the right in the Bear Mountain Trail parking area.

**The hike:** Doe Mountain is the flat red mesa to the southwest. Cross the trail and walk up the Doe Mountain Trail, which starts as an old jeep road heading directly toward a large ravine splitting the northwest side of the mesa. After a few hundred yards, the road becomes a foot trail and turns right as the slope becomes steeper. A single long switchback takes the trail back into the ravine, which it climbs to reach the rim of Doe Mountain. The trail ends, and most hikers turn back here. This hike continues cross country along the rim to the right (southwest). The walk is easy, and the reward is a series of views in all directions. The rim is about 1.8 miles long, and nearly level. Join the trail to return to the trailhead.

# HIKE 51  *FAY CANYON ARCH*

**General description:** A day hike in the Red Rock-Secret Mountain Wilderness. (see map on p. 121)
**General location:** 5 miles northwest of Sedona.
**Maps:** Wilson Mountain 7.5-minute USGS, Coconino National Forest.
**Difficulty:** Easy.
**Length:** 0.7 mile one way.
**Elevation:** 4,600 to 4,900 feet.
**Special attractions:** Natural arch, red rock canyon with very easy access.
**Water:** None.
**Best season:** All year.
**Information:** Sedona Ranger District, Coconino National Forest.
**Finding the trailhead:** From Sedona drive to the west end of town on AZ 89A, then turn right (north) on the paved Dry Creek Road (FR 152C). After 2.8 miles, turn left (southwest) at a signed junction, remaining on FR 152C. Continue 1.6 miles, then turn left (southwest) again. FR 152C becomes graded dirt after the second junction. After 0.5 mile, turn right (north) into the Fay Canyon parking area.

**The hike:** The Fay Canyon Trail is signed, and the trail starts out as an easy walk through pinyon-juniper forest along an old jeep trail. The only difficulty is a few false trails near the beginning. About 0.5 mile from the trailhead, watch for an unmarked trail going right (northeast) toward the canyon wall. This trail climbs steeply about 0.2 mile to Fay Canyon Arch, which is difficult to see until you are very close. The arch was formed from a massive fin in the Schnebly Hill formation, and stands close to the cliff behind it so there is little skylight shining through.

It is also worthwhile to continue on the main trail up Fay Canyon. It fades out about one mile from the trailhead, at a fork in the canyon, so this side trip would add two miles to the hike.

# HIKE 52  *BOYNTON CANYON*

**General description:** A day hike in the Red Rock-Secret Mountain Wilderness.
**General location:** 5 miles northwest of Sedona.
**Maps:** Wilson Mountain 7.5-minute USGS, Coconino National Forest.
**Difficulty:** Easy.
**Length:** 2.4 miles one way.
**Elevation:** 4,500 to 5,100 feet.
**Special attractions:** Red rock canyon, close up views of Bear Mountain.
**Water:** None.
**Best season:** All year.
**Information:** Sedona Ranger District, Coconino National Forest.
**Finding the trailhead:** From Sedona drive to the west end of town on AZ 89A, then

*Fay Canyon Arch frames a view of Bear Mountain in the Red Rock-Secret Mountain Wilderness.*

turn right (north) on the paved Dry Creek Road (FR 152C). After 2.8 miles, turn left (southwest) at a signed junction, remaining on FR 152C. Continue 1.6 miles, then turn right (north) onto the signed Boynton Canyon Road. Go 0.3 mile, then park at the Boynton Canyon Trailhead on the right. If you go too far you'll reach the entrance to a private resort. There is no access to the trail from the resort.

**The hike:** This is a very popular hike and it skirts a large resort for the first mile, so don't expect a wilderness experience. The upper part of Boynton Canyon is spectacular and makes up for the initial section of the hike.

The signed Boynton Canyon Trail climbs along the north side of the canyon to avoid the resort, then drops into the canyon and follows the drainage to the northwest. In another half mile or so, the canyon and trail turn toward the southwest, and the noises of the resort are left behind. The head of the canyon is formed by massive walls of Coconino sandstone on the east face of Bear Mountain. The trail becomes fainter near the end as it winds through cool pine-fir forest. A final short climb leads out of the dense forest to a viewpoint on the brushy slope above.

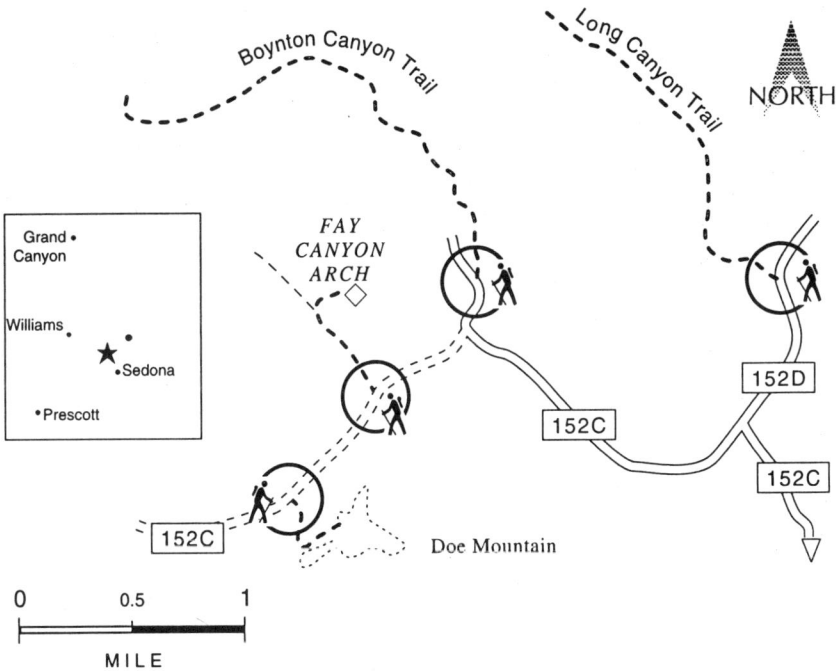

# HIKE 53 *LONG CANYON*

**General description:** A day hike in the Red Rock-Secret Mountain Wilderness.
**General location:** 5 miles northwest of Sedona.
**Maps:** Wilson Mountain 7.5-minute USGS, Coconino National Forest.
**Difficulty:** Easy.
**Length:** 2 miles one way.
**Elevation:** 4,600 to 4,900 feet.
**Special attractions:** Less visited red rock canyon.
**Water:** None.
**Best season:** All year.
**Information:** Sedona Ranger District, Coconino National Forest.
**Finding the trailhead:** From Sedona drive to the west end of town on AZ 89A, then turn right (north) on the paved Dry Creek Road (FR 152C). After 2.8 miles turn right (north) at the signed junction with the paved Long Canyon Road (FR 152D). Continue one mile to the trailhead parking on the left. (The road continues to a private subdivision.)

**The hike:** As with several other hikes in the Dry Creek area, this trail starts out as an old jeep trail. The mouth of Long Canyon is over a mile from the trailhead, so

*The giant desert centipede can inflict a painful bite without causing serious injury. They may be found under rocks and in crevices.*

the first section of the hike is through open pinyon-juniper flats, with tantalizing views of the canyon walls ahead, as well as Mescal Mountain to the south. Contrast this quiet area with the first part of the Boynton Canyon Trail.

About one mile from the canyon entrance, the trail begins to fade as the canyon walls close in. Several forks in the canyon lead up to the foot of the tall white cliffs at the base of Secret and Maroon Mountains, and offer possibilities for cross-country exploration. If you end the hike when the trail starts to fade, you'll be turning back about two miles from the trailhead.

# HIKE 54 *SECRET CANYON*

**General description:** A day hike or overnight backpack trip in the Red Rock-Secret Mountain Wilderness.
**General location:** 5 miles northwest of Sedona.
**Maps:** Wilson Mountain 7.5-minute USGS, Coconino National Forest.
**Difficulty:** Moderate.
**Length:** 4 miles one way.
**Elevation:** 4,700 to 5,100 feet.
**Special attractions:** Remote red rock canyon.
**Water:** Upper Secret Canyon.
**Best season:** All year.
**Information:** Sedona Ranger District, Coconino National Forest.
**Finding the trailhead:** From Sedona drive to the west end of town on AZ 89A, then turn right (north) on the paved Dry Creek Road (FR 152C). After two miles turn right

*Each species of yucca has a symbiotic species of moth, which carries out pollination for the yucca.*

(northeast) on the dirt FR 152. The condition of this road varies widely; some years it is rocky and very rough, and other years it is fairly good. The condition depends on the weather and the amount of recent maintenance. If you have a low clearance vehicle, plan an alternate hike in case FR 152 is impassable. Drive 3.2 miles to the Secret Canyon trailhead on the left side of the road. The parking area is small; if you miss it or it's full, drive to the end of the road to park, and then backtrack 0.8 mile.

**The hike:** Secret Canyon is the longest and most remote canyon in the Dry Creek Basin and is nearly as long as its much more famous neighbor, Oak Creek. It also has permanent water in the upper section, a rarity in the red rock area.

The Secret Canyon Trail crosses Dry Creek and then passes the wilderness boundary only a few yards from FR 152. The trail crosses Secret Canyon Wash several times; if either the wash or Dry Creek is flooding, then this hike will be impassable. Normally, however, Secret Canyon is dry in the lower section, and the hike is easy through the pinyon-juniper-cypress forest. The old jeep trail ends at a small clearing about two miles from the trailhead, and the trail becomes a foot trail. It contours along the north side of the drainage for a short distance, giving good views of Secret Canyon before dropping back into the bed. The canyon walls become much narrower here and are formed by the Mogollon Rim on the north and Maroon and Secret Mountains on the south. There is normally water (and poison ivy) in this section and a number of small

## HIKES 54, 55, 56 AND 57 *SECRET CANYON/BEAR SIGN CANYON/DRY CREEK/VULTEE ARCH*

*MOGOLLON RIM*

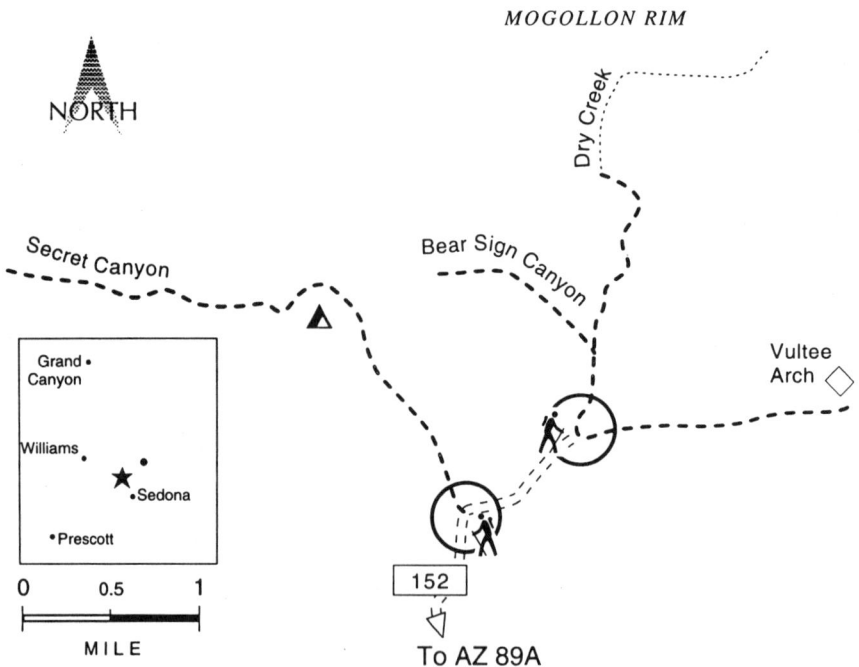

campsites on the ponderosa pine benches either side of the creek. About four miles from the trailhead, the hike ends as the trail fades out. Only those willing to do difficult cross-country hiking should continue above this point.

# HIKE 55 *BEAR SIGN CANYON*

**General description:** A day hike in the Red Rock-Secret Mountain Wilderness. (see map on p. 124)
**General location:** 6 miles northwest of Sedona.
**Maps:** Wilson Mountain 7.5-minute USGS, Coconino National Forest.
**Difficulty:** Easy.
**Length:** 2 miles one way.
**Elevation:** 4,800 to 5,100 feet.
**Special attractions:** Red rock canyon, easy hike.
**Water:** Seasonal in Bear Sign Canyon.
**Best season:** All year.
**Information:** Sedona Ranger District, Coconino National Forest.
**Finding the trailhead:** From Sedona drive to the west end of town on AZ 89A, then turn right (north) on the paved Dry Creek Road (FR 152C). After two miles, turn right (northeast) on the dirt FR 152. The condition of this road varies widely; some years it is rocky and very rough, and other years it is fairly good. The condition depends on the weather and the amount of maintenance. If you have a low clearance vehicle, plan an alternate hike in case FR 152 is impassable. Drive four miles to the end of the road.

**The hike:** Start out on the signed Dry Creek Trail. (Two trails begin at this trailhead. The Dry Creek Trail goes north, and the Vultee Arch Trail goes east.) Hike 0.6 mile north, then turn left (northwest) at Bear Sign Canyon. Bear Sign is the first side canyon on the left. The trail continues a little over one mile up Bear Sign Canyon before beginning to fade out. It is possible to go further, but the canyon becomes much rougher. There are great views of the cliffs of the Mogollon Rim, and after wet periods the creek will be running.

# HIKE 56 *DRY CREEK*

**General description:** A trail and cross-country day hike in the Red Rock-Secret Mountain Wilderness. (see map on p. 124)
**General location:** 6 miles northwest of Sedona.
**Maps:** Wilson Mountain 7.5-minute USGS, Coconino National Forest.
**Difficulty:** Moderate.
**Length:** 3.4 miles one way.
**Elevation:** 4,800 to 7,000 feet.
**Special attractions:** Remote red rock canyon, route to the Mogollon Rim.
**Water:** Seasonal in Dry Creek.

**Best season:** All year.

**Information:** Sedona Ranger District, Coconino National Forest.

**Finding the trailhead:** Follow the directions for Bear Sign Canyon to reach the Dry Creek trailhead.

**The hike:** Follow the Dry Creek Trail north out of the parking area. After 0.6 mile, Bear Sign Canyon branches left; continue north on the trail along Dry Creek. The informal trail fades out after about one mile, and this makes a good destination for an easy day hike.

Continue cross country another mile up the bed of Dry Creek. As the canyon heads against the impressive cliffs and ramparts of the Mogollon Rim, the canyon itself opens up a bit. Look east for glimpses of brushy ridges descending from the rim, which offer the possibility of a route to the top. Turn right (east) up the side canyon that enters Dry Creek just below the 5,600-foot contour on the topographic map. Follow this side canyon until it becomes difficult to continue, then turn right (southeast) and walk up the brushy ridge to reach the Mogollon Rim. Return the way you came.

An alternative plan, which requires a car shuttle, is to hike across the plateau to the west rim of Oak Creek Canyon, then down the AB Young Trail. To do this, walk cross country east through the rim forest to the top of East Pocket Knob. Alternatively, you can follow a road north to FR 231, then turn right (east) and follow it to the summit. From the fire tower on the summit, follow the cairned but faint AB Young Trail east. (See the AB Young Trail—Hike 69—for details).

*Coffee Pot Rock and Brins Mesa are seen in this aerial view looking north toward the Dry Creek area from over Sedona.*

# HIKE 57  *VULTEE ARCH*

**General description:** A day hike in the Red Rock-Secret Mountain Wilderness. (see map on p. 124)
**General location:** 6 miles northwest of Sedona.
**Maps:** Wilson Mountain 7.5-minute USGS, Coconino National Forest.
**Difficulty:** Easy.
**Length:** 2.2 miles one way.
**Elevation:** 4,800 to 5,400 feet.
**Special attractions:** Natural arch, cool pine and fir forest.
**Water:** None.
**Best season:** All year.
**Information:** Sedona Ranger District, Coconino National Forest.
**Finding the trailhead:** Follow the directions for Bear Sign Canyon (Hike 55) to reach the Dry Creek trailhead.

**The hike:** Go east from the parking lot on the trail up Sterling Canyon. This is an easy walk though pleasant pinyon-juniper-cypress forest, and the canyon is nearly straight. About two miles from the trailhead, watch for Vultee Arch on the left (north). It is a small arch and hard to spot. Right where Sterling Canyon takes a turn to the southeast, follow a trail left (north) out of the bed to reach the arch. It was named after the president of Vultee Aircraft who was killed in a plane crash nearby.

It's also interesting to continue up Sterling Canyon to its head. At the top, it is possible to descend to Oak Creek on the Sterling Pass Trail (see Hike 70 for details).

# HIKE 58  *BRINS MESA*

**General description:** A trail and cross-country day hike in the Red Rock-Secret Mountain Wilderness (see map on p. 130).
**General location:** 4 miles northwest of Sedona.
**Maps:** Wilson Mountain 7.5-minute USGS, Coconino National Forest.
**Difficulty:** Easy.
**Length:** 2.9 miles one way.
**Elevation:** 4,600 to 5,500 feet.
**Special attractions:** Views of Dry Creek, Wilson Mountain, and Sedona area.
**Water:** None.
**Best season:** All year.
**Information:** Sedona Ranger District, Coconino National Forest.
**Finding the trailhead:** From Sedona drive to the west end of town on AZ 89A, then turn right (north) on the paved Dry Creek Road (FR 152C). After two miles turn right (northeast) on the dirt FR 152. The condition of this road varies widely; some years it is rocky and very rough, and other years it is fairly good. The condition depends

on the weather and the amount of recent maintenance. If you have a low clearance vehicle, plan an alternate hike in case FR 152 is impassable. Drive 2.2 miles, then turn right into the trailhead parking area.

**The hike:** A small metal sign at the east side of the parking area marks the start of the Brins Mesa Trail. About 1.1 miles from the trailhead, the unsigned Soldier Pass Trail turns right (south). Stay left on the Brins Mesa Trail. For nearly two miles, the trail follows a normally dry wash, crossing the bed as necessary. The forest is mixed pinyon, juniper, and Arizona cypress, and views are limited until the trail climbs onto Brins Mesa. After crossing the flat mesa, the trail drops abruptly off the southeast side. Leave the trail here and go left, walking cross country (there is actually a faint trail) along the southeast edge of the mesa. Brins Mesa tilts up to the northeast, and the view gets better as you continue. At the northeast end of the mesa, about 0.5 mile from the trail, work your way onto a red outcrop. This is the end of the hike, a point offering close-up views of Wilson Mountain and the sandstone spires at the head of Mormon Canyon. You're standing on the Schnebly Hill formation, which is responsible for most of the red sandstone cliffs and rock formations in the Sedona-red rock area. The Schnebly Hill formation was deposited in a coastal tidal flat environment, and repeated exposure to the air oxidized traces of iron in the rock to create the red color. The buff-colored cliffs above, forming the impressive west face of Wilson Mountain, are Coconino sandstone, which was deposited in a dry, sand dune desert. Capping the rim of Wilson Mountain are gray layers of basalt rocks laid down in volcanic lava flows. The hard basalt protects the softer rocks below, so that erosion by water has shaped Wilson Mountain into a flat-topped mesa. In contrast, Capitol Butte to the southwest lacks a basalt cap and has eroded into a dome shape.

Return to the trail by walking directly down the center of the mesa, through the open meadow. You'll intercept the Brins Mesa Trail before you reach the end of the meadow; turn right (northwest) to return to the trailhead.

# HIKE 59 *DEVILS BRIDGE*

**General description:** A day hike in the Red Rock-Secret Mountain Wilderness.
**General location:** 3 miles northeast of Sedona.
**Maps:** Wilson Mountain 7.5-minute USGS, Coconino National Forest.
**Difficulty:** Easy.
**Length:** 0.7 mile one way.
**Elevation:** 4,600 to 4,900 feet.
**Special attractions:** Natural arch.
**Water:** None.
**Best season:** All year.
**Information:** Sedona Ranger District, Coconino National Forest.
**Finding the trailhead:** From Sedona drive to the west end of town on AZ 89A, then turn right (north) on the paved Dry Creek Road (FR 152C). After two miles turn right (northeast) on the dirt FR 152. The condition of this road varies widely; some years it is rocky and very rough, and other years it is fairly good. The condition depends

*A hiker enjoys the view from Brins Mesa, with Sedona and Munds Mountain in the background.*

on the weather and the amount of recent maintenance. If you have a low clearance vehicle, plan an alternate hike in case FR 152 is impassable. Drive 1.2 miles, then turn right into the signed Devils Bridge parking area.

**The hike:** For about 0.4 mile, the Devils Bridge Trail parallels a wash on its south side, and is confused by numerous old jeep trails. As you hike look for Devils Bridge at the top of a red sandstone ledge above and to the southeast, after which it is easier to stay on the correct trail. The last 0.3 mile of the trail is steeper as it leaves the wash and climbs directly to the west side of the bridge.

Devils Bridge is actually a natural arch, since it doesn't span a stream course. Natural arches are usually formed by the weathering of both sides of a narrow fin of sandstone.

# SEDONA

The early ranchers and cowboys referred to the Sedona area as Hells Hole because of its color and the difficulty of travel by horse before trails and roads were constructed. Settlers were attracted to Oak Creek because of its permanent stream. Originally called Oak Creek Crossing, the tiny settlement changed its name to Sedona after the Post Office balked at the length of the name. Sedona Schnebly, the town's

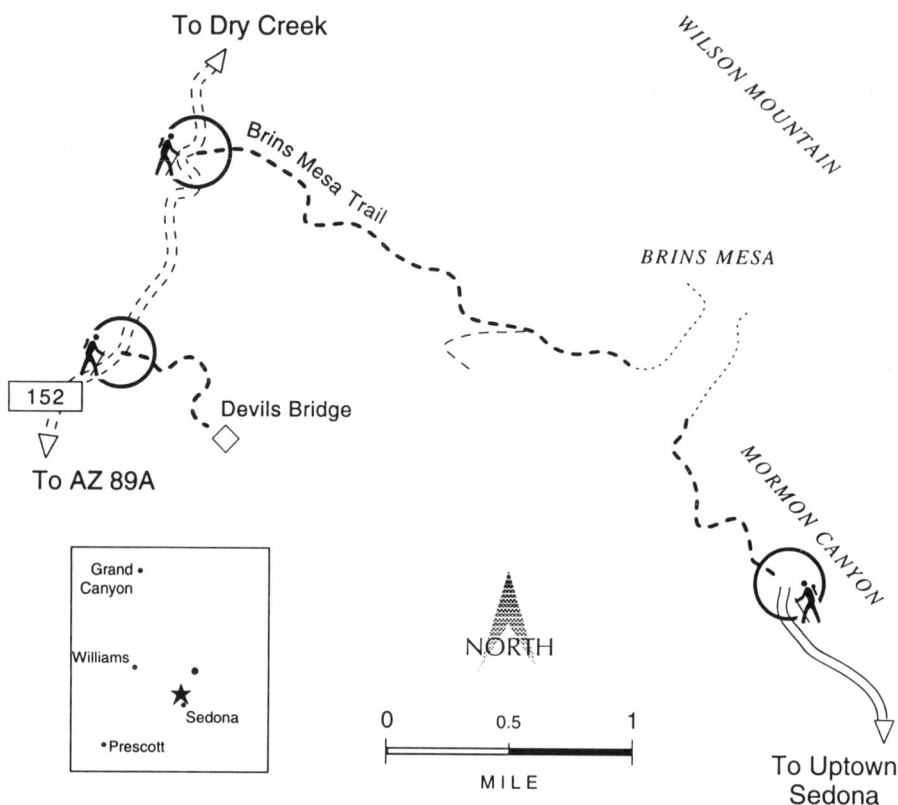

To Dry Creek

WILSON MOUNTAIN

Brins Mesa Trail

BRINS MESA

152

Devils Bridge

To AZ 89A

MORMON CANYON

Grand Canyon

Williams

★ Sedona

Prescott

NORTH

0          0.5          1

MILE

To Uptown Sedona

namesake, was the wife of an early rancher. Sedona is surrounded by the spectacular red rock area of the Coconino National Forest, and there are many excellent hiking trails.

# HIKE 60 *MORMON CANYON*

**General description:** A trail and cross-country day hike near Sedona.
**General location:** Northeast Sedona.
**Maps:** Wilson Mountain 7.5-minute USGS, Coconino National Forest.
**Difficulty:** Easy.
**Length:** 2.1 miles one way.
**Elevation:** 4,400 to 4,900 feet.
**Special attractions:** Towering sandstone cliffs and spires.
**Water:** None.
**Best season:** All year.

**Information:** Sedona Ranger District, Coconino National Forest.

**Finding the trailhead:** From the intersection of AZ 179 and AZ 89A in Sedona go north on AZ 89A. In uptown Sedona turn left (northwest) onto Jordon Road. Continue to the end of the street, which turns into an unmaintained dirt road, FR 633. Avoid private drives, continue to the locked gate, and park nearby.

**The hike:** Follow the road past the shooting range to the signed Brins Mesa Trail. This trail works its way through the Arizona cypress forest along the west side of Mormon Canyon. Arizona cypress is easily identified by its juniper-like scaly needles and its curling red bark. It is a relict survivor of past climate change, and now grows only in isolated pockets below the western Mogollon Rim and in the Mazatzal Mountains. As the trail starts to climb toward Brins Mesa, visible on the skyline to the north, watch for a cairned route that turns off to the right (northeast). Leave the trail and follow the cairns across the red sandstone ledges of the Schnebly Hill formation. The route descends into the bed of Mormon Canyon and follows it upstream. Without much difficulty you can get very close to the beautiful cliffs of Wilson

## HIKE 60  *MORMON CANYON*

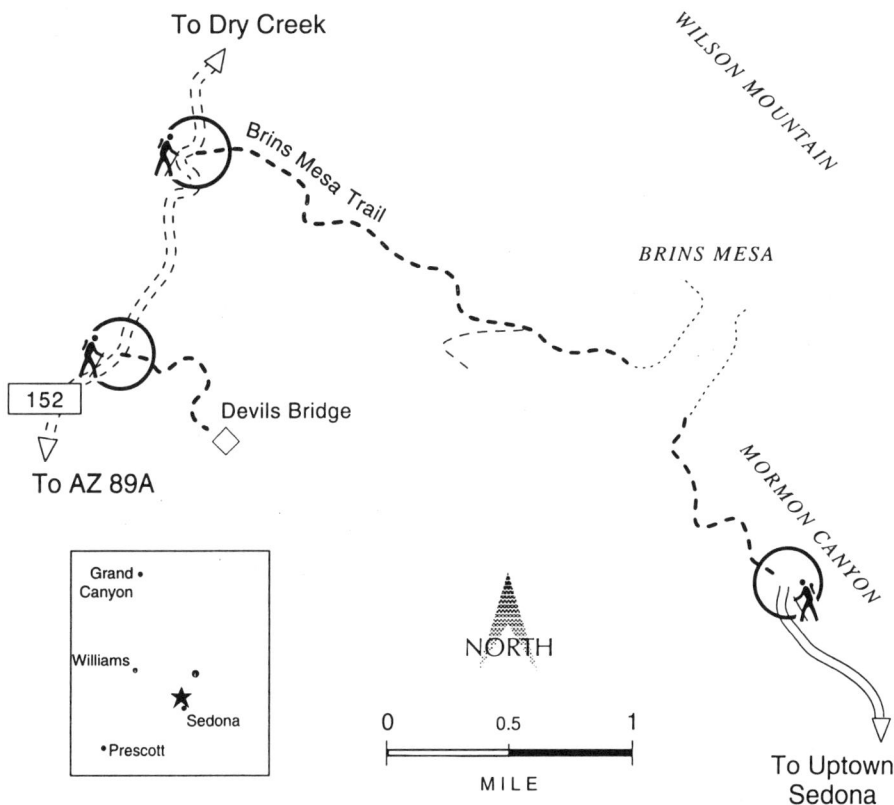

To Dry Creek

*Brins Mesa Trail*

*WILSON MOUNTAIN*

*BRINS MESA*

152

Devils Bridge

*MORMON CANYON*

To AZ 89A

Grand Canyon

Williams

★ Sedona

Prescott

NORTH

0    0.5    1

MILE

To Uptown Sedona

*Looking across Lee and Wilson Mountains in an aerial view toward the San Francisco Peaks from near Sedona.*

Mountain. The head of Mormon Canyon offers a surprisingly remote feeling considering its proximity to busy Sedona.

# HIKE 61 *EAGLES NEST TRAIL*

**General description:** A day hike in Red Rock State Park.
**General location:** 5 miles southwest of Sedona.
**Maps:** Sedona 7.5-minute USGS, Red Rock State Park brochure.
**Difficulty:** Easy.
**Length:** 2-mile loop.
**Elevation:** 3,800 to 4,100 feet.
**Special attractions:** Oak Creek.
**Water:** At visitor center.
**Best season:** All year.
**Information:** Red Rock State Park.
**Finding the trailhead:** From Sedona go west on AZ 89A to the paved lower Red Rock Loop Road, which is signed for Red Rock State Park. Turn left (south) and continue 2.9 miles, then turn right (southeast) on the paved, signed Red Rock State Park road. Continue past the entrance station to the end of the road at the visitor center.

**The hike:** Red Rock State Park was recently opened, based on a 1986 purchase of the

Smoke Trail Ranch. The ranch was the vacation retreat of Jack Fry, the president of Trans World Airlines. Purposes of the park include the preservation of the riparian habitat of Oak Creek and environmental education. A number of short hiking trails have been built along Oak Creek and on the red sandstone bluffs overlooking the creek.

From the visitor center follow the main trail downhill toward Oak Creek. Turn right at a junction, and cross Oak Creek on a low bridge at Sentinel Crossing. Notice the flood debris piled up from the huge flood of winter 1993. On the far side of the creek, turn right (west) on the signed Kisva Trail. Continue a short distance, then turn left (south) on the signed Eagles Nest Trail. This trail crosses an irrigation ditch then climbs away from the creek via several short switchbacks. At the signed junction with the Coyote Ridge Trail, turn right (south). The Eagles Nest Trail eventually turns northwest and works its way onto a ridge with a fine view of Oak Creek in the foreground and Cathedral Rock in the distance. Continue north as the trail descends to Oak Creek, crosses the ditch, and turns southeast to follow the creek. At the junction with the Kisva Trail, you've completed the loop. Retrace your steps to return to the visitor center.

## HIKES 61 AND 62 *EAGLES NEST TRAIL/ APACHE FIRE TRAIL*

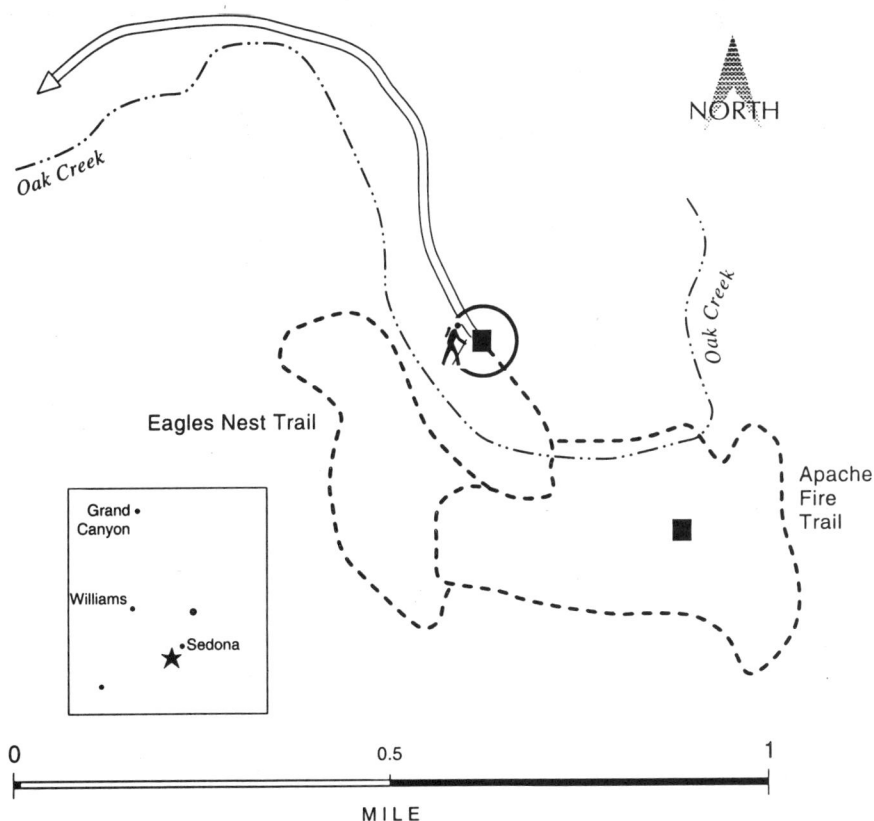

# HIKE 62 *APACHE FIRE TRAIL*

**General description:** A day hike in Red Rock State Park.
**General location:** 5 miles southwest of Sedona. (see map on p. 133)
**Maps:** Sedona 7.5-minute USGS, Red Rock State Park brochure.
**Difficulty:** Easy.
**Length:** 1.8-mile loop.
**Elevation:** 3,800 to 4,000 feet.
**Special attractions:** Oak Creek.
**Water:** At visitor center.
**Best season:** All year.
**Information:** Red Rock State Park.
**Finding the trailhead:** From Sedona go west on AZ 89A to the paved lower Red Rock Loop Road, which is signed for Red Rock State Park. Turn left (south) and continue 2.9 miles, then turn right (southeast) on the paved, signed Red Rock State Park road. Continue past the entrance station to the end of the road at the visitor center.

**The hike:** From the visitor center follow the main trail downhill toward Oak Creek, and cross Oak Creek on the bridge at Kingfisher Crossing. On the far side of the creek turn left (east) on the signed Apache Fire Trail. A side trail goes to the House of Apache Fire, which was built by Jack and Helen Fry in 1946. They named their

*An old wagon wheel on the Apache Fire Trail in Red Rock State Park on lower Oak Creek.*

vacation retreat house for the smoke from the campfires of the Yavapai Apache they employed in the construction. Back on the Apache Fire Trail, continue a short distance past the junction with the Javelina Trail. The trail works its way along the foot of the steeper bluffs above, then encounters another signed junction. Turn left (west) on the Coyote Ridge Trail, which continues to contour west. There are good views of Oak Creek and its lush habitat of Fremont cottonwood trees and other riparian vegetation. At the Eagles Nest Trail junction turn right (north), and follow the trail down toward Oak Creek. After crossing an irrigation ditch turn right (east) on the Kisva Trail. Next, turn left (north) and cross Oak Creek on the low bridge at Sentinel Crossing. Here there is an excellent view of the House of Apache Fire reflected in the creek. On the north side of Oak Creek turn right on the Smoke Trail, then left on the main trail to the visitor center.

# HIKE 63 *COURTHOUSE BUTTE*

**General description:** A day hike in the Munds Mountain Wilderness.
**General location:** 5 miles south of Sedona.
**Maps:** Sedona 7.5-minute, Munds Mountain 7.5-minute USGS, Coconino National Forest.
**Difficulty:** Easy.
**Length:** 3.1-mile loop.
**Elevation:** 4,300 to 4,500 feet.
**Special attractions:** Close-up views of Bell and Courthouse Rocks.
**Water:** None.
**Best season:** All year.
**Information:** Sedona Ranger District, Coconino National Forest.
**Finding the trailhead:** From the junction of AZ 89A and AZ 179 in Sedona go south 5.2 miles on AZ 179. Aptly named Bell Rock is to the left (east) of the highway. Park at any of several parking areas on the east side of the highway, just north of Bell Rock.

**The hike:** Don't let the crowds of motorized tourists at the trailhead put you off. You'll soon leave them and the roar of the highway behind. The unsigned trail starts as an old jeep trail going east around the north side of Bell Rock. After about 0.5 mile the jeep trail veers northeast and descends into a drainage, then crosses it. At this point turn right (east) and stay in the drainage, following a foot trail that climbs gradually toward the pass east of Courthouse Rock. From the pass follow the trail as it descends the drainage to the southeast. About 0.5 mile from the pass, the trail meets an unsigned trail that crosses the dry stream bed. Turn right (west) on this trail and continue around Courthouse Rock. The trail comes out onto a flat where the view is more open and stays just at the base of Courthouse Rock. Numerous trails branch left toward the subdivision; go right at each junction. Back near the highway, you'll pass the cottonwood trees of Bell Rock Spring (not reliable) and then turn northwest along the base of Bell Rock. The last part of the hike joins an old road paralleling the highway and completing the loop.

# HIKE 63 *COURTHOUSE BUTTE*

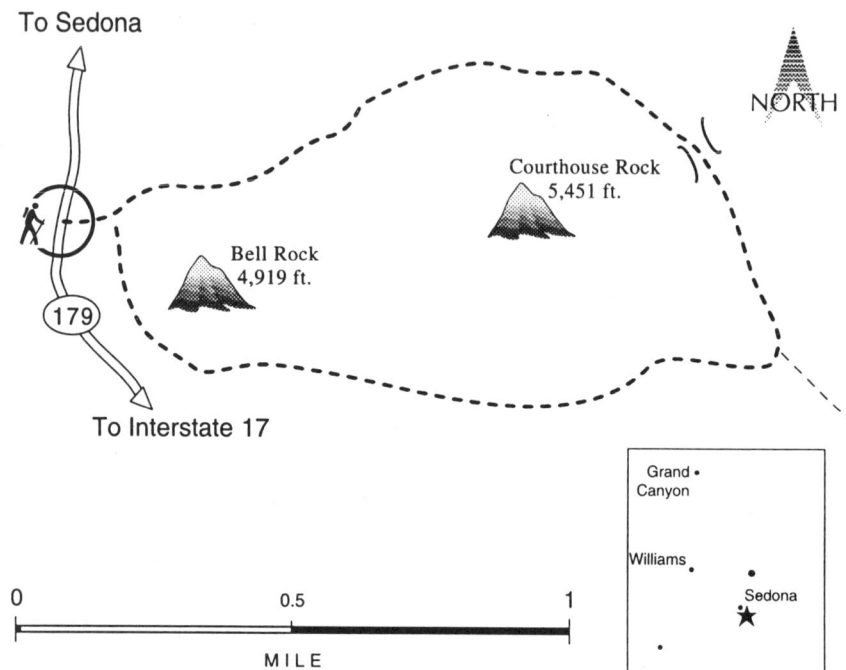

To Sedona

NORTH

Courthouse Rock
5,451 ft.

Bell Rock
4,919 ft.

179

To Interstate 17

| 0 | 0.5 | 1 |

MILE

Grand •
Canyon

Williams •
•
Sedona
★
•

# OAK CREEK CANYON

Sliced out of the Mogollon Rim, Oak Creek Canyon is very accessible from AZ 89A, which traverses its length from Sedona to Flagstaff. The canyon is about twenty miles long, and the permanent flow of Oak Creek adds to its charm. Numerous Forest Service campgrounds, picnic areas, and private resorts can be found along the highway. In the pioneer days, travel along the canyon was much more difficult. The easiest route to Flagstaff for supplies was via the canyon rims, so the early settlers built several horse trails up the steep walls of the canyon. Once on the rim, the horse would be hitched to a wagon (left there from the last trip), and the all-day journey to town for supplies would resume.

# HIKE 64 *PUMPHOUSE WASH*

**General description:** A cross-country day hike near Oak Creek Canyon. (see map on p. 138)
**General location:** 11 miles south of Flagstaff.
**Maps:** Mountainaire 7.5-minute USGS, Coconino National Forest.
**Difficulty:** Moderate.

*Cathedral Rock near Oak Creek.*

**Length:** 3.3 miles one way.
**Elevation:** 6,500 to 5,600 feet.
**Special attractions:** Narrow sandstone canyon.
**Water:** Seasonal in Pumphouse Wash.
**Best season:** Spring through fall.
**Information:** Sedona Ranger District, Coconino National Forest.
**Finding the trailhead:** This hike is most enjoyable when done one-way with a car shuttle. To reach the end of the hike from Flagstaff drive south about fifteen miles on AZ 89A to the signed Pumphouse Wash bridge. Park a car at the pullout just south of the bridge. To reach the start of the hike drive north four miles on AZ 89A, and turn right (east) on maintained dirt FR 237. Park just off the highway.

**The hike:** Walk southeast down the pine forested slope into an unnamed side canyon that drains into Pumphouse Wash. The bed of Pumphouse Wash is about 0.5 mile from the highway. Turn right and walk down Pumphouse as it makes its way southeast. The canyon becomes deeper as it cuts its way through the rim formations of dark basalt rock, exposing the buff Coconino sandstone below. A sharp turn to the southwest marks the approximate halfway point. Here the canyon is about five hundred feet deep. In the fall, the dark greens of the firs and pines growing in the canyon are supplemented by the bright yellow, orange, and red foliage of deciduous trees. Potholes carved in the sandstone bed of the canyon sometimes hold water. Several small bends in the canyon at the three-mile point mark the end of the canyon as it joins Oak Creek at the highway bridge.

# HIKES 64, 65, 66, 67, 68 AND 69 *PUMPHOUSE WASH / COOKSTOVE TRAIL/HARDING SPRING TRAIL/THOMAS POINT TRAIL/WEST FORK TRAIL/AB YOUNG TRAIL*

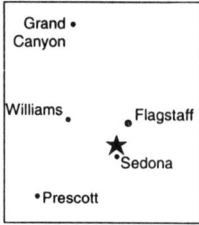

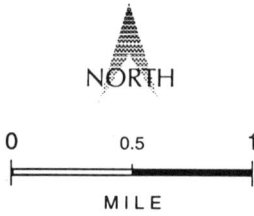

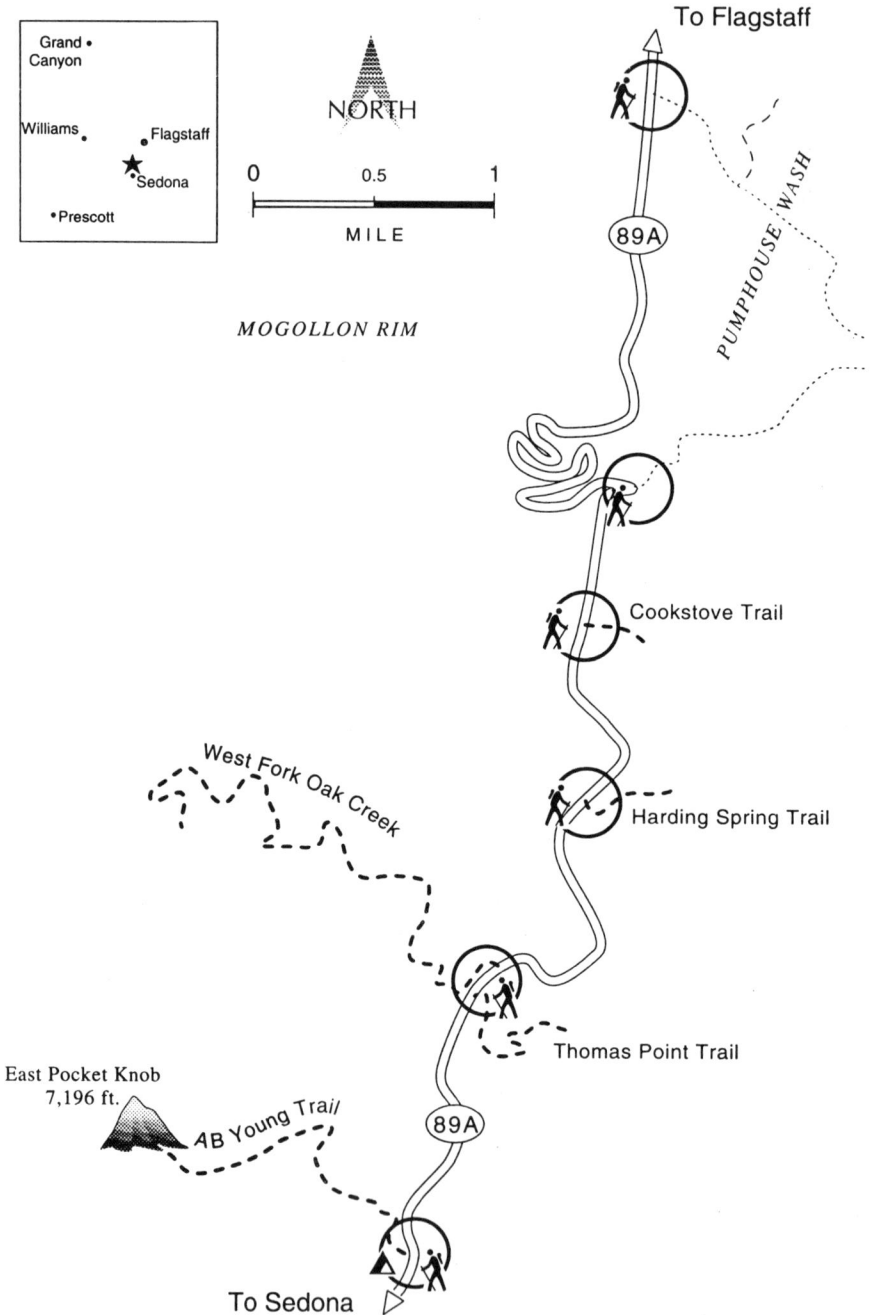

Grand Canyon

Williams

Flagstaff

Sedona

Prescott

NORTH

0    0.5    1

MILE

*MOGOLLON RIM*

To Flagstaff

89A

PUMPHOUSE WASH

Cookstove Trail

West Fork Oak Creek

Harding Spring Trail

Thomas Point Trail

East Pocket Knob
7,196 ft.

AB Young Trail

89A

To Sedona

Pumphouse Wash is the true head of Oak Creek Canyon and would be considered part of it except that the permanent flow of Oak Creek comes from Sterling Canyon. The source is Sterling Spring, which is about 0.3 mile up Sterling Canyon from the end of Pumphouse Wash.

# HIKE 65 *COOKSTOVE TRAIL*

**General description:** A day hike in Oak Creek Canyon.
**General location:** 13 miles north of Sedona.
**Maps:** Mountainaire 7.5-minute USGS, Coconino National Forest.
**Difficulty:** Easy.
**Length:** 0.5 mile one way.
**Elevation:** 5,500 to 6,300 feet.
**Special attractions:** Views of upper Oak Creek Canyon, access to Mogollon Rim.
**Water:** None.
**Best season:** Spring through fall.
**Information:** Sedona Ranger District, Coconino National Forest.
**Finding the trailhead:** From Sedona drive about thirteen miles north on AZ 89A to the north end of Pine Flat Campground, and park along the highway.

**The hike:** The trail, which is not shown on the topographic map, starts just north of the campground on the east side of the highway. It climbs directly up the ridge just south of Cookstove Draw. Although the trail is steep, it has been maintained in recent years and is in good shape. There are good views of upper Oak Creek Canyon, which is heavily forested with ponderosa pine, Gambel oak, and Douglas-fir. Alligator junipers are also common and are easily identified by their bark, which is broken into deep squares like an alligator's hide. Some alligator junipers reach massive size. The trail, originally built for fire-fighting access, reaches the rim after an 800-foot climb. It is possible to hike the rim to the south and descend via the Harding Spring Trail (see Hike 66).

# HIKE 66 *HARDING SPRING TRAIL*

**General description:** A day hike in Oak Creek Canyon.
**General location:** 12 miles north of Sedona.
**Maps:** Mountainaire 7.5-minute USGS, Coconino National Forest.
**Difficulty:** Easy.
**Length:** 0.7 mile.
**Elevation:** 5,400 to 6,200 feet.
**Special attractions:** Cool, shaded hike, views of upper Oak Creek Canyon, access to Mogollon Rim.
**Water:** None.
**Best season:** Spring through fall.
**Information:** Sedona Ranger District, Coconino National Forest.

**Finding the trailhead:** From Sedona drive about twelve miles north on AZ 89A to the turnoff to Cave Springs Campground. (The campground sign may be missing when the campground is closed for the winter. In this case look for the "Troutdale" sign at the same place.) The turnoff is on the left (west); park in the pullout just to the north.

**The hike:** Although the trail is not shown on the topographic map, the trailhead is signed and is across the highway to the east. The trail immediately starts to climb. (Ignore the other trail, which doesn't.) Originally built by the early settlers as a route to move their cattle to and from the plateau above, the Harding Spring Trail is still in good shape. The dense, cool forest offers welcome shade, so this is a good hike for a hot day. It is possible to hike the rim north and descend on the Cookstove Trail (Hike 65), or hike south and descend on the Thomas Point Trail (Hike 67). The upper ends of these other routes can be difficult to find—refer frequently to the topographic map, or hike them from their trailheads so you will know where they top out.

# HIKE 67 *THOMAS POINT TRAIL*

**General description:** A day hike in Oak Creek Canyon. (see map on p. 138)
**General location:** 11 miles north of Sedona.
**Maps:** Munds Park 7.5-minute USGS, Coconino National Forest.
**Difficulty:** Easy.
**Length:** 0.8 mile one way.
**Elevation:** 5,300 to 6,300 feet.
**Special attractions:** Excellent views of Oak Creek Canyon and the lower West Fork.
**Water:** None.
**Best season:** Spring through fall.
**Information:** Sedona Ranger District, Coconino National Forest.
**Finding the trailhead:** From Sedona drive about eleven miles north on AZ 89A, then turn left into the Call of the Canyon parking lot.

**The hike:** From the parking lot follow the unsigned trail, which is not shown on the topographic map, south through the old orchard for about one hundred yards. It will then turn east toward the highway. Look for a trail with a small rusty sign on the east side of the road. The Thomas Point Trail climbs south through shady ponderosa-oak forest for about 0.3 mile, then turns a corner onto a much drier, south-facing slope. Here, because of the increased temperature and evaporation, the chaparral plants dominate: scrub oak, mountain mahogany, and manzanita. There are fine views down the canyon to the flat-topped mesa of Wilson Mountain. A switchback leads to a point overlooking the mouth of the West Fork, then the trail turns east again and climbs into a pine saddle. The trail finishes by following the ridge east one hundred yards to the rim, where views are limited because of the thick forest.

# HIKE 68  *WEST FORK TRAIL*

**General description:** A day hike near Oak Creek Canyon. (see map on p. 138)
**General location:** 11 miles north of Sedona.
**Maps:** Dutton Hill 7.5-minute, Wilson Mountain 7.5-minute, Munds Park 7.5-minute USGS, Coconino National Forest.
**Difficulty:** Easy.
**Length:** 3 miles one way.
**Elevation:** 5,300 to 5,600 feet.
**Special attractions:** Deep, scenic canyon with lush riparian forest.
**Water:** West Fork.
**Best season:** Spring through fall.
**Information:** Sedona Ranger District, Coconino National Forest.
**Finding the trailhead:** From Sedona drive about eleven miles north on AZ 89A, then turn left into the Call of the Canyon parking lot.

**The hike:** The West Fork is an easy but extremely popular hike. This is not the place to go to escape crowds, especially on weekends when it is common to see twenty or thirty cars in the parking lot. For solitude, try the Thomas Point Trail (Hike 67) on the opposite side of Oak Creek. Note that the Forest Service prohibits camping in the lower West Fork due to heavy use. Stay on the trail and do not pick flowers or otherwise disturb this fragile environment. Use caution; there is a lot of poison ivy along the trail.

Follow the trail (not shown on the topographic map) that starts from the information sign at the west end of the parking lot. It crosses to the west side of Oak Creek then parallels the creek for about 0.2 mile. Watch for the opening of the West Fork to the right (west). When the trail turns toward the West Fork, it passes a Forest Service information sign and register. The trail turns west into the mouth of the canyon, and soon the sounds of the busy highway are left behind, replaced by the pleasant murmur of the creek and the whisper of the wind in the trees. Buttresses of Coconino sandstone tower on the left, while the canyon floor is filled with a tall pine-fir forest.

The trail crosses the creek many times and ends about three miles up the canyon. Walking is very easy to this point, which is the end of the hike. It is possible to continue up the West Fork to its head, which will require almost continuous wading in the creek and occasional swimming to cross deep pools. There is a serious danger of flash flooding; do not continue unless you have a stable weather forecast and are prepared to handle the deep pools.

Another possible hike for the adventurous, experienced canyon hiker is to climb to the south rim of the canyon, then hike to East Pocket Knob and use the AB Young Trail (Hike 69) to descend back into Oak Creek Canyon. There is a route up the nameless canyon just west of West Buzzard Point.

*An aerial view looking up the West Fork of Oak Creek. The Thomas Point Trail is visible in the foreground.*

# HIKE 69 *AB YOUNG TRAIL*

**General description:** A day hike in Oak Creek Canyon. (see map on p. 138)
**General location:** 9 miles north of Sedona.
**Maps:** Munds Park 7.5-minute, Wilson Mountain 7.5-minute USGS, Coconino
National Forest.
**Difficulty:** Moderate.
**Length:** 2.2 miles one way.
**Elevation:** 5,200 to 7,200 feet.
**Special attractions:** The best views of Oak Creek Canyon, access to the west rim.
**Water:** None.
**Best season:** Spring through fall.
**Information:** Sedona Ranger District, Coconino National Forest.
**Finding the trailhead:** From Sedona drive about nine miles north on AZ 89A to
the Bootlegger Campground. Park in the highway pullout to the north of the camp-
ground entrance.

**The hike:** Walk through the campground and cross Oak Creek. Turn left (south) on
the trail that parallels the creek and watch for the signed junction with the AB Young
Trail. This is a good, maintained trail that turns sharply right and starts climbing to
the northwest. The broad-leafed trees in the riparian habitat along the creek are soon
left behind as the trail climbs through pine forest. After a short distance, the trail
begins switchbacking directly up the steep slope. The dry southwest exposure supports dense chaparral brush, and the view becomes more open and expansive as you
climb. Just below the rim, the trail veers north in a long, final switchback. Turn
southwest and follow the cairned trail, which is fainter, along the pine-forested rim
for about 0.6 mile. Here the trail turns west and follows a gentle ridge the final 0.3
mile to East Pocket Knob and the end of the trail at the Forest Service fire tower. With
permission from the lookout, climb the tower for a panoramic view of the Mogollon
Rim and Oak Creek Canyon.

The AB Young Trail was originally built to move cattle to and from the rim country, then improved by the Civilian Conservation Corps in the 1930s. The CCC, along
with several other conservation agencies, built thousands of miles of trails in the
national forests and parks during the depression era.

# HIKE 70 *STERLING PASS TRAIL*

**General description:** A day hike in Oak Creek Canyon. (see map on p.145)
**General location:** 6 miles north of Sedona.
**Maps:** Munds Park 7.5-minute, Wilson Mountain 7.5-minute USGS, Coconino
National Forest.
**Difficulty:** Moderate.
**Length:** 0.8 mile one way.
**Elevation:** 4,800 to 6,000 feet.

**Special attractions:** Close up views of the cliffs on the north side of Wilson Mountain.
**Water:** None.
**Best season:** Spring through fall.
**Information:** Sedona Ranger District, Coconino National Forest.
**Finding the trailhead:** From Sedona drive about six miles north on AZ 89A to the Manzanita Campground. The trail starts from the left (west) side of the highway just north of the campground, but the parking is very limited. You may have to park at the pullouts south of the campground, then walk through the campground to reach the trailhead.

**The hike:** The Sterling Pass Trail is not shown on the topographic map. It climbs steeply up a drainage after leaving the highway, through a fine stand of ponderosa pines. It skirts a dry water fall, then begins a series of short, steep switchbacks. There are occasional glimpses of the massive cliffs which form the north side of Wilson Mountain. The hike ends at Sterling Pass, the sharp notch between the Mogollon Rim and Wilson Mountain. With a car shuttle, it would be possible to continue this hike by descending west to the Dry Creek trailhead. See the Vultee Arch Trail (Hike 57) for more information.

# HIKE 71 *NORTH WILSON MOUNTAIN TRAIL*

**General description:** A day hike in Oak Creek Canyon.
**General location:** 5 miles north of Sedona.
**Maps:** Munds Park 7.5-minute, Wilson Mountain 7.5-minute USGS, Coconino National Forest.
**Difficulty:** Difficult.
**Length:** 4.2 miles one way.
**Elevation:** 4,700 to 7,100 feet.
**Special attractions:** Views of Oak Creek Canyon, Dry Creek, and the Mogollon Rim.
**Water:** None.
**Best season:** Spring through fall.
**Information:** Sedona Ranger District, Coconino National Forest.
**Finding the trailhead:** From Sedona drive about five miles north on AZ 89A to the Encinosa Picnic Area. Park in the pullout on the right (west) side of the highway a few yards north of the picnic area turnoff.

**The hike:** The trailhead is signed, although the North Wilson Mountain Trail is not shown on the topographic map. The trail starts climbing immediately through mixed chaparral, ponderosa pine, and oak forest. When the trail reaches the ridge above the picnic area, it turns to the south and follows the ridge a short distance, giving good views of Oak Creek Canyon. After leaving the ridge, the trail climbs southwest up a heavily wooded drainage. The shade of the large ponderosa pines is a welcome relief on hot days. As the trail nears the base of the massive Coconino sandstone cliffs, it crosses the drainage and begins to switchback up the slope to the east. There are more fine views when the trail reaches the ridge at the top of this slope. Now the

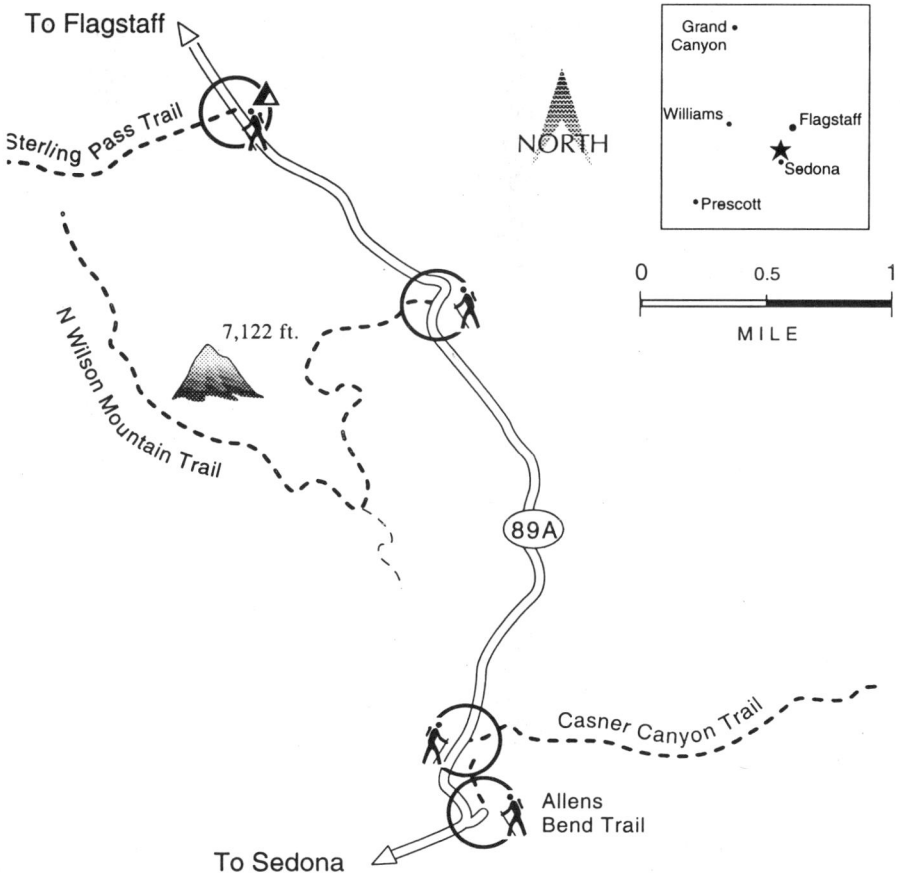

# HIKE 70, 71, 72 AND 73 *STERLING PASS TRAIL/NORTH WILSON MOUNTAIN TRAIL/CASNER CANYON TRAIL/ ALLENS BEND TRAIL*

To Flagstaff

Sterling Pass Trail

N Wilson Mountain Trail

7,122 ft.

NORTH

Grand Canyon

Williams

Flagstaff

Sedona

Prescott

0      0.5      1

MILE

89A

Casner Canyon Trail

Allens Bend Trail

To Sedona

trail turns to the south again and follows the ridge onto the First Bench of Wilson Mountain, a broad volcanic plateau, level with the east rim of Oak Creek Canyon.

Near the south end of the bench, the North Wilson Trail meets the Wilson Trail. Turn right (west) here and follow the Wilson Trail as it climbs Wilson Mountain itself. Several switchbacks lead through the basalt cliffs near the rim, and the trail comes out into a shallow drainage that it follows to reach a saddle on the wooded summit plateau. The actual summit is a small knob just to the north of this saddle.

Continue northwest on the trail, which the map shows ending just west of the 7,076-foot point. But the trail continues to the north end of Wilson Mountain where the vista includes Sterling Pass, upper Dry Creek, and the Mogollon Rim. The view of the maze of red, buff, and gray cliffs is well worth the long hike.

# HIKE 72 *CASNER CANYON TRAIL*

**General description:** A day hike in Oak Creek Canyon (see map on p. 145).
**General location:** 2.5 miles north of Sedona.
**Maps:** Munds Park 7.5-minute USGS, Coconino National Forest.
**Difficulty:** Moderate.
**Length:** 1.8 miles one way.
**Elevation:** 4,400 to 6,000 feet.
**Special attractions:** Seldom hiked trail, views of lower Oak Creek Canyon.
**Water:** None.
**Best season:** All year.
**Information:** Sedona Ranger District, Coconino National Forest.
**Finding the trailhead:** From Sedona drive about 2.4 miles north on AZ 89A, and park on the right (east) side of the highway at a closed road. This trailhead is 0.3 mile north of the turnoff to Grasshopper Point Picnic Area.

**The hike:** The trail follows the closed road down to Oak Creek, then crosses the creek and heads up the bed of Casner Canyon. There is no trail across the creek because of damage from the massive flood in 1993. The key is to locate the mouth of Casner Canyon on the east side of the creek, downstream from the point where the creek is first reached; the topographic map may be useful. After following the bed of Casner Canyon for a few hundred yards, the trail climbs out onto the north slope. It turns northwest into an unnamed side canyon below Indian Point, then climbs to reach the rim at the head of this side canyon. Most of the trail is on a dry, south-facing slope, and the low chaparral brush allows good views. This a good trail to hike on weekends and holidays when other trails are crowded.

# HIKE 73 *ALLENS BEND TRAIL*

**General description:** A day hike on Oak Creek Canyon. (see map on p. 145)
**General location:** 2 miles north of Sedona.
**Maps:** Munds Park 7.5-minute USGS, Coconino National Forest.
**Difficulty:** Easy.
**Length:** 0.3 mile one way.
**Elevation:** 4,400 feet.
**Special attractions:** Oak Creek.
**Water:** Oak Creek.
**Best season:** All year.
**Information:** Sedona Ranger District, Coconino National Forest.
**Finding the trailhead:** From Sedona drive about two miles north on AZ 89A and turn right (east) into the Grasshopper Point Picnic Area.

**The hike:** The unsigned trail, which is not shown on the topographic map, starts from the north end of the parking lot, and follows the west bank of Oak Creek. There are several sections of elaborate trail construction near the beginning, then the trail comes out onto a wider bench. Watch for poison ivy, which is very common along Oak Creek. The trail ends near an old road that comes down from the highway above. Although short, the Allens Bend Trail is a pleasant, shady walk along the rushing waters of Oak Creek. It also provides an alternate access to the Casner Canyon Trail (Hike 72), which crosses the creek at the end of this trail.

In this area, the red rocks near the creek are sandstones and limestones of the Supai formation. The Supai begins to outcrop here and forms the inner gorge of Oak Creek Canyon below this point.

# MOGOLLON RIM

East of Oak Creek Canyon, the Mogollon Rim turns southeast to form the eastern boundary of the Verde Valley. At Fossil Creek, the Rim resumes its general eastward direction. A series of long, spectacular canyons cut into the Rim; most are wild and remote and are protected as wilderness areas. Several of the following hikes are in these canyons; others are on the southeast portion of the Coconino Plateau.

# HIKE 74 *APACHE MAID TRAIL*

**General description:** A day hike in the Wet Beaver Creek Wilderness (see map on p. 149).
**General location:** 16 miles southeast of Sedona.
**Maps:** Casner Butte 7.5-minute USGS, Coconino National Forest.
**Difficulty:** Moderate.
**Length:** 3.5 miles one way.
**Elevation:** 3,900 to 5,100 feet.
**Special attractions:** Permanent stream, views of Wet Beaver Creek.
**Water:** Wet Beaver Creek.
**Best season:** All year.
**Information:** Beaver Creek Ranger District, Coconino National Forest.
**Finding the trailhead:** From Sedona drive about fourteen miles southeast on AZ 179, go under the I-17 interchange, then drive another 2.1 miles on the Beaver Creek road (FR 618). Turn left (east) on the signed, dirt road and go 0.2 mile to the Wet Beaver Creek trailhead.
**The hike:** This hike starts on the Bell Trail, which follows the north side of Wet Beaver Creek. Stands of Fremont cottonwood and other riparian vegetation crowd the creek, but there are several short side trails down to the water. One of several permanent streams flowing through the canyons below the Mogollon Rim, Wet Beaver Creek is very popular during hot weather. As you continue up the canyon, notice how the slope to the left, which is sunnier and drier, features a nearly pure stand of juniper trees. On the other hand, the slope to the right faces north and is cooler and moister, and supports a mixed stand of juniper and pinyon. Evidently the pinyon pines require just a bit more moisture, and possibly cooler temperatures, than

the junipers. Very slight changes in climate can have a dramatic effect on plant and animal communities.

After 2.1 miles, turn left (northeast) on the signed Apache Maid Trail, which starts climbing the north slope of the canyon. (For more information on the Bell Trail, see the *Hiker's Guide to Arizona*.) The juniper forest is open, and the first section of the trail provides good views down Wet Beaver Creek. A series of switchbacks lead up to the base of Casner Butte, then the trail crosses the drainage to the north and angles up to the Mogollon Rim. Here the view ranges from the San Francisco Peaks in the north to the Verde Valley in the west and southwest. Originally built for access to the Apache Maid fire tower, the remainder of the trail is faint and difficult to follow, so the hike ends here.

# HIKE 75 *BUCKHORN TRAIL*

**General description:** A day hike to the Mogollon Rim.
**General location:** 9 miles northeast of Camp Verde.
**Maps:** Walker Mtn. 7.5-minute USGS, Coconino National Forest.
**Difficulty:** Moderate.
**Length:** 2.4 miles one way.
**Elevation:** 4,100 to 5,200 feet.
**Special attractions:** Expansive views of the Verde Valley, rarely traveled trail.
**Water:** None.
**Best season:** All year.
**Information:** Beaver Creek Ranger District, Coconino National Forest.
**Finding the trailhead:** From Camp Verde drive east about three miles on the paved FH 9 (General Crook Trail), then turn left (north) on the graded, dirt FR 618. Continue 5.5 miles, then turn right (east) on FR 9201M. This unmaintained road is just past the sign for Wickiup Draw. Go 1.1 miles to the third closed road on the left (north). The trailhead is not signed, and there is minimal parking.

FR 9201M can also be reached from the north. Take the AZ 179 exit from I-17, then go southeast on FR 618, which is paved to the Beaver Creek Campground. FR 9201M is 8.1 miles from the interstate, and just before the Wickiup Draw sign.

**The hike:** Initially, the Buckhorn Trail is an old jeep road that the Forest Service has closed by bulldozing a pile of dirt across its beginning. The trail leads northeast across a flat, then climbs onto a juniper-covered mesa. It is a pleasant walk about 1.3 miles to a fence line, where the trail turns southeast and starts to climb along a ridge crest. The view becomes wider as the ridge gains elevation and narrows. Pinyon pines begin to compete with the junipers. Finally, the ridge runs into the slopes below the Mogollon Rim, and the trail grows steep and rocky. Mercifully, this section is short, and the trail soon reaches a saddle on the ridge leading to Hollingshead Point. Above this saddle the trail becomes difficult to follow, so the hike ends here. It is possible to continue cross country another mile to the actual Mogollon Rim.

The Verde Valley (*verde* means green in Spanish) to the west was named by the members of the Spanish expedition under Coronado that explored Arizona in the early 1540s. After their long, hot journey from Mexico City through the Sonoran

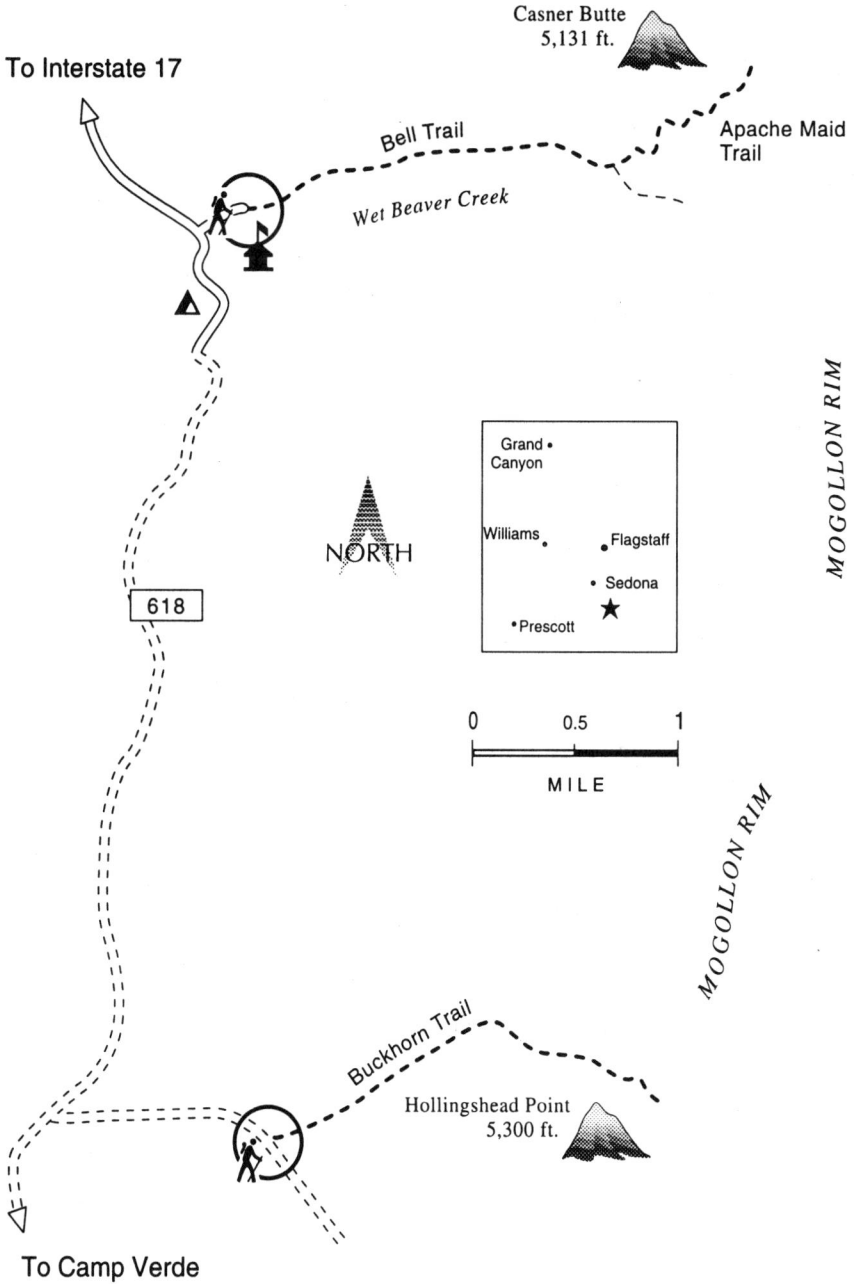

Casner Butte
5,131 ft.

To Interstate 17

Bell Trail

*Wet Beaver Creek*

Apache Maid
Trail

MOGOLLON RIM

618

NORTH

Grand
Canyon

Williams

Flagstaff

Sedona

Prescott

★

0     0.5     1

MILE

MOGOLLON RIM

Buckhorn Trail

Hollingshead Point
5,300 ft.

To Camp Verde

MOGOLLON RIM

desert, the Verde Valley with its river and several permanent streams must have been a relief. The valley and the surrounding canyons contain numerous cliff dwellings, pueblos, and other ruins left by the Sinagua people about nine hundred years ago. Examples are preserved in Montezuma Castle and Tuzigoot National Monuments.

# HIKE 76  *TRAMWAY TRAIL*

**General description:** A day hike in the West Clear Creek Wilderness.
**General location:** 58 miles southeast of Flagstaff.
**Maps:** Calloway Butte 7.5-minute USGS, Coconino National Forest.
**Difficulty:** Moderate.
**Length:** 0.4 mile one way.
**Elevation:** 6,700 to 6,000 feet.
**Special attractions:** Access to spectacular West Clear Creek.
**Water:** West Clear Creek.
**Best season:** Spring through fall.
**Information:** Long Valley Ranger District, Coconino National Forest.
**Finding the trailhead:** From Flagstaff drive about fifty miles southeast on the Lake Mary Road (FH 3), then turn right (west) on FR 81. Stay on this graded dirt road three miles, then turn right (west) on FR 81E. After 3.6 miles turn right (south) on FR 693. In 1.2 miles turn left at a fork and continue 0.3 mile to the end of the road. The last few miles of road may be impassable during wet weather, and a high clearance vehicle is recommended.

You may also reach FR 81 from Camp Verde by driving about thirty miles east on the General Crook Trail (FH 9). Turn left (north) on AZ 87 and continue eleven miles, then turn left (northwest) on the Lake Mary-Happy Jack Road (FH 3). Go seven miles, then turn left on FR 81.

**The hike:** The short but spectacular trail descends into the gorge of West Clear Creek, affording fine views both up and down the canyon. It follows the route of an old aerial tramway. The Kaibab limestone makes up the rocks near the rim. This fossil-rich layer was deposited in a shallow ocean, and forms the edge of the Mogollon Rim in this area. Below the Kaibab limestone, the cross-bedded Coconino sandstone appears, with its layers of overlapping petrified sand dunes.

The trail ends at the bottom of the canyon. It is possible to hike cross country upstream and climb out via the Maxwell Trail (Hike 77). Downstream, West Clear Creek continues for twenty-five miles to the Bull Pen Ranch trailhead. This is a long backpack trip that requires swimming and floating your pack across numerous pools. It should be attempted only in warm weather by experienced canyon hikers.

# HIKE 77  *MAXWELL TRAIL*

**General description:** A day hike in the West Clear Creek Wilderness.
**General location:** 58 miles southeast of Flagstaff.
**Maps:** Calloway Butte 7.5-minute USGS, Coconino National Forest.

**150**

To FH 3

81E

NORTH

Grand •
Canyon

Williams •          • Flagstaff

                         • Sedona

                            ★

• Prescott

693

81E

Tramway Trail

Maxwell
Trail

*West Clear Creek*

*Willow Creek*

*Clover Creek*

0          0.5          1

M I L E

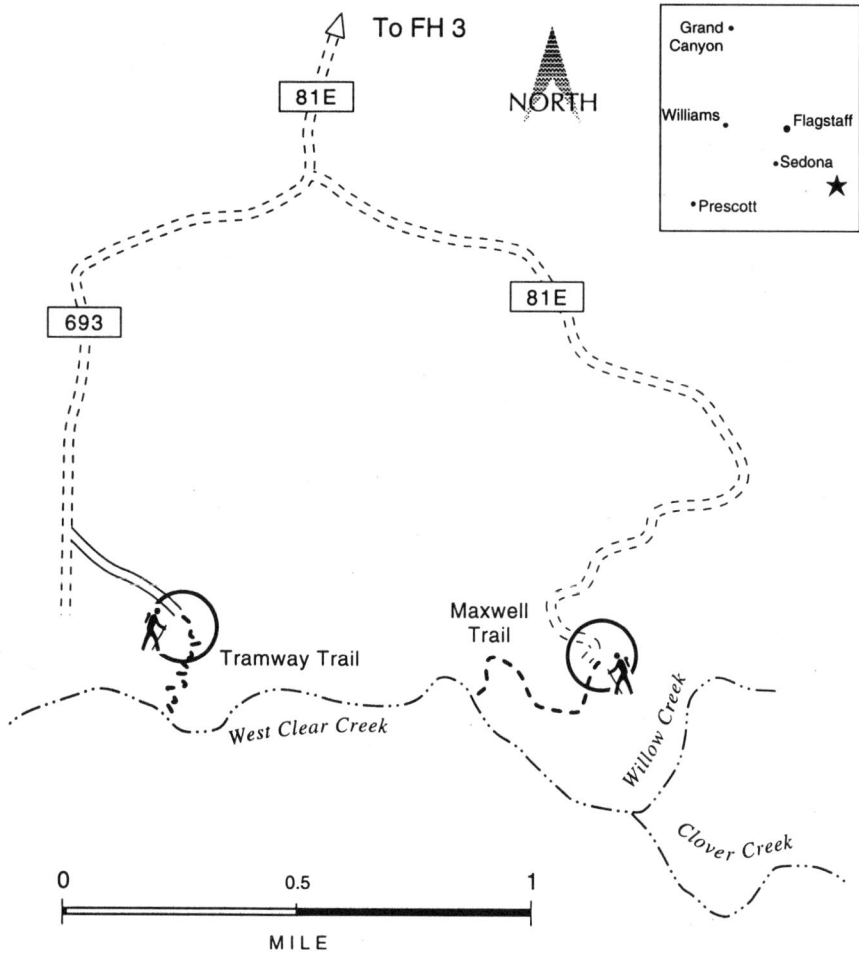

**Difficulty:** Moderate.
**Length:** 0.5 mile one way.
**Elevation:** 6,700 to 6,000 feet.
**Special attractions:** Access to upper West Clear Creek.
**Water:** West Clear Creek.
**Best season:** Spring through fall.
**Information:** Long Valley Ranger District, Coconino National Forest.
**Finding the trailhead:** From Flagstaff drive about fifty miles southeast on the Lake Mary Road (FH 3), then turn right (west) on FR 81. Stay on this graded dirt road three miles, then turn right (west) on FR 81E. After 3.6 miles turn left on FR 81E. Turn right at all later forks to stay on FR 81E to its end. The last few miles of road may be impassable during wet weather, and a high clearance vehicle is recommended.

*West Clear Creek Canyon seen from near the Tramway and Maxwell Trails.*

You may also reach FR 81 from Camp Verde by driving about thirty miles east on the General Crook Trail (FH 9). Turn left (north) on AZ 87 and continue eleven miles, then turn left (northwest) on the Lake Mary-Happy Jack Road (FH 3). Go seven miles, then turn left on FR 81.

**The hike:** The Maxwell Trail descends in a series of switchbacks, then traverses to the west for a short distance before resuming the steep descent to the canyon bottom. The creek, which flows all year, sports a lush riparian habitat—a strong contrast with the dry plateau at the trailhead. It is possible to explore cross country up or down stream from the end of the trail.

# HIKE 78  *WILLOW CROSSING TRAIL*

**General description:** A day hike on the Mogollon Rim.
**General location:** 56 miles southeast of Flagstaff.
**Maps:** Calloway Butte 7.5-minute USGS, Coconino National Forest.
**Difficulty:** Easy.
**Length:** 0.8 mile one way.
**Elevation:** 6,700 to 6,500 feet.
**Special attractions:** Natural arch.
**Water:** None.
**Best season:** Spring through fall.
**Information:** Long Valley Ranger District, Coconino National Forest.
**Finding the trailhead:** From Flagstaff drive about fifty-three miles southeast on the Lake Mary Road (FH 3), then turn right (west) on FR 196. (FR 196 is not well marked; it is 13.2 miles south of the Happy Jack Ranger Station.) Stay on this graded dirt road 1.9 miles, then turn right onto FR 122A, an unmaintained dirt road. After only 0.1 mile turn left (west) and continue on FR 122A. Continue another 0.7 mile on FR 122A across a shallow valley, then turn right (northwest) on FR 122A. (The main road continues straight ahead; do not take this road.) Drive 1.1 miles to a point where the road reaches the bottom of a drainage, then turn sharply right (north) on FR 122A, and go 0.7 mile to the end of the road in a grassy valley just beyond a gate. The last few miles of the road may be impassable during wet weather.

You may also reach FR 196 from Camp Verde by driving about thirty miles east on the General Crook Trail (FH 9). Turn left (north) on AZ 87 and continue eleven miles, then turn left (northwest) on the Lake Mary-Happy Jack Road (FH 3). Go three miles, then turn left (west) on FR 196.

**The hike:** The Willow Crossing Trail is not shown on the topographic map, but a sign marks the beginning of the trail. It follows the drainage in a gentle descent through tall ponderosa pines for about 0.4 mile. As the side canyon becomes steeper, the trail abandons it for the ridge to the west, and then stays on the ridge to the canyon bottom. Watch for poison ivy. Here the trail turns north to cross the normally dry creek bed, then climbs the west side of the canyon to reach the rim. (The trail continues another 0.6 mile to end at FR 9366M, but this area has been heavily logged

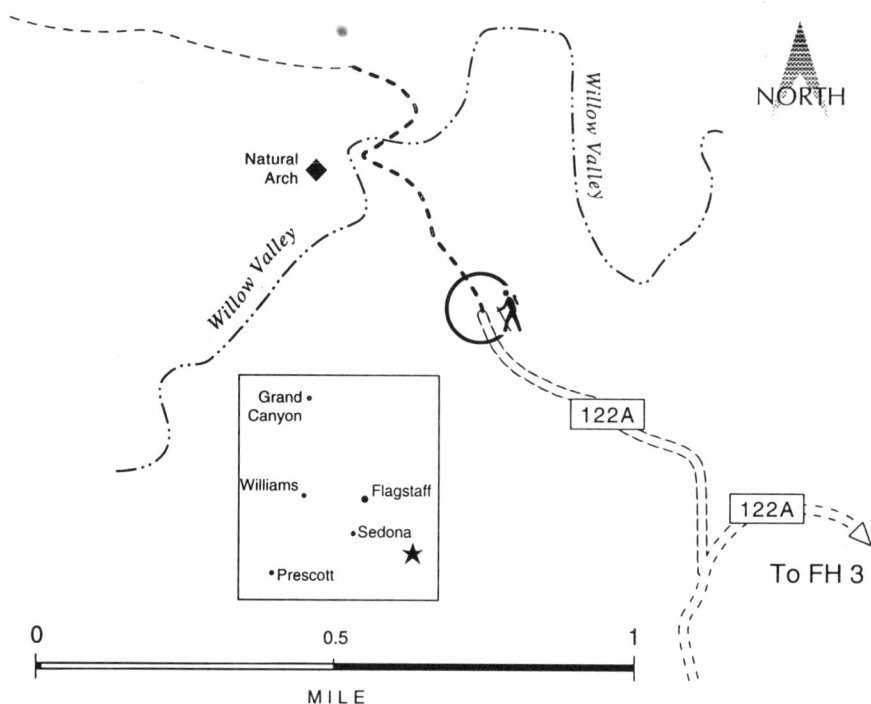

and is disappointing after Willow Valley.) After retracing your steps to the bottom of Willow Valley, go downstream a few yards and look for the natural arch on the west wall. It is not easily seen from the trail.

Willow Valley is seldom visited and invites cross-country exploration both up and downstream. The experienced canyon hiker can walk downstream to West Clear Creek and the Maxwell Trail, a boulder-hopping distance of about nine miles.

# HIKE 79  *HORSE CROSSING TRAIL*

**General description:** A day hike in East Clear Creek.
**General location:** 70 miles southeast of Flagstaff.
**Maps:** Blue Ridge Reservoir 7.5-minute USGS, Coconino National Forest.
**Difficulty:** Easy.
**Length:** 0.7 mile one way.
**Elevation:** 6,900 to 6,400 feet.
**Special attractions:** Historic trail, access to East Clear Creek.
**Water:** East Clear Creek.
**Best season:** Spring through fall.
**Information:** Blue Ridge Ranger District, Coconino National Forest.

**Finding the trailhead:** From Flagstaff drive about fifty-five miles southeast on Lake Mary Road (FH 3) to Clints Well. Turn left (north) on AZ 87. From Clints Well continue north on AZ 87 nine miles, then turn right (southeast) on signed FR 95. Continue four miles on this graded road, then turn left (northeast) on FR 513B, which is signed for the Horse Crossing Trail. Drive two miles on this unmaintained road and park at the signed Horse Crossing trailhead on the right.

Clints Well can also be reached from Camp Verde by driving thirty miles east on the General Crook Trail (FH 9), then turning left (north) on AZ 87 and continuing eleven miles.

**The hike:** The Horse Crossing Trail is shown incorrectly on the topographic map. From the trailhead it descends to the south through the fine pine-oak forest, then follows a gentle ridge for the final descent. East Clear Creek drains north from the Mogollon Rim and forms a major barrier to travel on the Coconino Plateau. A number of crossings were established by the early settlers, and some, like Horse Crossing, survive today. Others have been replaced by high-speed logging roads, but East Clear Creek is still crossed by roads in only three places.

This delightful creek runs all year, making the canyon bottom easy to explore. It is possible to hike upstream about three miles to Kinder Crossing. East Clear Creek is much easier to hike than West Clear Creek, although it is still cross country and requires a lot of wading. It is best hiked in warm weather, when the occasional deep pools are irresistible swimming holes instead of chilly obstacles.

*East Clear Creek flows all year and is accessible via several historic trails that provided routes across the canyon before the days of the automobile.*

**155**

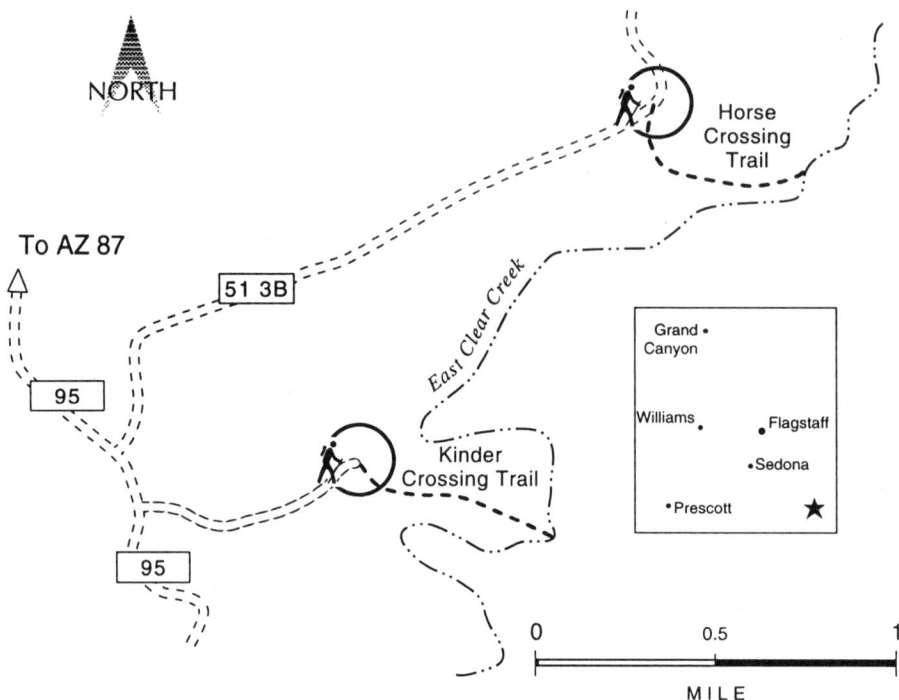

# HIKE 80 *KINDER CROSSING TRAIL*

**General description:** A day hike in East Clear Creek.
**General location:** 70 miles southeast of Flagstaff.
**Maps:** Blue Ridge Reservoir 7.5-minute USGS, Coconino National Forest.
**Difficulty:** Easy.
**Length:** 0.6 mile one way.
**Elevation:** 7,000 to 6,500 feet.
**Special attractions:** Historic trail, access to East Clear Creek.
**Water:** East Clear Creek.
**Best season:** Spring through fall.
**Information:** Blue Ridge Ranger District, Coconino National Forest.
**Finding the trailhead:** From Flagstaff drive about fifty-five miles southeast on Lake Mary Road (FH 3) to Clints Well. Turn left (north) on AZ 87. From Clints Well continue north on AZ 87 nine miles, then turn right on signed FR 95. Continue 4.2 miles on this graded road, then turn left (east) on the signed, unmaintained road to the Kinder Crossing Trail. Continue 0.6 mile to the end of the road.

Clints Well can also be reached from Camp Verde by driving thirty miles east on the General Crook Trail (FH 9), then turning left (north) on AZ 87 and continuing eleven miles.

**The hike:** The Kinder Crossing Trail descends into East Clear Creek by following the ridge to the east, reaching the creek at the confluence of East Clear Creek and Yeager Canyon. There is a large and very inviting swimming hole at the confluence. After cooling off it is fun to explore the canyon. It is possible to hike cross country downstream about three miles to Horse Crossing.

# HIKE 81  *U-BAR TRAIL*

**General description:** A day hike near the Mogollon Rim.
**General location:** 80 miles southeast of Flagstaff.
**Maps:** Blue Ridge Reservoir 7.5-minute, Dane Canyon 7.5-minute USGS, Coconino National Forest.
**Difficulty:** Moderate.
**Length:** 7 miles one way.
**Elevation:** 7,000 to 7,600 feet.
**Special attractions:** Historic trail and cabins.
**Water:** Barbershop Canyon, Dane Canyon and Dane Spring.
**Best season:** Spring through fall.
**Information:** Blue Ridge Ranger District, Coconino National Forest.
**Finding the trailhead:** From Flagstaff drive about fifty-five miles  southeast on Lake Mary Road (FH 3) to Clints Well. Turn left (north) on AZ 87 go north nine miles, then turn right (southeast) on signed FR 95. Continue 11.1 miles on this graded road, then turn left on FR 139A. After just over 0.1 mile, turn left on an unsigned, rough road (park low clearance vehicles here). The road drops into Houston Draw and ends at Pinchot Cabin, the trailhead, in 0.5 mile.

Clints Well can also be reached from Camp Verde by driving thirty miles east on the General Crook Trail (FH 9), then turning left (north) on AZ 87 and continuing eleven miles.

**The hike:** This hike is part of the Cabin Loop, a system of trails that connects three historic cabins in the rim country. Other trails in the Cabin Loop could be combined with the U-Bar Trail to make a three- or four-day backpack trip. (None of the trails in this system are shown on the topographic maps.) Pinchot Cabin is named for Gifford Pinchot, the first Chief of the Forest Service. It was used for many years as a fire guard station. The trail system provided the main transportation routes through this remote country during the early days of ranching and forestry. Most of the trails have been lost during the development of the forest road system, but several, including the U-Bar, have recently been relocated and restored. This trail differs from most in this book in that it follows roads for part of the distance, and is in a multiple-use area. Sections of the trail are cross country, but are well marked by tree blazes.

Initially, the U-Bar Trail route follows the road past the cabin and up the hill to the east. Note the fresh tree blazes. The entire trail is blazed with the same style

# HIKES 81 AND 82  *U-BAR TRAIL/HOUSTON BROTHERS TRAIL*

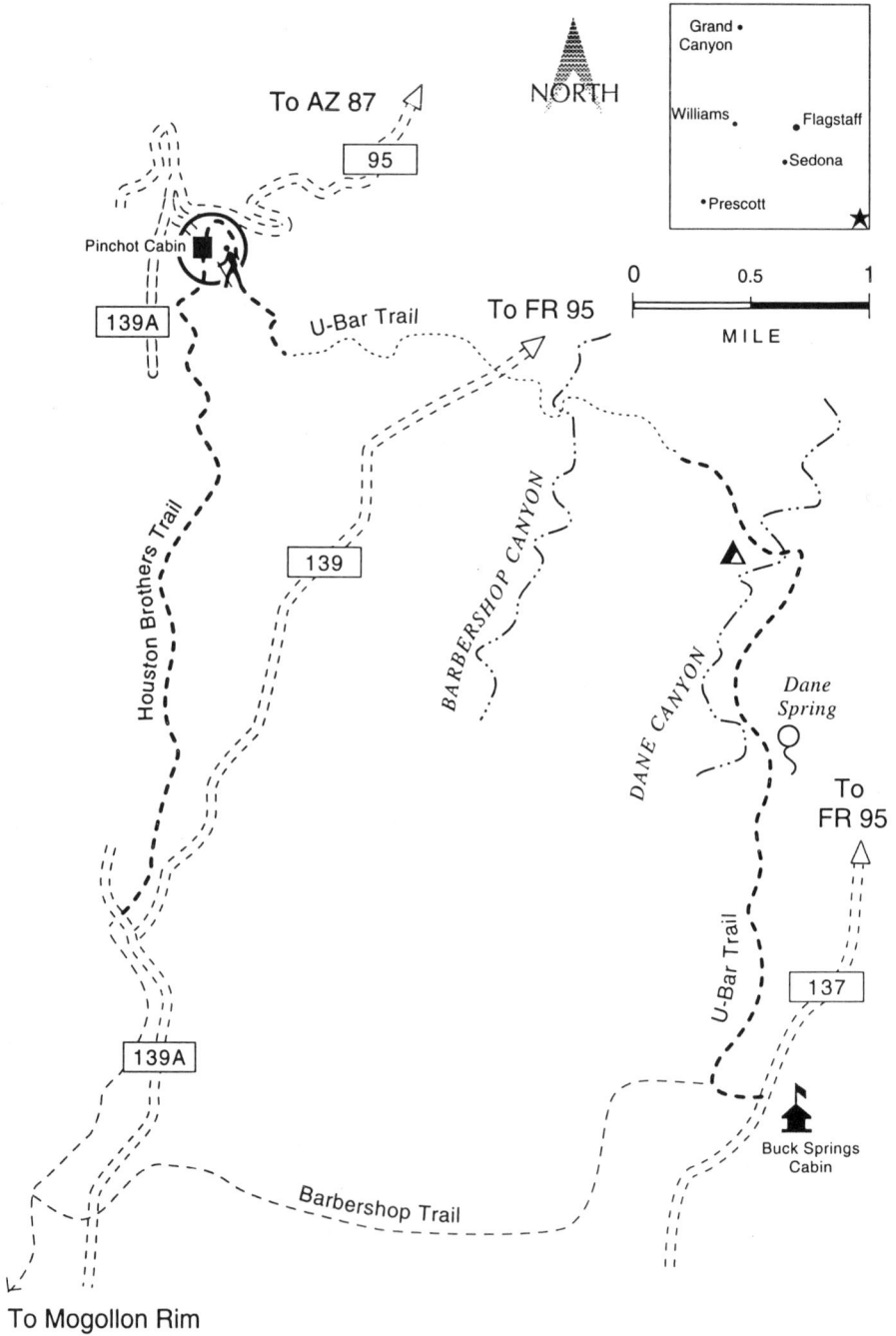

To AZ 87

95

NORTH

Grand •
Canyon

Williams •            • Flagstaff

• Sedona

• Prescott

★

Pinchot Cabin

139A

U-Bar Trail

To FR 95

0          0.5          1

MILE

Houston Brothers Trail

139

BARBERSHOP CANYON

DANE CANYON

*Dane Spring*

To
FR 95

U-Bar Trail

137

139A

Barbershop Trail

Buck Springs
Cabin

To Mogollon Rim

*The ruins of an old cabin at Dane Spring along the U-Bar Trail.*

blazes. After 0.8 mile, turn right (south) onto another road (note the blaze and right arrow), and continue 0.2 mile to a third road intersection. The trail crosses the road and continues east into the forest, ignoring both roads. In this section there is no trail, but walking through the forest is easy and pleasant if you follow the blazes carefully. The trick is to walk from blaze to blaze, always keeping the last blaze in sight. If the route is lost, return to the last known blaze and locate the next one before continuing. Also, watch for very old, historic blazes.

The route crosses Dick Hart Draw, then meets another road in 0.6 mile. The route now turns left (north) and follows the road past a large steel water tank. After about 0.3 mile the route turns sharply right (east) and leaves the road. After another 0.5 mile the route crosses a graded dirt road (FR 139), and a sign calls out the U-Bar Trail. The route veers slightly left as it crosses the road—follow the blazes carefully. The U-Bar route leads southeast out onto a point, then descends through a gate.

After the fence, the trail becomes obvious as it descends into Barbershop Canyon, which is 0.5 mile from FR 139. Serious trail construction was done on this section. Barbershop Canyon has a fine little permanent stream, and this would make a good goal for hikers wanting an easy day. For those on a backpack trip, there is very limited camping in the canyon bottom. It would be better to carry water about 0.2 mile up to the east rim where there is unlimited camping.

The trail, still distinct, climbs the east wall of the canyon and crosses a faint road. After this, the trail becomes a blazed route again. About 0.7 mile from Barbershop Canyon, the route crosses a road at right angles and a sign marks the U-Bar trail.

On the east side of the main road, the U-Bar Trail follows an unmaintained road past a small meadow bordered by pines and aspens, and McClintock Spring. About 0.4 mile from the sign, the road joins another road, and the route continues across the road and descends into Dane Canyon. The historic trail is distinct again in this section. Dane Canyon has a permanent stream and offers plentiful campsites on grassy meadows. A lush forest of Douglas-fir and ponderosa pine covers the canyon walls, spiced by an occasional aspen, limber pine, or white fir.

After crossing the creek, the trail climbs east out of the canyon and then turns south along the east rim. This is one of the prettiest sections of the trail, as it stays below the heavily logged ridgetop. About 1.6 miles from Dane Canyon, the U-Bar Trail reaches Dane Spring and the ruins of an old cabin. This is an excellent goal for a more ambitious day hike.

The trail continues south along the east side of a shallow drainage, then crosses the drainage and climbs to cross a road on a ridge top. It descends into the next drainage to end at the junction with the Barbershop Trail, 1.5 miles from Dane Spring. Turn left (east) on the Barbershop Trail to reach a trailhead at Buck Springs Cabin in an additional 0.5 mile. With a car shuttle, this could be done as a one-way hike.

# HIKE 82  *HOUSTON BROTHERS TRAIL*

**General description:** A day hike near the Mogollon Rim. (see map on p. 158)
**General location:** 80 miles southeast of Flagstaff.
**Maps:** Blue Ridge Reservoir 7.5-minute, Dane Canyon 7.5-minute USGS, Coconino National Forest.
**Difficulty:** Moderate.
**Length:** 3.7 miles one way.
**Elevation:** 7,000 to 7,600 feet.
**Special attractions:** Historic trail and cabins.
**Water:** Aspen Spring, Houston Draw.
**Best season:** Spring through fall.
**Information:** Blue Ridge Ranger District, Coconino National Forest.
**Finding the trailhead:** Follow the directions under the U-Bar Trail (Hike 81) to reach the trailhead at Pinchot Cabin.

**The hike:** This hike is part of the Cabin Loop, a system of trails that connects three historic cabins in the rim country. Other trails in the Cabin Loop could be combined with the Houston Brothers Trail to make a three- or four-day backpack trip. (None of the trails in this system are shown on the topographic maps.) The trailhead is signed and starts along the east side of Houston Draw.

Water is usually present in the creek, and the valley bottom makes for a pleasant hike. There is little sign of the heavy logging that has taken place on the ridges, and large ponderosa pines and graceful aspens line the grassy meadows. Just under two miles from the trailhead, the trail passes Aspen Spring, where a road comes down to the trail. A mile of hiking through open meadows leads to McFarland Spring. Nearing the head of Houston Draw, the forest changes to mixed fir and pine, with

*The historic Houston Brothers Trail in the Mogollon Rim country follows beautiful Houston Draw through stands of ponderosa pine and quaking aspen.*

white and Douglas-fir providing a more alpine feeling. The trail crosses FR 139A, a maintained gravel road that marks the end of the hike, 3.7 miles from the trailhead.

The second half of the trail closely follows FR 139A and is a blazed route. Very little of the trail remains; if you decide to hike this section, carefully follow the blazes, which are often too far apart. If you lose the trail turn directly east and walk to FR 139A, which is never more than 0.2 mile away.

# SIERRA PRIETA MOUNTAINS

The "pretty mountains," as the name means in Spanish, are well-named. They lie west and northwest of Prescott, and their northernmost outlier is rugged Granite Mountain. Prescott was the capital of the Territory of Arizona, and the surrounding mountains were known for their gold and silver mines.

# HIKE 83 *GRANITE MOUNTAIN TRAIL*

**General description:** A day hike or overnight backpack in the Sierra Prieta Mountains.
**General location:** 8.5 miles northwest of Prescott.
**Maps:** Iron Springs 7.5-minute, Jerome Canyon 7.5-minute USGS, Prescott National Forest.

**Difficulty:** Moderate.

**Length:** 3.2 miles one way.

**Elevation:** 5,600 to 7,200 feet.

**Special attractions:** Views, rugged granite terrain, good trail.

**Water:** None.

**Best season:** Spring through fall.

**Information:** Bradshaw Ranger District, Prescott National Forest.

**Finding the trailhead:** From Prescott drive northwest about 4.5 miles on the paved Iron Springs Road, then turn right (north) on the signed, paved Granite Basin Road. Continue four miles past the campground and the lake to the end of the road and the signed trailhead.

**The hike:** The Granite Mountain Trail follows a drainage uphill through a forest of juniper, pinyon pine, oak, and ponderosa pine. To the right, there are occasional views of Granite Mountain, the destination for this hike. After 1.3 miles, the trail reaches Blair Pass, which is the signed junction with the Cedar Spring and Little Granite Mountain trails. Turn right (north) to continue on the Granite Mountain Trail. After following a broad ridge a short distance, the trail begins to ascend the rocky slopes in a series of switchbacks. Rock climbers sometimes take an unmarked turnoff to-

## HIKE 83  *GRANITE MOUNTAIN TRAIL*

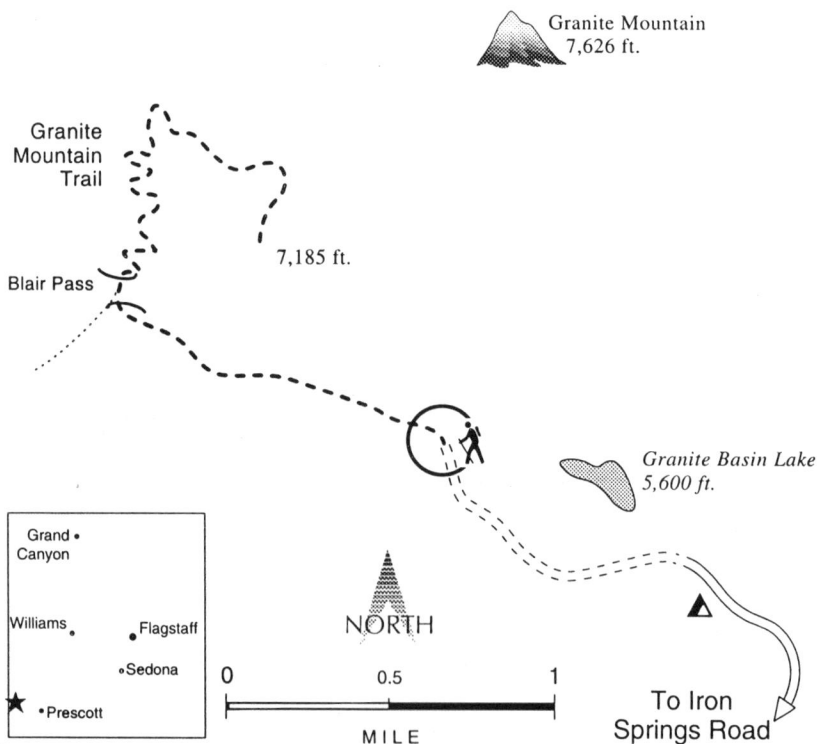

Granite Mountain
7,626 ft.

Granite Mountain Trail

7,185 ft.

Blair Pass

Granite Basin Lake
5,600 ft.

Grand Canyon

Williams

Flagstaff

Sedona

Prescott

NORTH

0        0.5        1

MILE

To Iron Springs Road

ward the prominent granite cliff above. Granite Mountain Wall offers some of the best technical climbing in the area.

The terrain here faces to the south and the increased heat and dryness causes the pines to give way to chaparral and juniper. Chaparral is not a single plant, but an association of three shrubs that commonly grow together in the upper Sonoran life zone. The red-barked bush is manzanita; the brush with the oak-like prickly leaves is scrub oak; and the plant with longish leaves, curled under at the edges and fuzzy underneath, is mountain mahogany. Chaparral provides vital cover and habitat for wildlife.

The reward for the steady climb is expanding views. Little Granite Mountain forms a conspicuous landmark to the south; beyond are the pine-forested slopes of the Sierra Prieta Mountains. After reaching a saddle, the trail turns east and climbs the beautiful west ridge of Granite Mountain, passing through stately groves of ponderosa pine and winding around granite slabs. Some of the slabs look almost glacial in origin. When the trail reaches the summit plateau, it turns south and ends at a view point above the Granite Mountain Wall. Granite Basin Lake, Prescott, and the northern Bradshaw Mountains are all visible. Although this is not the true summit of the mountain, the views are still excellent.

# MINGUS MOUNTAIN

The western boundary of the Verde Valley is formed by the Black Hills and the Verde Rim, trending north-northwest to south-southeast. The rim was formed by faulting, which caused it to rise high above the Verde Valley to the east. Minerals, especially copper, were concentrated by the fault and were mined at Jerome. The highest section is Mingus Mountain, which rises to nearly 8,000 feet. There are a number of trails, remnants of the pre-road transportation system, ascending the pine covered slopes of these mountains. All offer superb views of the surrounding mountains and valleys.

# HIKE 84 *NORTH MINGUS TRAIL*

**General description:** A day hike on Mingus Mountain (see map on p. 166).
. **General location:** 28 miles east of Prescott.
**Maps:** Hickey Mountain 7.5-minute, Cottonwood 7.5-minute USGS, Prescott National Forest.
**Difficulty:** Moderate.
**Length:** 3 miles one way.
**Elevation:** 6,000 to 7,400 feet.
**Special attractions:** Scenic hike through historic mining district, views of Verde Valley and Mogollon Rim.
**Water:** Mescal Spring.
**Best season:** Spring through fall.
**Information:** Verde Ranger District, Prescott National Forest.
**Finding the trailhead:** From Prescott drive about twenty-eight miles east on AZ

89A, over Mingus Mountain. Watch for a Prescott National Forest sign as you descend the east side of the mountain, then turn right (east) on an unsigned, unmaintained dirt road just past this sign. (This turnoff is about four miles west of Jerome.) Low-clearance vehicles should park at the highway. Go through the gate and continue 0.5 mile to Mescal Spring, and park. Mescal Spring is marked by a large cement tank that catches water piped down a few feet from the actual spring.

**The hike:** Walk up the jeep road, which forks right and climbs steeply (it is shown as a foot trail on the topographic map). The little-used jeep road does a switchback then contours around a basin. This section of the road is very easy and pleasant. It crosses a ridge just as it enters another basin. Watch carefully for the cairned but unsigned foot trail that goes up this ridge. This junction is 1.2 miles from Mescal Spring. Although it is possible to reach this point in a high-clearance vehicle, there is no parking. The rocky but well-maintained trail climbs through a fine stand of ponderosa pine then starts switchbacking up the north ridge of Mingus Mountain. The view starts to open up as the trail gains elevation. About 1.4 miles from the jeep road, the trail reaches a shallow saddle and the signed junction with Trail 105A. Continue south, directly up the steep ridge, on Trail 105. The trail soon resumes switchbacking, and passes through a small aspen grove near the rim. The trail reaches the rim about 0.4 mile from the trail junction. The forest is thick here, but by walking around good views can be found. A large section of the Mogollon Rim, the Verde Valley, and the red-rock country of Sedona and Sycamore Canyon are visible. A trailhead is located 0.5 mile south, but the rim makes a good destination for the hike.

# HIKE 85 *MINGUS RIM LOOP*

**General description:** A day hike on Mingus Mountain.
**General location:** 25 miles east of Prescott.
**Maps:** Cottonwood 7.5-minute USGS, Prescott National Forest.
**Difficulty:** Moderate.
**Length:** 3.2-mile loop.
**Elevation:** 6,700 to 7,800 feet.
**Special attractions:** Scenic loop along and below the rim of Mingus Mountain.
**Water:** None.
**Best season:** Summer through fall.
**Information:** Verde Ranger District, Prescott National Forest.
**Finding the trailhead:** From Prescott drive about twenty-five miles east on AZ 89A to the highway summit, then turn right (south) on the graded Mingus Mountain road (FR 104). The turnoff is about five miles from Jerome. Go 2.4 miles to the east end of the Mingus Mountain Campground, and park at the view point. This trailhead is also signed for Trail 106.

**The hike:** After checking out the view descend east on Trail 106. The steep trail leaves the cool pine forest behind as it rapidly descends in a series of switchbacks.

*Panoramic views of the Verde Valley from the North Mingus Trail are a prime attraction of this hike.*

## HIKES 84 AND 85 *NORTH MINGUS TRAIL/MINGUS RIM LOOP*

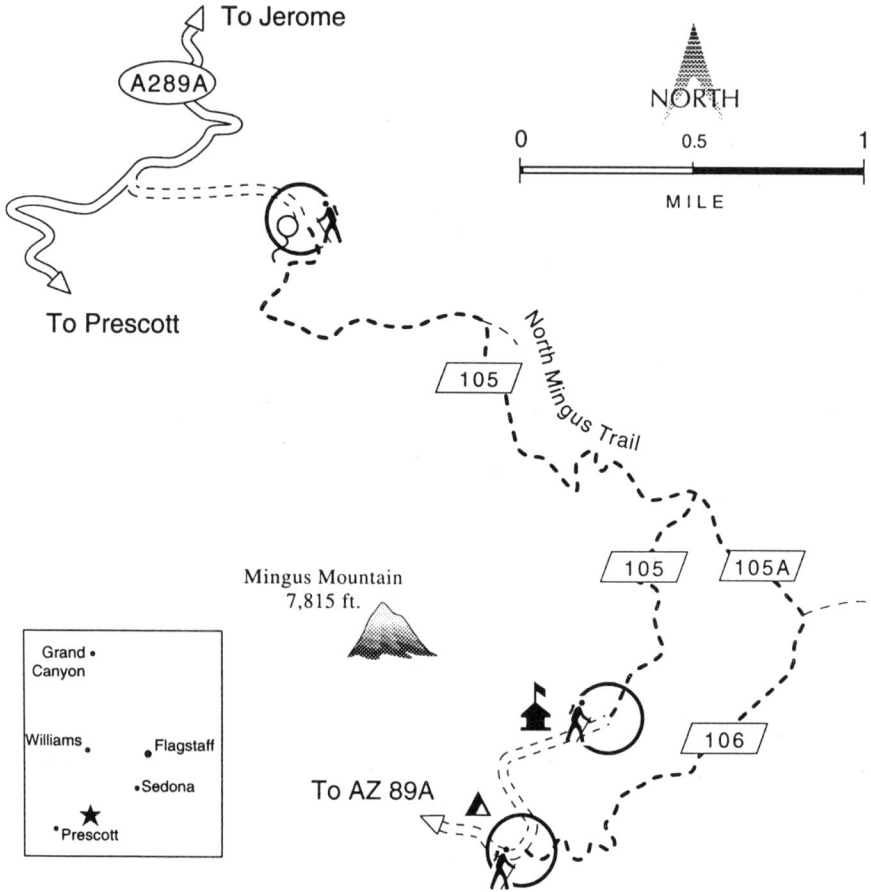

Soon the trail starts a more gentle descent to the north as it traverses a chaparral slope. The chaparral country is difficult to penetrate without a trail, but provides vital wildlife cover under the dense brush.

The trail enters a shadier section of pine forest and meets Trail 105A (not shown on the topographic map) about 1.4 miles from the trailhead. This junction is signed; turn left (north) on Trail 105A and follow it as it gradually climbs 0.6 mile to another saddle, where it meets Trail 105. Turn left (south) and follow the trail as it climbs 0.4 mile to the north rim of Mingus Mountain in a series of switchbacks. Walk south another 0.5 mile to the trailhead (a hang glider launch site), then follow the main road another 0.7 mile to the Mingus Mountain Campground and the trailhead.

# HIKE 86  *YAEGER CANYON LOOP*

**General description:** A day hike on Mingus Mountain.
**General location:** 22 miles east of Prescott.
**Maps:** Hickey Mountain 7.5-minute USGS, Prescott National Forest.
**Difficulty:** Moderate.
**Length:** 6-mile loop.
**Elevation:** 6,000 to 7,200 feet.
**Special attractions:** Loop hike on good trails, views of Prescott Valley.
**Water:** None.
**Best season:** Spring through fall.
**Information:** Verde Ranger District, Prescott National Forest.
**Finding the trailhead:** From Prescott drive about twenty-two miles east on AZ 89A to the unmarked trailhead. To find the trailhead note your mileage as you pass the Prescott National Forest boundary sign at the foot of Mingus Mountain; the trailhead is on the right 1.7 miles past the sign. Turn sharply right on the dirt road, and park on either side of the normally dry creek.

**The hike:** The hike starts on the Little Yaeger Canyon Trail, which is signed and begins from the southeast side of the parking area. Several switchbacks through pinyon-juniper forest lead to the top of a gentle ridge, where ponderosa pines begin to take over. The trail climbs more gradually through a small saddle, then meets the Allen Springs Road 1.6 miles from the trailhead. Turn left (east) and walk down the road 0.2 mile to the signed Trail 111, then turn left (north) onto this trail.

Still in pine-oak forest, Trail 111 drops slightly as it traverses a side canyon of Little Yaeger Canyon, then begins to work its way up the head of the canyon. There is sometimes water in the bed of the canyon near its head. The trail comes out onto a pine flat on the southwest ridge of Mingus Mountain. Turn left on a signed trail 1.8 miles from the Allens Springs Road. (This side trail also goes right to the Allen Springs Road.) Continue 0.1 mile to the end of trail 111 at a three-way trail junction. Forest Trail 530 continues straight ahead, while Trail 28 crosses from right to left.

Turn left (west), and follow Trail 28 to the rim where there is a good view of Little Yaeger Canyon and the rim of Mingus Mountain. The trail descends to the southwest in a series of switchbacks, and the trailhead is visible along the highway. When the trail reaches the bottom of Yaeger Canyon it turns left on the old highway road bed. It stays on the left (east) side of the creek and doesn't cross on the old highway bridge. The trailhead is reached 2.3 miles from the end of Trail 111.

# HIKE 86  *YAEGER CANYON LOOP*

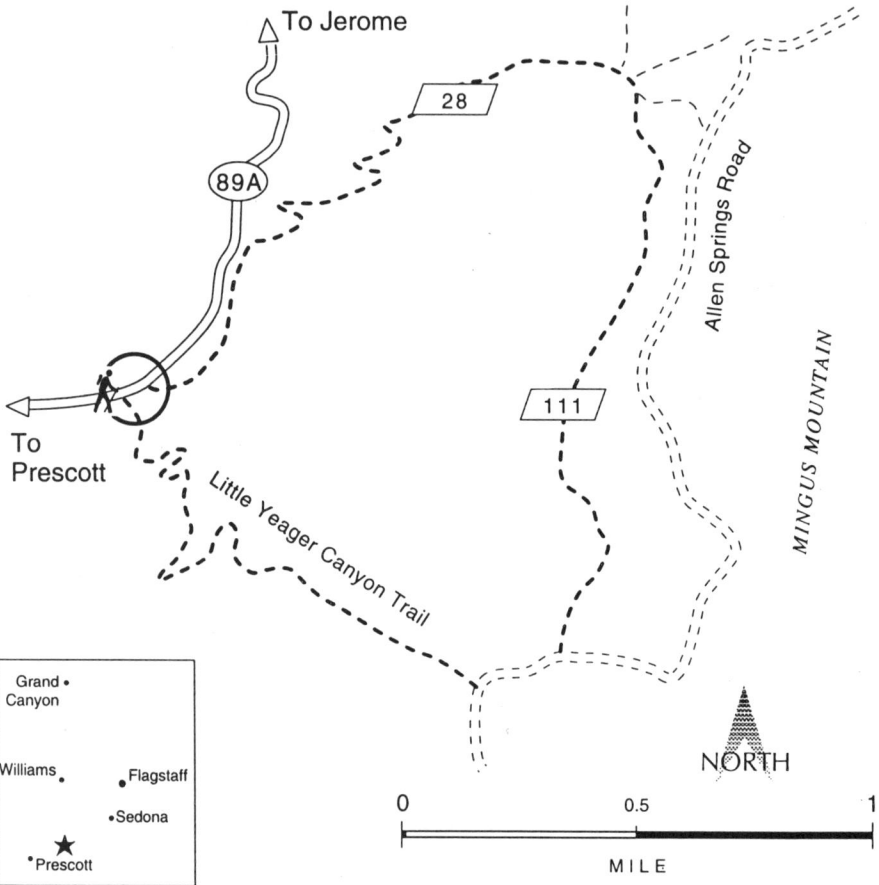

To Jerome

28

89A

To
Prescott

111

Allen Springs Road

MINGUS MOUNTAIN

Little Yeager Canyon Trail

Grand
Canyon

Williams

Flagstaff

Sedona

Prescott

NORTH

0            0.5            1

MILE

*This variety of mistletoe is a parasite on ponderosa pine, seen here on the Yaeger Canyon Loop on Mingus Mountain.*

# AFTERWORD

## Wilderness

It doesn't take long for a hiker to begin to appreciate wild country. Although hiking in semi-urban settings can be pleasant, natural settings are more enjoyable. The idea behind the wilderness conservation movement is to preserve the opportunity for primitive, nonmotorized recreation and to protect wild plants and animals in their wild settings.

Aldo Leopold of the USDA Forest Service began to promote the idea of preserving wild country within the national forests in the 1920s, and a few years later the agency began designating wilderness and primitive areas. Roads and other permanent man-made structures were excluded from such areas, although trails and activities considered compatible such as hunting, fishing, grazing, and limited mining were allowed. Most of the lands within the national parks were also managed as wilderness. Initially, this protection was under the control of the land management agencies, which could rescind the wilderness designation at any time. Congress decided to take the wilderness concept further when it passed the Wilderness Act in 1964, establishing the National Wilderness Preservation System. Most of the existing designated Wilderness and Primitive Areas on the national forests were included in the system. Since then, conservationists have added many deserving areas to the wilderness system.

In the 1960s, when I started hiking in Arizona, there were only a few protected wilderness areas. Interests such as ranching, mining, and even tourism fought to prevent any wilderness protection. As time passed, more people began to appreciate wild country as a priceless asset to the state. Now Arizona is a leader in wilderness protection. In recent years many wild areas in Arizona have been protected by congress as national wilderness areas administered by the Forest Service or the Bureau of Land Management. Other wilderness areas have been protected in National Monuments adminstered by the National Park Service. Private organizations such as The Nature Conservancy have also become managers of wild areas on private trust lands.

We owe this change to the dedication of the hard working people in the convervation groups, government agencies, and U.S. Congress who believe in protecting what remains of the American wilderness.

While protecting roadless areas is vital, the emphasis is now changing to the protection of intact ecosystems. As we learn more about plant and animal habitats, we find that survival of individual species is linked to the health of other plants and animals as well as the quality of the air and water. Instead of protecting a few isolated wild areas and ignoring the consequences of unrestricted human activities on the rest of the land, we have to consider entire watersheds and entire forests and consider how proposed activities will affect them.

–Bruce Grubbs

# RESOURCES

## Local Hiking Clubs And Conservation Groups

Arizona Mountaineering Club, P.O. Box 1695, Phoenix, AZ 85001, no phone.

Central Arizona Hiking Club, 1026 N. 9th St., Phoenix, AZ 85006, no phone.

Earth First!, P.O. Box 5871, Tucson, AZ 85703, no phone.

Maricopa Audubon Society, 4619 E. Arcadia Ln., Phoenix, AZ 85018, no phone.

The Nature Conservancy, 300 E. University Blvd., Suite 230, Tucson, AZ 85705, (602) 622-3861.

Sierra Club, Grand Canyon Chapter, 516 E. Portland St., Phoenix, AZ 85004, no phone.

## Private Organizations

Meteor Crater Enterprises, 603 N. Beaver St., Flagstaff, AZ 86001, (602) 774-8350.

## Public Agencies

Arizona State Land Department, 3650 Lake Mary Rd., Flagstaff, AZ 86001, (602) 774-1425.

Arizona State Parks, 1300 W. Washington, Phoenix, AZ 85007, (602) 542-4174.

Bureau of Land Management, Arizona State Office, 3707 N. 7th St., Phoenix, Arizona 85014, (602) 241-5509.

Bureau of Land Management, Phoenix District Office, 2015 W. Deer Valley Rd., Phoenix, AZ 85027, (602) 863-4464.

Coconino National Forest, 2323 E. Greenlaw Ln., Flagstaff, AZ 86001, (602) 556-7400.

Beaver Creek Ranger District, H.C. 64, Box 240, Rimrock, AZ 86335, (602) 567-4510.

Blue Ridge Ranger District, H.C. 31, Box 300, Happy Jack, AZ 86024, (602) 477-2255.

Long Valley Ranger District, P.O. Box 68, Happy Jack, AZ 86024, (602) 354-2216.

Mormon Lake Ranger District, 4825 S. Lake Mary Rd., Flagstaff, AZ 86001, (602) 556-7474.
Peaks Ranger District, 5079 N. Highway 89, Flagstaff, AZ 86004, (602) 526-0866.

Sedona Ranger District, P.O. Box 300, Sedona, AZ 86336, (602) 282-4119.

Flagstaff Planning Division, 211 W. Aspen, Flagstaff, AZ 86001, (602) 779-7632.

Grand Canyon National Park, P.O. Box 129, Grand Canyon, AZ 86023, (602) 638-2474.

Kaibab National Forest, Supervisor's Office, 800 South 6th St., Williams, AZ 86046, (602) 635-2681.

Chalender Ranger District, 501 W. Bill Williams Ave., Williams, AZ 86046, (602) 635-2676.

Tusayan Ranger District, P.O. Box 3088, Tusayan, AZ 86023, (602) 638-2443.

Williams Ranger District, Rt. 1, Box 142, Williams, AZ 86046, (602) 635-2633.

Prescott National Forest, Supervisor's Office, 344 S. Cortez St., Prescott, AZ 86303, (602) 771-4700.

Bradshaw Ranger District, 2230 E. Hwy 69, Prescott, AZ 86301, (602) 445-7253.

Chino Valley Ranger District, P.O. Box 485, Chino Valley, AZ 86323, (602) 636-2302.

Verde Ranger District, P.O. Box 670, Camp Verde, AZ 86322, (602) 567-4121.

Red Rock State Park, HC - Box 886, Sedona, AZ 86336, (602) 282-6907.

Sunset Crater National Monument, 2717 N. Steves Blvd., Suite 3, Flagstaff, AZ 86004, (602) 556-7042.

U.S. Geological Survey, Distribution Branch, Box 25286, Denver Federal Center, Denver, CO 80225.

Walnut Canyon National Monument, 2717 N. Steves Blvd., Suite 3, Flagstaff, AZ 86004, (602) 526-3367.

Wupatki National Monument, 2717 N. Steves Blvd., Suite 3, Flagstaff, AZ 86004, (602) 556-7040.

# FURTHER READING

*A Guide to Exploring Oak Creek and the Sedona Area.* Aitchison, Stewart. RNM Press, Salt Lake City, Utah, 1989.
*Biography of a Small Mountain.* Ashworth, Donna. Small Mountain Books, Flagstaff, Arizona, 1991.
*Ecology of Western Forests.* Kricher, John C., and Morrison, Gordon. Houghton Mifflin, New York, 1993.
*Guide to the Natural Areas of New Mexico, Arizona, and Nevada.* Perry, John and Jane Greverus. Sierra Club Books, San Francisco, California, 1985.
*Medicine for Mountaineering.* Wilkerson, James A. The Mountaineers, Seattle, Washington, 1985.
*Outdoor Emergency Care.* Warren Bowman, M.D. National Ski Patrol. 1993. 546 pp.
*Red Rock Sacred Mountain: the canyon and peaks from Sedona to Flagstaff.* Aitchison, Stewart. Voyager Press, Stillwater, Minnesota, 1992.
*Sierra Club Naturalist's Guide to the Deserts of the Southwest.* Larson, Peggy. Sierra Club Books, San Francisco, California, 1977.
*The Complete Walker III.* Fletcher, Colin. Alfred A. Knopf, New York, 1989.
*The Hiker's Guide to Arizona.* Aitchison, Stewart, and Grubbs, Bruce. Falcon Press, Helena, Montana, 1992.
*Wild Country Companion.* Harmon, Will, Falcon Press, Helena, Montana, 1994. 208 pp.

# HIKER'S CHECKLIST

This checklist may be useful for ensuring that nothing essential is forgotten. Of course, it contains far more items than are needed on any individual hiking trip.

## Clothing

Shirt
Pants
Extra underwear
Swim suit
Walking shorts
Belt or suspenders
Windbreaker
Jacket or parka
Rain gear
Gloves or mittens
Sun hat
Watch cap or balaclava
Sweater
Bandanna

## Footwear

Boots
Extra socks
Boot wax
Camp shoes

## Sleeping

Tarp or tent with fly
Groundsheet
Sleeping pad
Sleeping bag

## Packing

Backpack
Day pack
Fanny pack

## Cooking

Matches or lighter
Waterproof match case
Fire starter
Stove
Fuel
Stove maintenance kit
Cooking pot(s)
Cup
Bowl or plate
Utensils
Pot scrubber
Plastic water bottles
Collapsible water containers

## Food

Cereal
Bread
Crackers
Cheese
Margarine
Dry soup
Packaged dinners
Snacks
Hot chocolate
Tea
Powdered milk
Powdered drink mixes

## Navigation

Maps
Compass

### Emergency/Repair

Pocket knife
First aid kit
Snakebite kit
Nylon cord
Plastic bags
Wallet or ID card
Coins for phone calls
Space blanket
Emergency fishing gear
Signal mirror
Pack parts
Stove parts
Tent parts
Flashlight bulbs, batteries
Scissors
Safety pins

### Miscellaneous

Fishing gear
Photographic gear

Sunglasses
Flashlight
Candle lantern
Sunscreen
Insect repellent
Toilet paper and trowel
Binoculars
Trash bags
Notebook and pencils
Field guides
Book or game
Dental and personal items
Towel
Water purification tablets
Car key
Watch
Calendar

### Car

Extra water
Extra food
Extra clothes

---

# ABOUT THE AUTHOR

Bruce Grubbs has been hiking in the Southwest for more than twenty-five years, as well as cross-country skiing and technical mountaineering. He fought forest fires for the Forest Service and the Bureau of Land Management for eleven seasons, then became an active partner in a hiking and ski shop in Flagstaff for eight years. He presently flies for a commuter airline and lives in Flagstaff.

# Out Here there's No One to Ask Directions

# Let Falcon Be Your Guide

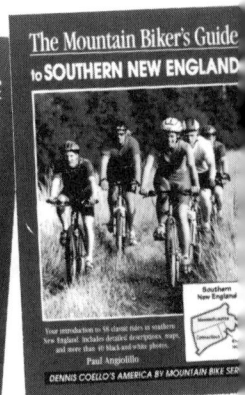

The **FALCON**GUIDES series consists of recreational guidebooks designed to help you safely enjoy the great outdoors. Each 6 x 9" softcover book features up-to-date maps, photos, and detailed information on access, hazards, side trips, special attractions, and more. So whether you're planning you first adventure or have enjoyed the outdoors for years, a **FALCON**GUIDE makes an ideal companion.

For more information about these and other Falcon Press books, please visit your local bookstore, or call or write for a free catalog.

Falcon Press • P.O. Box 1718 • Helena, Montana 59624
**1-800-582-2665**

FALCON